BASIC KNOWLEDGE AND CONDITIONS ON KNOWLEDGE

Basic Knowledge and Conditions on Knowledge

Mark McBride

https://www.openbookpublishers.com

© 2017 Mark McBride

This work is licensed under a Creative Commons Attribution 4.0 International license (CC BY 4.0). This license allows you to share, copy, distribute and transmit the work; to adapt the work and to make commercial use of the work providing attribution is made to the authors (but not in any way that suggests that they endorse you or your use of the work). Attribution should include the following information:

Mark McBride, *Basic Knowledge and Conditions of Knowledge*. Cambridge, UK: Open Book Publishers, 2017, https://doi.org/10.11647/OBP.0104

In order to access detailed and updated information on the license, please visit https://www.openbookpublishers.com/product/537#copyright

Further details about CC BY licenses are available at http://creativecommons.org/licenses/by/4.0/

All external links were active at the time of publication unless otherwise stated and have been archived via the Internet Archive Wayback Machine at https://archive.org/web

Digital material and resources associated with this volume are available at https://www.openbookpublishers.com/product/537#resources

The National University of Singapore supported this Open Access publication with a Start Up Grant (WBS No: R-241-000-126-133).

ISBN Paperback: 978-1-78374-283-7
ISBN Hardback: 978-1-78374-284-4
ISBN Digital (PDF): 978-1-78374-285-1
ISBN Digital ebook (epub): 978-1-78374-286-8
ISBN Digital ebook (mobi): 978-1-78374-287-5
DOI: 10.11647/OBP.0104

Cover image: Milickie Ponds Nature Reserve. Barycz Valley Landscape Park. Lower Silesian Voivodeship, Poland. Photo by Bartosz Dworski CC BY-SA 3.0, https://commons.wikimedia.org/wiki/File:Dolina_Baryczy_1.jpg

Cover design: Heidi Coburn

All paper used by Open Book Publishers is SFI (Sustainable Forestry Initiative), PEFC (Programme for the Endorsement of Forest Certification Schemes) and Forest Stewardship Council(r)(FSC(r) certified.

Printed in the United Kingdom, United States, and Australia
by Lightning Source for Open Book Publishers (Cambridge, UK)

Contents

Publication Details	vi
Acknowledgements	viii
Introduction	1

PART ONE — EXPLORING BASIC KNOWLEDGE

Overview of Part One	29
1. Reflections on Moore's 'Proof'	33
2. First Reflections on the Problem of Easy Knowledge	55
3. The Problem of Easy Knowledge: Towards a Solution	77
4. Evidence and Transmission Failure	95
5. A Puzzle for Dogmatism	117
Interim Review	125

PART TWO — CONDITIONS ON KNOWLEDGE: CONCLUSIVE REASONS, SENSITIVITY, AND SAFETY

Overview of Part Two	139
6. Conclusive Reasons	143
7. Sensitivity	159
8. Safety	181
9. Safety: An Application	199
Conclusion	207
Bibliography	213
Index	225

Publication Details

Each numbered chapter in this book has been published in a peer-reviewed journal. Details are provided below.

Between the point of publication of the articles and publication of this monograph, many further changes have been made, such that even those chapters not designated as published in shorter form are different from the published versions. In all cases, however, the integrity of the published version has been preserved.

1. Reflections on Moore's 'Proof'

Published as "The Dogmatists and Wright on Moore's 'Proof'", *International Journal for the Study of Skepticism*, 2 (2012), 1–20, https://doi.org/10.1163/221057011X554133

2. First Reflections on the Problem of Easy Knowledge

Shorter version published as "Zalabardo on Easy Knowledge", *Journal of Philosophical Research*, 38 (2013), 177–88, https://doi.org/10.5840/jpr2013389

3. The Problem of Easy Knowledge: Towards a Solution

Published as "Davies on Easy Knowledge", *International Journal for the Study of Skepticism*, 4 (2013), 1–20, https://doi.org/10.1163/22105700-03011093

4. Evidence and Transmission Failure

Published in *Logos & Episteme: An International Journal of Epistemology*, 2 (2011), 557–74, https://doi.org/10.5840/logos-episteme2011245, available at: https://logos-and-episteme.proiectsbc.ro/?q=taxonomy/term/222

5. A Puzzle for Dogmatism

Published in *Logos & Episteme: An International Journal of Epistemology*, 2 (2011), 295–302, https://doi.org/10.5840/logos-episteme20112238, available at: https://logos-and-episteme.proiectsbc.ro/?q=node/91

6. Conclusive Reasons

Published as "Is Knowledge Closed Under Known Entailment? The Strange Case of Hawthorne's 'Heavyweight Conjunct' (and Other Strange Cases)", *Theoria: A Swedish Journal of Philosophy*, 2 (2009), 117–28, https://doi.org/10.1111/j.1755-2567.2009.01036.x

7. Sensitivity

Published as "Sensitivity and Closure", *Episteme: A Journal of Individual and Social Epistemology*, 11 (2014), 181–97, https://doi.org/10.1017/epi.2014.5

8. Safety

Published as "Saving Sosa's Safety", *Logos & Episteme: An International Journal of Epistemology*, 3 (2012), 637–52, https://doi.org/10.5840/logos-episteme20123413, available at: http://logos-and-episteme.proiectsbc.ro/sites/default/files/SAVING SOSA'S SAFETY.pdf

9. Safety: An Application

Published as "Reply to Pardo: Unsafe Legal Knowledge?", *Legal Theory*, 17 (2011), 67–73, https://doi.org/10.1017/S1352325211000048

Acknowledgements

For financial assistance, I am grateful to support from the National University of Singapore Start Up Grant (WBS No: R-241-000-126-133) in helping to make this book possible. It has been a pleasure to work with my editor at Open Book Publishers, Alessandra Tosi. More generally, I am delighted to be a part of this exciting Open Access press, whose vision for academic publishing I share. Philosophically, thanks to Martin Davies for extended, and stimulating, discussion, both during and after my time at Oxford. As well as learning about the topics considered in this book from Martin, I learnt how to become a better philosopher. Thanks also to other philosophers who have helped along the way. Further thanks to Chris Tucker (who, after the fact, disclosed his status as referee for this book) for extended written comments, and discussion. Finally, and most importantly, thanks to my family for their support during the writing of this book: Jackie, Edna, and Johnny (and crew).

Introduction*

This book explores two sets of issues in contemporary epistemology. The first part explores issues surrounding the category of basic knowledge (or justification) — that is, at a first pass, knowledge (or justification) which is immediate, in the sense that one's justification for the known proposition doesn't rest on any justification for believing other propositions.[1] The second part investigates issues surrounding knowledge-closure and various conditions, namely conclusive reasons, sensitivity and safety, which some philosophers have claimed are necessary for knowledge. Each part of the book is substantial (there are five chapters in the first part and four in the second), and the two sets of issues — while evidently of independent interest — are interrelated in several ways (on which more below). The Conclusion, which includes a prospectus for further work, ties the safety condition on knowledge (Chapters Eight and Nine) back to the notion of failure of transmission of epistemic warrant (an absolutely central notion in Part One).

Before getting to the substance of the book, some terminological remarks are in order. Knowledge is taken to be a propositional attitude. Thus our focus is on so-called 'knowledge-that', as contrasted with other potential forms of knowledge — most saliently, perhaps, so-called 'knowledge-how'.[2] 'Justification' and 'warrant', unless

---

* All footnotes are the author's own unless otherwise stated.
1 Our chief focus in this book is on empirical knowledge (and extensions of it through inference/deduction), though inevitably, at times, consideration of non-empirical knowledge becomes salient.
2 For a good overview of knowledge-how, and its contested relationship with knowledge-that, see Fantl (2012).

© 2017 Mark McBride, CC BY 4.0   https://doi.org/10.11647/OBP.0104.01

otherwise stated, are used interchangeably in this book to refer to that which makes it epistemically appropriate to believe a proposition, and this is commonly referred to as *propositional* justification or warrant. Thus — using the 'warrant' nomenclature — if S has propositional warrant for a proposition, p, we can talk of S having warrant *to* believe p (or warrant *for* (believing) p). Also, S has *doxastic* warrant for p iff S has propositional warrant for p and S believes p *on the basis of* his propositional warrant for p. If this is the case, one can talk of S having a warrant*ed* belief in p (or, perhaps, being warrant*ed in* believing p). My choice of which term to use on any particular occasion is determined by the term most commonly used in the debate into which I'm entering. Relatedly, I assume, consistently with there being degrees of belief or credences, that there is a workable notion of binary belief. Unless otherwise stated, when I refer to 'belief(s)' in this book, I am making reference to this binary notion.

1. Starting Points

The starting points for our enquiry are G. E. Moore's (1939) 'Proof' of an external world and Crispin Wright's (1985) discussion of sceptical arguments and, especially, his introduction of the notion of transmission failure. The following argument can be extracted from Moore's paper:[3]

(WARRANT FOR 1) I am having a visual experience as of having hands.

(MOORE)

(1) I have hands.

(2) If I have hands an external world exists.

(3) An external world exists.

My interest is not primarily in this argument and its logical properties but in *reasoning with* the argument. This reasoning involves inference, a mental activity, in contrast with the argument itself, which is an

---

3   In this book I do not enter into the exegetical question of how best to interpret Moore (1939).

ordered set of propositions. On the distinctions between argument and inference, the logical and the psychological, and for strong views on the *disconnect* between the distinctions' *relata*, see Harman (1986, 2010), who "reject[s] the idea that deductive rules like *modus ponens* are in any way rules of inference" (2010: 152).

As it is formulated here, (WARRANT FOR 1) is a proposition about Moore's experience. According to one interpretation of the argument, this proposition is a premise and the transition from this premise to (1) involves inductive inference. According to another interpretation, the visual experience described in (WARRANT FOR 1) makes it epistemically appropriate to believe (1) — and the transition from experience to belief is not one of inference. Whichever way the epistemic support for (1) is understood, the critical question is whether this support is transmitted across the simple *modus ponens* inference to the anti-sceptical conclusion (3). Wright suggests that the (MOORE) argument does not provide a satisfying response to the sceptic (1985: 437):

> Once the hypothesis is seriously entertained that it is as likely as not, for all I know, that there is no material world as ordinarily conceived, my experience will lose all tendency to corroborate the particular propositions about the material world which I normally take to be certain.

Thus, Wright continues (437): "Only if Moore already has grounds for [(3)] does [(WARRANT FOR 1)] tend to support [(1)]."[4]

Wright's purpose is not, of course, to promote scepticism; he notes that scepticism could be avoided "if it could be reasonable to accept a group III proposition [e.g. (3)] *without reason*; that is, without evidence" (1985: 459). In later work (e.g. 2004) he refers to the envisaged unearned warrant as 'entitlement'.[5] If we have an unearned and non-evidential warrant for (3), then (WARRANT FOR 1) does support (1). But, Wright says, it would be a mistake to think that this evidential support is transmitted across the inference from (1) to (3) (1985: 436–37):

> It simply is not true that whenever evidence supports a hypothesis, it will also support each proposition which follows from it. The important

---

4   For more on this, see Davies (2004: 215, 217).
5   Such entitlement would seem to be a form of *a priori default warrant*. For Wright's latest word on entitlement, see his (2014).

class of exceptions illustrated are cases where the support offered to the hypothesis is conditional upon its being independently reasonable to accept one in particular of its consequences.

Thus, on Wright's account, there is failure of transmission of epistemic warrant from premise to conclusion in cases with the structure of the (MOORE) argument. Warrant is not transmitted from the premise (1) to the conclusion (3) because the support for (1), provided by the visual experience as of having hands, is conditional or dependent on its being antecedently and independently reasonable to accept (3).[6]

Authors writing about warrant transmission and transmission failure often present principles concerning the (non-)transmission of warrant, and such principles will be mentioned at many points in this book. I do not *definitively* commit to any particular such principles. Throughout, I simply explore these principles, taking them — in particular, the results they mandate — to be answerable to a more general notion of epistemic circularity. Plausibly, it is because the (MOORE) argument exhibits a kind of epistemic circularity that it does not provide a satisfying response to the sceptic. There would be no evident circularity, and no correspondingly obvious explanation for the unsatisfying character of the (MOORE) argument, if our warrant to believe (1) ('I have hands') did not rest or depend on a warrant — whether earned or unearned — to believe or assume (3) ('An external world exists').

2. Immediate Justification and Basic Knowledge

We shall say that a subject has immediate or basic justification for believing p iff that subject is justified in believing p, and that justification doesn't rest or depend on any justification for believing other supporting propositions. This account of immediate justification is related to the notion of epistemic antecedence.[7] I prefer to leave the notion intuitive, and not to commit to a substantive analysis thereof. However, should I need to commit to a substantive analysis of epistemic antecedence,

---

6   For more on this, see Davies (2004: 217–21) and McGlynn (2014). See Moretti and Piazza (2013) for a good survey of *transmission issues*.

7   The very idea that there could be genuine instances of this to-be-explained notion of epistemic antecedence is seemingly called into question by some philosophers (cf. Chapter Four).

let me tentatively endorse James Pryor's (2000: 525): "Your justification [i.e. warrant] for believing $p1$ is antecedent to your justification [i.e. warrant] for believing $p2$ just in case your reasons for believing $p1$ do not *presuppose or rest on* your reasons for believing $p2$. Your reasons for believing $p1$ can not *beg the question* whether $p2$." It should be noted that the *analysans* contains several interrelating notions — presuppose; rest; reasons — which may themselves call for further analysis.[8] I shall make use of a notion of epistemic dependence, related to Pryor's notion of epistemic antecedence as follows: your warrant to believe p is antecedent to your warrant to believe q just in case your warrant to believe p does not depend on your warrant to believe q. A notion of epistemic antecedence more demanding than Pryor's would require, in addition, that warrant to believe q does depend on warrant to believe p.

I explore a contrasting notion of *temporal* antecedence in Chapter Two — a notion which some philosophers (e.g. Zalabardo 2005) seem, upon analysis of their work, to take to be *the* important notion of antecedence in these debates. Here I offer several quick notes about the relationship between temporal antecedence and epistemic dependence (and the theses I come to put on display will be implicitly utilised in Chapter Two). First:

(TE1) If warrant for p is temporally antecedent to warrant for q, then it's not the case that warrant for p is epistemically dependent on warrant for q.

If one can have warrant *to* believe p without (yet) having warrant *to* believe q, then the warrant *to* believe p cannot be epistemically dependent on warrant *to* believe q. One could, though — it would seem — have a warrant*ed* belief p without (yet) having a warrant*ed* belief q, even though warrant *to* believe p is epistemically dependent on warrant *to*

---

[8] A cautionary note about terminology: Pryor (2004) uses the term 'liberal' — to contrast with 'conservative' — to refer to stances endorsing immediate justification of this kind. (Such stances are liberal in the sense of *not requiring* — as a conservative stance would — justification for believing the other supporting propositions. And Pryor's dogmatism is one such liberal stance.) Huemer (2001: ch.5), meanwhile, coined the term 'phenomenal conservatism' to refer to (and endorse: see, *inter alia*, 2006, 2007) a stance of a kind which Pryor would refer to as 'liberal'. (For a recent collection of essays on dogmatism and phenomenal conservativism, see Tucker (2013a).) I avoid these labels, and thus this potential confusion, in this book.

believe q. Pryor (2012: 271) describes a position (not his own), according to which warrant *to* believe p could be epistemically dependent on warrant *to* believe q, even though warrant*ed* belief in p would not need to be *based* on warrant*ed* belief in q (nor even on warrant *to* believe q).

Second:

> (TE2) It is not the case that: If warrant for p is temporally antecedent to warrant for q, then warrant for q is epistemically dependent on warrant for p.

One could have warrant *to* believe p without (yet) having warrant *to* believe q, even though warrant *to* believe q is not epistemically dependent on warrant *to* believe p. After all, warrant *to* believe q might be quite unrelated to warrant *to* believe p. Part of my aim in Chapter Two's engagement with Jose Zalabardo — when I next return to consider notions of *temporal* antecedence — is to argue that *epistemic* antecedence and dependence are *the* important notion in these debates.

So, returning squarely to the epistemic domain, let us suppose — as an example of immediate or basic justification — that the mere having of a visual experience as of having hands gives one *defeasible* perceptual justification to believe that one has hands. Pryor introduces the notion of defeasible justification in the following way (2000: 517): "Our perceptual justification for beliefs about our surroundings is always defeasible — there are always possible improvements in our epistemic state which would no longer support those beliefs". Similarly, defeasible justification is "justification that does not *guarantee* that our beliefs are correct" (2000: 518).[9] If a subject has knowledge on account of having immediate or basic justification then we shall say that the subject has *immediate* or *basic knowledge*.

Importantly, focusing on the preceding sentence, it is 'if' and not 'iff': I want to leave open, and later in the book explore, a different form of knowledge, explored by Stewart Cohen (2002, 2005), aptly called 'immediate' or 'basic', which, importantly, *is not* — better: *need not be* — arrived at on account of having immediate or basic justification. (It may be that the 'basic' terminology *sits easier* with this form of

---

9 Cf. Williamson (2000: 265–66) on the putative *both-ways* independence of defeasibility and *non-factiveness*.

knowledge than the 'immediate' terminology.) Cohen (2002: 310) calls knowledge delivered "prior to one's knowing that the source is reliable" *basic knowledge*.

How best to understand this Cohenian basic knowledge? Consider (Cohen 2002: 309):

> KR: a potential knowledge source K can yield knowledge for S only if S knows that K is reliable.

Allowing for basic knowledge involves rejection of KR. Here is my understanding of such a rejection: it allows for knowledge of a kind that can be yielded for S by a potential knowledge source K even if S does not know K is reliable. It is *not* saying that only knowledge that is *actually* yielded for S *prior to* S's knowing that its source is reliable can be basic knowledge. Instead, even when S *does* know that K is reliable, S can still continue to acquire basic knowledge from source K. S can still acquire knowledge that could have been yielded for S by K even if S did not know K is reliable. (Of course, it is also the case that, if S does know that K is reliable, then S can acquire knowledge based on S's knowledge that K is reliable.) In sum, I understand Cohen's basic knowledge as a modal notion: a case in which K yields for S knowledge that p and S happens to know that K is reliable *may still be a case of basic knowledge in Cohen's sense* if S's knowledge that p is of a kind that *could* be yielded for S by K even if S did not know K is reliable.

Assuming I'm right on all this, the pressing question would become: what would it be *in virtue of* that we could have Cohen's basic knowledge? A natural thought at this point would be, given Cohen's focus on knowledge, to appeal to a notion of epistemic antecedence or dependence for knowledge: we could have Cohen's basic knowledge *in virtue of* knowing p not being epistemically dependent on knowing K is reliable. Now Cohen doesn't provide us with such a notion, but we might — at this point — draw on Pryor's (2000: 525) "exten[sion of] th[e] notion of epistemic priority to knowledge":

> [Y]ou count as *knowing p1* antecedently to knowing *p2* just in case you know *p1* and *p2*, and *the justification* on which you base your belief in *p1* is antecedent to the justification on which you base your belief in *p2*.

Now Pryor (2000: 521) himself notes that "connections between justification and knowledge are complicated", so we must be cautious here. I suggest that a subject S who knows p and knows that the source of that knowledge is reliable (q) can have Cohenian basic knowledge if:

> the justification on which S bases his belief in p does not epistemically depend on the justification on which he bases his belief in q.

I also suggest that a subject S who knows p and does not know that the source of that knowledge is reliable (q) can have Cohenian basic knowledge if:

> the justification on which S bases his belief in p does not epistemically depend on any justification to believe q.

It seems implausible that a subject S who knows p and knows that the source of that knowledge is reliable (q) can have Cohenian basic knowledge if:

> the justification on which S bases his belief in p epistemically depends on the justification on which he bases his belief in q.

And it seems at best unclear that a subject S who knows p and does not know that the source of that knowledge is reliable (q) can have Cohenian basic knowledge if:

> the justification on which S bases his belief in p epistemically depends on a justification to believe q.

Now this is only a first pass, but I hope to have gone some way towards connecting epistemic antecedence and dependence for knowledge (Cohen's focus) with epistemic antecedence and dependence for justification/warrant (my chief focus, and Pryor's). Moreover, though I have not settled whether or not we can in fact have Cohenian basic knowledge in any particular case, I have given a view of what it is *in virtue of which* we might have it.

It remains to depict the relationship between this Cohenian basic knowledge and Pryorian basic knowledge. Suppose, then, that some knowledge *is* basic knowledge in Cohen's sense. Does it follow that the corresponding justification is an immediate justification in a Pryorian sense? The answer is 'no'. Cohen (2002: n. 4) asserts: "One could consistently hold that basic knowledge in my sense must be based on other beliefs, provided it need not be based on the belief that the belief source is reliable." (And we may take it if the knowledge is based on *knowledge* of, or *justification to believe*, other propositions, it would still be basic in Cohen's sense.) Straightforwardly then, this knowledge wouldn't be Pryorian basic knowledge, which involves justification which isn't based on *any* other beliefs (or on knowledge of, or justification to believe, *any* other propositions). Thus, Cohenian basic knowledge need not be Pryorian basic knowledge.

What about the converse entailment? Is it the case that Pryorian basic knowledge must be Cohenian basic knowledge? This time, the answer is 'yes'. Cohen (2002: n. 4) asserts: "[A]ny basic knowledge in the traditional foundationalist sense will be basic in my sense as well." Now while it's not entirely clear what Cohen means by 'traditional',[10] this assertion is an important clue as to Cohen's intentions. Pryorian basic knowledge is arrived at on account of immediate justification — justification not based on *any* other beliefs. *A fortiori*, then, it isn't based on "the belief that the belief source is reliable" (Cohen 2002: n. 4), which is the key to securing Cohenian basic knowledge. Thus, Pryorian basic knowledge must be Cohenian basic knowledge.

Thus, summing up, we have two forms of knowledge which can aptly be referred to as *basic* knowledge. As a conceptual matter, there is no bar to a piece of knowledge being both Pryorian and Cohenian basic knowledge. But Pryorian basic knowledge and Cohenian basic knowledge are *independent* of one another: Cohenian basic knowledge need not be Pryorian basic knowledge. They are not, however, *both-ways* independent of one another: Pryorian basic knowledge must be Cohenian basic knowledge. Pryorian and Cohenian basic knowledge are, then, logically distinct — in the sense of not being extensionally equivalent. These two forms of basic knowledge are at stake as we move through Part One of the book, and are contrasted further in the Interim Review. (I hereinafter take care, where there is a potential for confusion, to explicitly distinguish between these two forms of basic knowledge.)

---

10 Indeed, his introduction of 'evidentialist foundationalism' — a Pryorian thesis — muddies the water somewhat.

3. A Pattern of Objection

Having introduced immediate justification and basic knowledge, we can say that there would be no evident epistemic circularity in the (MOORE) argument if our perceptually based knowledge were to be Pryorian basic knowledge; that is, if the justification to believe (1) provided by the visual experience described in (WARRANT FOR 1) were to be immediate — not dependent on a justification to believe any other proposition, such as (3). According to the epistemological position known as dogmatism (Pryor, 2000, 2004), merely having a perceptual experience that represents the world as being a certain way provides immediate, though defeasible, justification to believe that the world is that way.[11] So the epistemological dogmatist cannot appeal to epistemic circularity to explain why the (MOORE) argument does not provide a satisfying response to the sceptic.

On the face of it, this is a problem for dogmatism; and the problem generalises. Stewart Cohen (2002, 2005) considers arguments such as the following:

(WARRANT FOR 1) The table looks red.

(TABLE)

(1) The table is red.

(2) If the table is red, then it is not white with red lights shining on it.

(3) The table is not white with red lights shining on it.

Here it might be said, by analogy with what Wright (1985) says about the (MOORE) argument, that it is only if one has antecedent warrant (perhaps unearned warrant) for (3) that the visual experience as of the table being red, described in (WARRANT FOR 1), supports (1). If this is, indeed, the structure of dependence of justification in the (TABLE) argument, then the argument involves a kind of epistemic circularity

---

11 See Wedgwood (2011: n. 4) for a "claim that the process of taking one's sensory experiences at face value is primitively rational [, which] is similar in spirit to the position that James Pryor (2000) has called 'dogmatism'."

and provides another example of transmission failure. This seems to fit well with the intuitive view that simply looking at the table and following through the (TABLE) argument is not an adequate way of assuring oneself that one is not being misled by tricky red lights. (Wright, 2003: 60–63, discusses this same example — but with a red wall instead of a red table.)

However, according to dogmatism, merely having a perceptual experience that represents the table as being red provides immediate, though defeasible, justification to believe (1) ('The table is red'). Specifically, this justification does not depend on an antecedent justification to believe (3) ('The table is not white with red lights shining on it'). So there is no epistemic circularity and no failure of transmission of warrant.[12] This is a problem for dogmatism — the problem of easy knowledge (Cohen, 2002: 313): "It seems very implausible to say that I could in this way come to know that I'm not seeing a white table illuminated by red lights."[13]

Cohen (2002, 2005) raises a second problem for views that allow immediate justification and basic knowledge: what I shall, for contrast purposes, refer to as *the problem of easy evidence*, or *bootstrapping*. Here, the question is whether a reasoner is in a position to know, by racking up enough pairs of the form <I am having a visual experience as of P, P> (e.g. <I am having a visual experience as of the table being red, The table is red>), that my visual perception is reliable. In this book, I bracket consideration of the problem of easy evidence or bootstrapping. Principally this is because I am presently inclined to follow Wright's (2007: 43–44) proposal:

> A pool of evidence should be regarded as providing inductive confirmation of a hypothesis only if it is reasonable to consider it as drawing upon a representative sample. And that in turn requires that a significant prior probability for the thesis that counterexamples would have shown up in the sample if there are any [*sic*]. But the body

---

12 Pryor (2004, 2012) suggests instead a dialectical failing. (For more exploration of this dialectical route, see Burge (2003) and Markie (2005).) Davies (2009), meanwhile — on whom we focus in Chapter Three — explores both epistemic and dialectical realms in consideration of these arguments. (For discussion of Davies, see Coliva (2010) and Pérez Otero (2013).) For a useful survey article, see Carter (2012).

13 For more on this, see Davies (2004: 236–37).

of 'confirming' data compiled by chalking up pairs of the form, <It appears visually to me that P, P>, in the way described has no chance of containing any counterexamples to the contention of the reliability of my visual appearances. So it provides no inductive support for that contention in any case, for purely general methodological reasons quite independent of Dogmatism.[14]

I would simply add: if, by contrast, the body of confirming data *does* have a chance of showing up counterexamples to the contention of the reliability of my visual appearances, it *can* provide inductive support for that contention. Now I do not, for one moment, pretend that this can be the end of the matter (for one thing, there has been a wealth of interesting, recent literature on this issue); it does, though, at least explain my motivation for not devoting extended treatment to the bootstrapping problem in the book.[15]

The problem of explaining why the (MOORE) argument does not provide a satisfying response to the sceptic about the external world, and the problem of explaining why the (TABLE) argument does not intuitively provide assurance that one is not the victim of a trick of the light, instantiate a *pattern of objection* to dogmatism, immediate justification, and basic knowledge. And, at a very general level, it is this pattern of objection which forms the core of Part One of the book.

4. The Backdrop of Foundationalism

Before turning to the second part of the book, a matter pertaining to the *backdrop* against which the book is written — in particular, the first part of the book — must be addressed. There are two reasons for delving into this. First, at a general level it is important to be clear about the scope of the issues addressed head-on in the book. Second, and relatedly, it is important to note a particular epistemological approach falling outside

---

14 Wright (2011: 36) has since qualified this claim somewhat (in response to conversation with Cohen), and it is an interesting question whether the qualification is necessary.

15 I note that William Alston (1989) called bootstrapping 'epistemically circular' reasoning — and Alston's usage has become popular. While I don't dissent from this terminology, I use 'epistemically circular' in a different sense in this book. Finally, see Cohen (2010) and Wedgwood (2013) for interesting recent remarks on bootstrapping.

the scope of the book, as the adoption of this approach would lend a very different view of issues central to the first part of the book.

In a nutshell, Part One of the book takes place against the backdrop of a form of *foundationalism*.[16] And it should be noted that on a (much more) *coherentist* epistemology, many of the issues opened up in this book — e.g. the problem of easy knowledge — may well take on a very different form, or even disappear. (Relatedly, on such an epistemology, it is not clear how there could be instances of epistemic antecedence or dependence between two propositions, of the kind which might underwrite instances of transmission failure.) This is all a little gnomic. To make it less gnomic I need to do three things: first, say a little more about foundationalism and coherentism; second, explain what I mean by 'backdrop'; and finally, explicate why it is an upshot of a (particular) coherentist approach that issues such as the problem of easy knowledge alter form, or even dissolve. Pursuing these issues — in particular, addressing the upshots of coherentism for issues in this book — will involve analysis of Ernest Sosa's (2009) position on the problem of easy knowledge.

First, then, what are foundationalism and coherentism? Foundationalism first. Pryor (2001: 100–01) succinctly states the matter thus:

> According to the foundationalist, the justification for all our beliefs ultimately traces back to a set of 'basic beliefs', which we have immediate justification for using.

(It is worth emphasising that Pryor is using 'immediate justification' in the sense delineated earlier in this introductory chapter.) We can take this to be *core foundationalism* — a thesis to which all foundationalists must be committed. Within the genus foundationalism we can follow Pryor in prising apart two species — *traditional* (or *robust*) and *modest*.

There appear to be two characteristics or hallmarks of traditional foundationalism; one is a claim pertaining to the *nature* of the basic beliefs, and one is a claim pertaining to the *security* with which such

---

16 See Pryor (2001: sec.2) for a good overview of, and extensive list of references for, foundationalism's development in recent epistemology. I shall be drawing on material from Pryor (2001) in what follows in the main text. See also Fumerton (2000/2010) for a good survey of foundationalism.

beliefs are held by the believer. The traditional foundationalist approach to the nature and security of basic beliefs can be summarised thus:

> Traditionally, foundationalism thought that these basic beliefs could only concern the nature of one's current thoughts and experiences. (And perhaps some *a priori* matters as well.) All our other empirical beliefs, including beliefs about our perceptual environment, had to rest inferentially on this austere foundation of beliefs about our current mental states. These basic beliefs were thought to be exceptionally secure. They were often claimed to be infallible and indubitable. According to many foundationalists, the reason why these beliefs were so secure was that we had a non-propositional 'direct apprehension' of the mental states the beliefs were about. (Pryor 2001: 101)

Traditional foundationalism came in for persuasive criticism on all counts; and philosophers of a foundationalist bent have, typically, responded not by rejecting core foundationalism, but by adopting a more modest version of foundationalism than that found in its traditional precursor. This modesty is evident in a weakening of the foregoing 'security claim':

> Newer forms of foundationalism are quite 'modest', in that they allow basic beliefs to be fallible, revisable, less than maximally justified, and so on. They only require that these basic beliefs be immediately justified [...] (Pryor 2001: 101)

Additionally, there has been a sea-change in the 'nature claim' as held by modest foundationalists: "Some of these new foundationalists allow beliefs about our perceptual environment to qualify as basic" (Pryor 2001: 101). Finally — crucial for our coming contrast with coherentism — to be a modest foundationalist is not to rule out "important epistemic roles for facts about coherence, e.g. they may allow facts about coherence to defeat or to strengthen one's justification of a belief, even a basic belief." (Pryor 2001: 101) What, then, makes modest foundationalism a genuine form of foundationalism? It is its commitment to the above-mentioned core foundationalism — its commitment to a set of basic beliefs for which we have immediate justification. It is this modest foundationalism which serves — in a sense to be explained — as the backdrop for Part One of the book (and hereinafter I use the term 'foundationalism' to refer to this modest form thereof).

Now to coherentism. It should be evident from the foregoing that our resulting taxonomy is going to be more complex than a simple foundationalism/coherentism divide according to which foundationalism allows *no* epistemic role for coherence: foundationalism, we have seen, *can* allow *some* epistemic role for coherence. Before getting to our ultimate taxonomy, let us, in broad-brush form, set out a working thesis of coherentism:

> According to the coherence theory of justification, also known as coherentism, a belief or set of beliefs is justified, or justifiably held, *just in case* the belief coheres with a set of beliefs, the set forms a coherent system or some variation on these themes [...] By a traditional account of coherence we will mean one which construes coherence as a relation of mutual support, consistency or agreement among given data (propositions, beliefs, memories, testimonies etc.) (My emphasis) (Olsson 2003/2012)[17]

Let us refer to an account of justification of this form as *pure* or *robust* coherentism. Its purity or robustness is arrived at by dint of the italicised 'just in case' in the above quotation. Finally, let us refer to an account of justification allowing a *significant role* for coherence — in the sense outlined in the above quotation — but not adopting the 'just in case' claim distinctive of pure/robust coherentism as *impure* or *modest* coherentism.[18] (It is regrettably not, I think, as simple a matter as replacing 'just in case' with 'if'/'only if' in the above quotation to arrive at impure or modest coherentism.) And just as modest foundationalism can be *supplemented by* a role for coherentism, let us, plausibly, assume that impure/modest coherentism can be *supplemented by* a role for foundationalism.

We are now in a position to state our tripartite taxonomy: (modest) foundationalism; impure/modest coherentism; and pure/robust coherentism. One thing should be readily apparent. Foundationalists *can* allow and impure/modest coherentists *do* allow a role for coherence in the epistemic justification of a belief or set of beliefs. The natural next question then becomes: what determines whether an account of epistemic

---

[17] Olsson (2003/2012) goes on to provide an illuminating analysis of coherentism in much more detail.

[18] Wright (2011) also adopts the 'pure'/'impure' coherentism distinction, though he puts a somewhat different gloss on it. (The gloss is not so different as to render impermissible, in this Introduction, quoting Wright when using the distinction.) We will shortly come to see an instance of impure or modest coherentism which Wright (2011) labels 'frictional coherentism'.

justification that allows a role for coherence in epistemic justification gets to be foundationalist or coherentist? As one might anticipate, there is no clean answer to this question. My working assumption is that the *significance* of the role ascribed to coherence determines this: the less significant, the more likely we are to have a foundationalist theory; the more significant, the more likely we are to have a coherentist theory.[19]

Now, with this taxonomy in hand, I can explain more fully what I mean by the 'backdrop' against which this book operates. I've said the book takes place against the backdrop of a form of *foundationalism*. We're now in a position to see two related things. First, given the form of foundationalism in question is modest (and not traditional/robust), this backdrop is not stipulating away *any possible* role for coherence in a theory of epistemic justification. Second, and relatedly, this backdrop is not stipulating away impure/modest coherentism. As regards 'backdrop' itself, what precisely do I mean in this context? I absolutely do not mean that (modest) foundationalism's *truth* is presupposed: on the contrary, much of the first part of the book is an exploration — a testing — of its viability. (Indeed, one of the chief interlocutors in Part One of the book is Wright — a philosopher who would not ascribe to foundationalism in the sense delineated here.) Instead I mean something a little more nebulous: the first part of the book takes seriously the viability of (modest) foundationalism (compatibly with which, it also, we have seen, takes seriously *a role* for coherence in epistemic justification). Limitations of space regrettably mean that something has to give, and a corollary of erecting this foundationalist backdrop to the book is that extended treatment is not given to pure/robust coherentism.[20]

Beyond the independent importance of making this backdrop clear, why spend so much time on this ostensibly merely terminological matter? Because, as I want to show now, this backdrop has important upshots for the broad shape of problems considered in the first part

---

19   Three points: (1) Regarding significance: it is notable that the two examples, reproduced in the main text, which Pryor gives of a role that a modest foundationalist can ascribe to coherence are *defeating* or *strengthening* (presumably pre-existent) justification. (2) I assume that the impure/modest coherentist can allow a role for factors which are neither coherentist nor foundationalist (that is, I assume that it is not the case that factors that are not coherentist are *ipso facto* foundationalist). Nothing crucial hangs on this, however. (3) With all this in hand, we can plausibly describe our taxonomy as *exclusive*; it will almost certainly not be *exhaustive*.

20   And so the antonym of 'takes seriously' is not 'takes unseriously'.

of the book. In particular, I want to show that if — and, importantly, *only if* — pure/robust coherentism is adopted, problems such as that of easy knowledge alter their form entirely.[21] Put differently: problems such as that of easy knowledge — and putative solutions thereto — take the form as presented in this book against the backdrop of (modest) foundationalism, a backdrop which *takes seriously* both modest foundationalism *and* impure/modest coherentism (plausible forms of which assign *a role* for foundationalism).

One good way into this is by introducing Sosa's (2009) recently articulated views. More specifically, I will do this by focusing on Sosa's stance on the problem of easy knowledge — a problem which receives extended scrutiny in Chapters Two and Three of the book. Cohen (2002: 309) introduces this problem by presenting the following proposition, with which we are already familiar:

> KR: a potential knowledge source K can yield knowledge for S only if S knows that K is reliable.

Sosa (2009: 211) nicely charts consideration of proposition KR as presenting us with a dilemma: to affirm KR is to "face the problem of vicious circularity"; to deny KR is to face the problem of easy evidence, or bootstrapping (and also the problem of easy knowledge as delineated above). Here, then, is the beginning of Sosa's (2009: 239–40) response to this dilemma:

> The right model for understanding reflective[22] justification is not the linear model whereby justification is a sort of liquid that flows through some pipe or channel of reasoning, from premises to conclusion. (Such flow is linear, unidirectional; the pipe or channel "transmits" the justification — or warrant, or epistemic status.) A better model is rather that of the web of belief, whereby the web is properly attached to the environment, whilst its nodes can also gain status through mutual support. Any given node is thus in place through its connections with other nodes, but each of them is itself in place through its connections with the other nodes, including the original given node.

---

21 It is worth pointing out that, just as traditional/robust foundationalism has fallen out of fashion on account of the extremeness of its stance, so too has pure/robust coherentism fallen out of fashion.

22 I assume broad familiarity with Sosa's (2007, 2009) difficult *animal/reflective* distinction, though I delve further into this distinction later.

Now there is much to be said about this suggestive passage. First, though — and most importantly for present purposes — by looking at the passage in context we can be fairly sure that, though Sosa is acknowledging *an* epistemic role for coherence, he is not elaborating a *pure* coherentist picture here. As Wright (2011: 38) puts it: "So Sosa's view, although his recourse to the metaphor of the web emphatically commits him to coherence as *a* source of justification, cannot be such a pure coherentism."[23] It will, at most, be impure/modest coherentism. We can drive this point home by noting Sosa's remark that the web be "properly attached to the environment".[24] Now, while there is nothing, so far, to commit Sosa's impure/modest coherentism to supplementation by foundationalism, when we come to piece together Sosa's position on KR such supplementation is hinted at by Sosa.

Before moving on to Sosa and KR — a topic with which we shall conclude our introduction of Part One of the book — let's pause to consider a pure coherentist picture with respect to the easy knowledge case and the above-noted dilemma arising from consideration of KR. Wright (2011: 38) eloquently, but suggestively, puts things thus:

> Notably, there is no easy knowledge problem for pure coherentism [...] The Dilemma is precisely a problem about how to understand the justificational architecture of [...] rational beliefs independently of considerations of their systematic integration into a larger system. The ground is cut from under the Dilemma by the pure coherentist's willingness to disavow that there is any such well-conceived species of [...] rationality.[25]

Now this is all just to vindicate my claim that *if* we adopt pure coherentism, then problems such as the problem of easy knowledge — and answers thereto — are not going to take the form they take in this book.

It remains for me to vindicate — or, better, take a first step towards vindicating — the corresponding *only if* claim. Inevitably, I must be

---

23 Wright (2011) adds, here, in a footnote (n. 14): "And is much the better for that, many would hold. It is pure coherentism that is open to the McDowellian complaint about 'frictionless spinning in the void'."

24 This indicates some impurity in the coherentism only on the plausible assumption — which I hereby make — that a pure coherentist is bound to deny that the web of belief (as a whole) needs to be properly attached to the environment (as a whole).

25 I have omitted here Wright's distinction between *access*- and *management*-rationality.

more cautious — less confident — about this claim. My strategy will be to show that Sosa's impure/modest coherentism addresses the problem of easy knowledge in much the form in which it is presented in this book. I will then perform an inference to the best explanation: *all* (plausible) impure/modest coherentist positions address the problem of easy knowledge in much the form it is presented in in this book.[26]

Wright (2011: 39) notes that:

> Sosa's tendency seems to be to try to address the Dilemma by, as it were, distributing the distinction in the two kinds of knowledge [animal and reflective] across the horns. So: there has to be some knowledge (the animal) for which KR fails if knowledge is to be possible at all; but there also has to be some knowledge for which KR holds if knowledge is to allow rational scrutiny and organisation under a fully responsible epistemic perspective.[27]

Yet Wright (39) is correct to point out that, at this stage, we can simply "present the Dilemma as one for reflective knowledge".[28] Thus, so far, we have nothing like the radically different form — dissolution — of the problem of easy knowledge as mandated by adoption of pure coherentism. How, then, *does* Sosa explain the accomplishment of a transition from mere animal knowledge that, say, the table is red, to reflective knowledge of the same proposition?[29]

---

26 Two points: (1) This inference is made more plausible by the sophisticated nature of Sosa's account of epistemic justification. (2) At n. 19, I acknowledged that our tripartite taxonomy will likely not be exhaustive. In particular, neither Wright nor *the sceptic* would seem to fall neatly into any of our three categories, but the claims just made about Sosa hold for the sceptic and Wright too. Thus to establish my 'only if' claim, I likewise perform a second inference to the best explanation: *all* (plausible) approaches to epistemic justification falling outside our tripartite taxonomy address the problem of easy knowledge in much the form it is presented in in this book.

27 This is similar to Cohen's (2002) approach to KR (detailed in Chapter Three) — an approach Cohen acknowledges to be drawing on Sosa's work.

28 In a rhetorical vein, Wright (2011: 39) continues: "How are we to advance from the animal knowledge that the wall is red to reflective knowledge that it is so? If reflective knowledge requires reflective knowledge of the presuppositions of its acquisition, how is the latter to be accomplished?"

29 Wright (39) pauses to consider an impure coherentist answer, which he labels *frictional coherentism*, which is — perhaps surprisingly — not pursued by Sosa. In broad outline it is a "pure coherentism restricted to *reflective* knowledge and warrant". In essence, on this answer, we would have no epistemic role for coherence at the level of animal knowledge, and then an exclusive epistemic role for coherence in transforming animal knowledge into reflective knowledge. The key point for

Sosa suggests (2009: 239):

> Consider [...] one's justification for a given commitment (or its status as epistemically appropriate): say a commitment that lies behind one's belief that one sees a red wall [e.g. that in the present instance the appearance of the wall displays the actual colour of the wall] — might one's reflective rational justification for that commitment gain a boost through one's now basing it in part (perhaps in some very small part) on the belief that one does see a red wall? How are we to understand such boost in reflective rational justification?

Now this is all somewhat suggestive in nature. Here is one way — pursued by Wright (2011) — of connecting these suggestive comments with Sosa's impure coherentist account of epistemic justification. It is noteworthy that the foregoing suggestive comments of Sosa's occur immediately before the above-quoted 'web-as-contrasted-with-pipeline' analogy is drawn by Sosa. It is thus natural to take Sosa's answer to the question of how to understand such 'boosting' to be provided (in part) by the 'web model'. As Wright (39–40) puts it:

> [T]he idea seems to be that once a suitable web of beliefs is in place, able to receive and integrate new animal knowledge and take it up into reflective awareness, a *modest degree* of transmission of warrant — not enough, presumably, to invite the charge of "easy warrant" — from immediately believed (animally known) premises to those of their deductive consequences that articulate presuppositions for the acquisition of that knowledge, becomes possible.

Let us assume this is an adequate interpretation of Sosa. The important point for present purposes is that this impure coherentist account addresses the problem of easy knowledge much as it is presented in this book.[30] More specifically, even though this impure coherentist account, on this view, assigns the foregoing 'boosting' role to coherence, the KR problem of understanding the 'justificational architecture' of beliefs independently of their coherence is still a live one. The impurity of this

---

present purposes is that, insofar as frictional coherentism is not *unrestricted* pure coherentism, the KR problem of understanding the 'justificational architecture' of beliefs independently of their coherence is still a live one.

30 It should be emphasised that Sosa is interested, in the chapter under consideration, in both what we have called the problem of easy knowledge and the problem of easy evidence, or bootstrapping.

coherentist account ensures that this is a live question; in contrast with the previously considered pure coherentist account on which it is not live. It remains for me to perform an inference to the best explanation, namely: this is so for *all* impure coherentist approaches.

I take myself to have done the three things I set out to do in this section, namely: to explicate further foundationalism and coherentism; to clarify what I mean by 'backdrop'; and finally, to explain why it is an upshot of a (particular) coherentist approach that issues such as the problem of easy knowledge alter form, or even dissolve. (In this final task I have also sketched a view of a sophisticated impure coherentist response to the problem of easy knowledge: Sosa's).

5. Conditions on Knowledge[31]

Part Two of the book proceeds to examine three putative conditions on knowledge which have received much scrutiny from epistemologists since their proposals: conclusive reasons (Dretske, 1971: 1):

> R is a conclusive reason for P if and only if, given R, $\sim\Diamond\sim P$ (or, alternatively, $\sim\Diamond (R.\sim P)$);

sensitivity (Nozick, 1981: 172):

> [S knows that p only if] if p weren't true, S wouldn't believe that p;[32]

and safety (Sosa, 1999: 378):

> Call a belief by S that p "safe" if: S would not believe that p without it being so that p.[33]

---

31 For a good survey article of recent debate over these conditions, see Comesaña (2007).

32 Recent discussion of the (conclusive reasons and) sensitivity condition as a live option as a necessary condition on knowledge is not vast, but cf. DeRose (1995, 2011), Adams and Clarke (2005), Black and Murphy (2007), Cross (2010). For signs of change, see Becker and Black (2012), though it is to be noted that only a small number of the essays therein end up defending sensitivity. Roush's recent work (2005, 2010, 2012) on the sensitivity condition bears a special mention here. However, as her account (2012: 244) is one which "uses probability rather than counterfactuals, and in which the sensitivity condition is neither a necessary nor a sufficient condition", it does not receive extended treatment in this book.

33 Safety, meanwhile, has proven more popular than sensitivity as a necessary condition on knowledge. Indeed, it is its very popularity which demands the inclusion of a chapter in this book focusing on it: Juan Comesaña's (2005) putative

Exploration of these conditions on knowledge is evidently of independent interest (and I say more about this in the Overview of Part Two of the book). For now, I want to introduce two issues of particular interest when considering links between the two parts of the book.

The first issue concerns the conclusive reasons and sensitivity conditions on knowledge — conditions I attempt to render in as plausible a form as possible in Chapters Six and Seven, respectively. These two closely related conditions, while not identical, each license a rejection of knowledge-closure. (The matter is slightly more complicated than this: Essentially, to show a necessary condition on knowledge is not *closed*, isn't quite yet to show *knowledge itself* is not *closed*.[34] But this complication can be bracketed for present purposes.) For example, while one has a conclusive reason for/sensitively believes the table is red, one *does not* have a conclusive reason for/sensitively believe what is known to be entailed by this proposition, *viz.* the table is not: white and cleverly lit by red lights. This (controversial) rejection of knowledge-closure — licensed by adoption of conclusive reasons/sensitivity as a necessary condition on knowledge — leads to a straightforward solution to the problem of easy knowledge (assuming rejection of KR):[35] we can have basic knowledge that the table is red, *without it following* that we can have (easy) knowledge that sceptical hypotheses don't obtain (by simple deduction or inference from said basic knowledge).

The problem of easy knowledge is one problem for dogmatism; a second is presented in Chapter Five. Rejection of knowledge-closure seems to promise a possible solution to that second problem as well — at least, for dogmatism about *knowledge*. But the second problem also arises

---

counterexample to safety is the chief focus of Chapter Eight. For some other recent putative counterexamples to safety as a necessary condition on knowledge, see Vogel (1987: 212, 1999: 165), Hawthorne (2004: 4–5), and Hudson (2007). And for an interesting recent discussion of "a safety theoretic conception of knowledge", see Hawthorne (2007). Finally, Comesaña (2007: n. 21) interestingly notes that "under the assumption that p is truly believed, if p is sensitive then it is safe (under the revised semantics of subjunctive conditionals [gestured at in Chapter Eight, n. 2 of this book]). Therefore, counterexamples to safety as a necessary condition on knowledge are also (further) counterexamples to sensitivity." But caution is in order: Sosa, on whose account of safety we focus in Chapter Eight, does not always formulate safety in terms of subjunctive conditionals.

34 See Chapter Seven, n. 6
35 The problem of easy knowledge only arises for theorists (like the dogmatist) who reject KR.

for dogmatism about *justification*, and here it is instead rejection of a corresponding justification-closure principle which promises a possible solution.[36]

Do, then, my tentative arguments against knowledge-closure in Chapters Six and Seven carry over to constitute arguments against justification-closure? (Interestingly, Wright (2011: 31–32), for example, reads Dretske to be rejecting knowledge- *and* justification-closure.) To establish that they do carry over I would need to claim that these conditions (conclusive reasons and sensitivity) *characterise* justification. ('Characterise' is a hedging term.) Suppose one claimed that conclusive reasons or sensitivity are necessary conditions on justification. But to show that a necessary condition on justification is not closed, isn't quite yet to show justification itself is not closed — for the premise may fail to meet other necessary conditions for justification. Still, in any actual case, there might be no reason to suppose that the premise, which meets conclusive reasons or sensitivity, *fails* to meet any other necessary condition for justification. (And in the Interim Review I consider whether the dialectical context of a defense of dogmatism is one such case.) Absent any such failure, one can reasonably suppose that the premise is justified and that one has an exception to justification-closure. The exception to justification-closure would be *explained* by the failure of closure for the necessary condition (conclusive reasons or sensitivity), even though failure of closure for the necessary condition does not (for the reason given) *logically guarantee* failure of justification-closure. (Such is typically the way with explanation.)

Now even amongst defenders of these conditions, it is difficult to discern unqualified endorsement of these 'carry over' claims. (Interpretation of Dretske and Nozick on this issue is difficult.) But, while it would be inadvisable for me to push any such claim too far,[37] I do believe it is worthy of serious consideration.[38]

---

36 And I take it that if dogmatism about justification is false, then dogmatism about knowledge is also false. Importantly, the Interim Review makes clear that knowledge-/justification-closure rejection is not the only possible solution for the dogmatist.

37 One reason is that I do not have a particularly substantive account of justification. This book simply takes justification to be that which makes it epistemically appropriate to believe a proposition.

38 Cf. Chapter Six, section 2.6, where I am prepared to talk of "conclusive reasons in some sense *justify[ing]* belief in propositions for subjects".

I pick up on, and discuss, these issues further in the Interim Review (and beyond). And this linkage between the two parts of the book should be kept in mind as the conclusive reasons and sensitivity conditions on knowledge are scrutinised in detail in Chapters Six and Seven.[39]

The second linkage issue connects the safety condition on knowledge — scrutinised in detail in Chapters Eight and Nine — with an absolutely central issue in the first part of the book: failure of transmission of (epistemic) warrant. Martin Smith (2009) has proposed an intriguing account of failure of transmission of *knowledge*[40] in terms of the safety condition. (In particular, Smith (2009: 172) claims "that a failure to transmit safety is a sufficient [but not necessary] condition for a failure to transmit knowledge.")[41] I take it if there is failure of transmission of warrant, there is failure of transmission of knowledge (insofar as warrant is a necessary condition on knowledge);[42] but the converse entailment does not hold (insofar as warrant may transmit, but some other necessary condition on knowledge may fail to do so). Thus, there can be failure of transmission of knowledge without failure of transmission of warrant. (If such a possibility obtains, that would mean that warrant would transmit, but not knowledge.) One might then ask: if Smith explains failure of *knowledge* transmission in terms of safety, how will that help us understand failure of *warrant* transmission, if the two — failure of knowledge and failure of warrant transmission — can come apart? The answer is that, while there is no entailment from the former to the latter, the former may well be playing an important explanatory role in many instances of the latter. I discuss

---

39 For a good survey article on closure principles, including an extensive list of references, see Kvanvig (2006). It is worth noting also that many 'closure' principles which we encounter in the book, insofar as they involve deduction or inference, are closely related to 'transmission' principles. For subtle distinctions between different versions of closure, and their relationships to problems in this area, see Blome-Tillmann (2006). And for a closure-based proposed solution to the problem of easy knowledge, see Black (2008).

40 Smith takes it to be something of an historical accident that 'transmission questions' are formulated in terms of warrant or justification, and not knowledge.

41 It is again possible — though not common amongst participants in these debates — to conceive of the *safety* condition as *characterising* warrant or justification. (Smith, for example, does not do so, but cf. section 2.3 of Chapter Eight, where I am prepared to talk of safety playing some form of justificatory role.)

42 And so, if there is not failure of transmission of knowledge, there is not failure of transmission of warrant.

Smith's proposal further in the Conclusion. For now it suffices to note that this second linkage between the two parts of the book should be kept in mind while the safety condition on knowledge is scrutinised in detail in Chapters Eight and Nine.

I have aimed to produce a straightforward and uncluttered text, and to present the main lines of argument with maximum clarity. As a consequence, a not insubstantial portion of the words in this book are to be found in footnotes. I hope that an initial reading of the main text of each individual chapter will provide a clear view of its claims and strategy. The footnotes are not, however, dispensable; they provide background and connections, elucidation, caveats, and concessions. Ultimately, my investigation of the viability of allowing for basic knowledge, and into various putative conditions on knowledge, is to be judged on the basis of the full text, and not just the main text, of this book.

PART ONE
EXPLORING BASIC KNOWLEDGE

Overview of Part One

In Part One of this book, immediate justification and basic knowledge (particularly as these are conceived by the dogmatist) are exposed to a pattern of objection. One instance of the pattern is along the lines that, if perception delivers basic knowledge of a proposition such as the proposition that I have hands, then it would seem to follow that Moore's 'Proof' provides an adequate response to the sceptic about the external world. At the very least, there would be no evident epistemic circularity in Moore's 'Proof'. This poses a problem for immediate justification and basic knowledge to the extent that Moore's 'Proof' does *not* seem to provide an adequate response to scepticism. Other instances of the pattern of objection are presented by arguments that raise Stewart Cohen's (2002, 2005) problem of easy knowledge.

In the first chapter, I consider two prominent responses to the question of what (if anything) is wrong with reasoning in accordance with the (MOORE) argument — (MOORE)-reasoning. Crispin Wright (1985, 2003) says that (MOORE)-reasoning involves epistemic circularity, that epistemic warrant is not transmitted from the premise (1) to the conclusion (3), and that by engaging in (MOORE)-reasoning one could not come to have, for the first time, a warranted belief that an external world exists. A dogmatist (Pryor, 2000, 2004) maintains, in contrast, that (MOORE)-reasoning does *not* involve epistemic circularity, that warrant *is* transmitted, and that (MOORE)-reasoning *can* provide a first-time warrant for (3). On the face of it, Wright has a ready answer to the question what is wrong with (MOORE)-reasoning, while the dogmatist faces the problem of explaining why something seems to be wrong with (MOORE)-reasoning, even though it is not epistemically circular and does transmit warrant — the *(MOORE)-transmit* problem. The advantage would therefore seem to lie with Wright's view rather than with that of the dogmatist; but I contest that assessment.

First, Martin Davies (2004) has proposed a solution to the (MOORE)-transmit problem. Even the dogmatist can agree that, within the context of the epistemic project of *settling the question* whether or not an external world exists (a project governed by suppositional doubt about whether an external world exists), one cannot rationally deploy one's perceptual justification to believe that one has hands (see Davies, 2009: 364–68).

Second, I argue that, on Wright's view, there is still a kind of transmission of epistemic warrant in (MOORE)-reasoning. According to Wright (1985, 2004), by engaging in (MOORE)-reasoning, one cannot come, for the first time, to have some justification or other to assume or believe the conclusion (3). But one can come, for the first time, to have at least partly perceptual and evidential justification to believe (3). Thus, (MOORE)-reasoning transmits evidential warrant and Wright faces the (MOORE)-transmit problem.

Third, I argue — though in a provisional spirit — that the (MOORE)-transmit problem is particularly challenging for Wright because it is not clear that he can adopt Davies's (2004) proposal. The proposition that an external world exists has, for Wright (2004; see also 1985), 'cornerstone' status, which may not be consistent with its being called into question or doubted, even suppositionally. The upshot is that this first exposure to the pattern of objection leaves dogmatism no worse off — and perhaps better off — than Wright's view.

In the second and third chapters, I turn to the problem of easy knowledge. Reasoning in accordance with the (TABLE) argument (referred to as the (EK) argument in these chapters) seems to allow us to proceed *too easily* from basic knowledge of a quotidian proposition (the proposition that a viewed table is red) to knowledge of a conclusion that rules out a disobliging hypothesis less general than a global sceptical hypothesis (the hypothesis that one is being misled by tricky red lighting). My focus in the second chapter is (one strand of) José Zalabardo's (2005) response to the problem of easy knowledge and, specifically, an argument to the conclusion that there is no such problem.

Zalabardo's argument concerns the relationship between transmission of epistemic warrant and closure of warrant under known entailment. It is a familiar point that failure of transmission of warrant from the premises to the conclusion of a valid argument — as in the (MOORE) argument, according to Wright — is consistent with closure of warrant. On Wright's view, we do have a warrant for the proposition that an external world exists, but it is an unearned, antecedent warrant, and not a warrant transmitted from the premises of the argument. On Zalabardo's view, in contrast, warrant *transmission* itself presupposes a *failure* of closure. Consequently, unless the (EK) argument constitutes an exception to the closure of warrant under known entailment, (EK)-reasoning does not transmit warrant and so there is no problem of acquiring too easy knowledge by inference from basic knowledge. I reject Zalabardo's radical solution to the problem of easy knowledge and, along the way, subject key notions — especially warrant and transmission — to close examination.

In the third chapter, I develop my own solution to the problem of easy knowledge — a solution that is available to the dogmatist. First, Davies's (2004) proposed solution to the (MOORE)-transmit problem extends to the problem of easy knowledge. Within the context of the epistemic project of settling the question whether or not the viewed table is white with red lights shining on it, one cannot rationally deploy one's perceptual justification to believe that the table is red. But second, Davies's proposal is incomplete. There are pairs of arguments that Davies has to classify together despite the fact that, intuitively, reasoning with one of the arguments is less epistemically unsatisfactory than reasoning with the other. Third, I make a proposal about the epistemic property that explains the intuitive difference. Thus, it seems, epistemic dogmatism, immediate justification, and basic knowledge can be defended despite exposure to the pattern of objection.

I turn to a general theoretical issue in the fourth chapter. An important notion in the literature that we have been considering (beginning from Wright, 1985) is that of warrant transmission failure — conceived, in this book, as related to *epistemic circularity*. (Somewhat confusingly, Davies (2004, 2009) sometimes says that the limitation of (MOORE)-reasoning and (EK)-reasoning in the context of the epistemic project of settling the question — a limitation that can be acknowledged by the dogmatist — provides a second account of transmission failure.) However, there are philosophers who can be taken to claim that there are no genuine instances of transmission failure and also that the impression that there are such instances is the product of a flawed conception of evidence. There are large and difficult issues here, and scepticism about transmission failure may flow naturally from lack of enthusiasm for notions of epistemic antecedence or dependence. Nonetheless I aim at least to begin the task of showing that transmission failure is a possibility on most plausible accounts of evidence.

The availability of the notion of transmission failure (related to epistemic circularity) does not, of course, advance the cause of dogmatism. The dogmatist needs to respond to the pattern of objection without appeal to epistemic circularity and, on the basis of the first three chapters, the prospects for such a response seem quite good. In the fifth chapter, however, I describe what seems to be a more serious puzzle confronting dogmatism. Possible responses are discussed in the Interim Review at the end of Part One.

1. Reflections on Moore's 'Proof'

Dogmatism, immediate justification, and basic knowledge are to be exposed to a pattern of objection. I begin from Wright's (1985) discussion of Moore's (1939) 'Proof', and his introduction of the notion of failure of warrant transmission (related to epistemic circularity). I argue, against the standard view, that Wright's position does not enjoy an advantage over dogmatism.

0.1   Suppose one has a visual experience as of having hands, and then reasons as follows:

(MOORE)

(1) I have hands.

(2) If I have hands an external world exists.

(3) An external world exists.

Suppose one's visual experience gives one defeasible perceptual warrant, or justification, to believe (1) — that is, one's experience makes it epistemically appropriate to believe (1).[1] And suppose one comes to believe (1) on the basis of this visual experience. The conditional premise

---

[1]   This experience can be — indeed often for Wright it is (e.g. 2004: 170) — taken to feature as a premise. If it is so taken we will construe the transition from having this experience to coming to believe one has hands as (inductively) inferential. This is relevant to Wright's — but not the dogmatists' — focus on the *claimability* of warrant. I think this potential disconnect can be safely bracketed here.

© 2017 Mark McBride, CC BY 4.0

(2) is knowable a priori.² And (3) can be established by *modus ponens* inference. If one reasons thus, say one is engaged in *(MOORE)-reasoning*.

What, if anything, is wrong with (MOORE)-reasoning? I consider two prominent responses to this question — the *dogmatists'* and Crispin Wright's. Each finds fault in (MOORE)-reasoning, but on different grounds.

0.2   Let's start with the following accounts of (non-)transmission of warrant:

(α) Non-transmission of warrant

Epistemic warrant is not transmitted from the premises of a valid argument to its conclusion if the putative support offered for one of the premises is conditional on its being antecedently and independently reasonable to accept the conclusion. (Davies 2004: 221)³

(β) Transmission of warrant

A valid argument [transmits warrant] if [...] to have warrant for its premises and then to recognise its validity is to acquire — perhaps for the first time — a warrant to accept the conclusion. (Wright 2003: 57)

Wright's principle (β) can be contrasted with a closure principle for (an inclusive notion of) warrant:

(WC) If one has warrant for p, and knows or justifiably believes that p entails q, then one has warrant for q.

On the face of it, the key difference between (β) and *(WC)* is that the latter says nothing about "for the first time". Acceptance of *(WC)* for an inclusive notion of warrant does not require acceptance of a closure principle for each more specific kind of warrant.⁴

---

2   This conditional need not — indeed for Wright it does not — feature as a premise.

3   Wright (2003: 57) has a similar sufficient condition for non-transmission. My ensuing claims go through, *mutatis mutandis*, operating with Wright's condition for non-transmission.

4   Further understanding of why, for Wright, *(WC)* is exceptionless while (β) has exceptions must await the introduction of Wright's notion of *entitlement* (see 1.2 *infra*). Endorsement of *(WC)*, coupled with rejection of a closure principle specifically for evidential justification, is relevant to Wright's response to the *leaching* problem (see 2.2 *infra*) — the problem providing the stimulus for my claims to come.

0.3 Dogmatists, like James Pryor (2000),[5] can be taken to employ a notion of *negative entitlement*: in order for one's visual experience to generate warrant for (1), there is *no need* to have antecedent warrant for (3); in the absence of defeaters one has an entitlement — negative in nature — not to adopt the attitude of doubt towards (3).[6] For the dogmatist, then, there is (or can be) warrant transmission in (MOORE)-reasoning: by recognising the entailment from (1) to (3) the dogmatist is in a position to ground a belief in (3) on the very warrant that grounds his belief in (1). If there is (or need be) no transmission failure in a piece of (1)-(3) reasoning, the dogmatist must explore other avenues for finding error in (MOORE)-reasoning.

Wright, meanwhile, employs a notion of *positive entitlement*: in order for one's visual experience to generate warrant for (1), there *is need* to have antecedent warrant for (3); and we do in fact have antecedent warrant — an entitlement — for (3).[7,8] So warrant *is* — in the absence of defeaters — generated for (1); it is just not transmissible to (3). For Wright, then, there is transmission failure in (MOORE)-reasoning and, resultantly, no alternative avenues need be explored for finding error in (MOORE)-reasoning.

In sum, philosophers locating the defectiveness of (MOORE)-reasoning in transmission failure, as Wright does, typically take (MOORE)-reasoning to suffer from a form of *epistemic circularity*: it is only if one already has warrant for (3) that one can have a warrant for

---

5   Other candidate dogmatists are Burge (1993, 2003), Davies (2004, 2009), Peacocke (2003), and Pollock (1986). As a positive matter, dogmatists take the warrant one gets for (1) on the basis of one's visual experience to be *immediate* — that is, it does not rest on antecedent warrant for any other propositions.

6   The thesis preceding the semi-colon and the thesis following it are *both-ways* independent. Indeed, Pryor himself only explicitly commits to what precedes the semi-colon — the notion of negative entitlement is Davies's (2004) (cf. Dretske (2000)). At this point in the chapter no particular substantive notion of entitlement itself is yet operative (cf. 1.2 *infra* where Wright's notion is introduced). I characterise negative entitlement as the conjunction of these two theses, but this is merely stipulative. Moreover, one might endorse the thesis preceding the semi-colon while maintaining one in fact has antecedent warrant for (3) — see Silins (2007).

7   Again, the thesis preceding the semi-colon and the thesis following it are *both-ways* independent. I characterise positive entitlement as the conjunction of these two theses, but this is merely stipulative.

8   Cf. Cohen (1999: 76) and White (2006: 552–53) for such views. Cohen's notion of non-evidential rationality, in particular, bears clear similarities to Wright's notion of non-evidential warrant (see 1.2 *infra*).

(1). If (MOORE)-reasoning suffers from transmission failure in this way, we can say that propounding (MOORE) cannot offer a new route to its conclusion. As dogmatists deny that it's only if one already has warrant for (3) that one can have a warrant for (1), for them warrant for (1) can cross over the conditional to provide a first-time warrant for (3).

1. The Standard View

1.1 Nevertheless, the dogmatist thinks (MOORE)-reasoning can be problematic: is it really this easy to get warrant for the falsity of a global sceptical hypothesis? Assume, then — with the dogmatist and Wright — that something (at least) *seems* wrong with (MOORE)-reasoning. Consequently, it's a strength of any account of the structure of perceptual warrant(s) that it can give a plausible account of *why* something seems wrong with (MOORE)-reasoning. Call the particular problem of giving a plausible account of why something seems wrong with (MOORE) reasoning *given it can transmit warrant*, the (MOORE)-transmit problem.

I want to focus on the (MOORE)-transmit problem. It's seemingly faced by the dogmatist, but not by Wright: in (MOORE)-reasoning warrant is (or can be) transmitted according to the dogmatist, but cannot be transmitted according to Wright. Call this view of the (MOORE)-transmit problem *the standard view*. My claim is that the standard view is wrong. The (MOORE)-transmit problem is not just the dogmatist's problem, it's Wright's too: there's a sense in which there's transmission of warrant in (MOORE)-reasoning for Wright. And I make a stronger claim: not only is the (MOORE)-transmit problem Wright's problem (*contra* the standard view), it's furthermore more troubling for Wright than for the dogmatist. So, at least, I shall argue.

Why is opposing the standard view important? Assume answering the (MOORE)-transmit problem is not straightforward. Then, if the standard view is correct, a strength of Wright's account of the structure of perceptual warrant(s) is that it doesn't face the (MOORE)-transmit problem. If the standard view is correct, then to that extent we would have some motivation to adopt Wright's account over the dogmatist's. If it's wrong, however, this motivation disappears.

1.2 To fully understand the standard view note that, for Wright, (3) lies outside the domain of cognitive achievement: it's "outside the domain of what may be known, reasonably believed, or doubted" (1985: 470–71). Wright so concludes upon consideration of the following pattern of sceptical argument (437–38):[9]

> (a) All our evidence for particular propositions about the material world [...] depends for its supportive status on the prior reasonableness of accepting [(3)].
>
> (b) For this reason [(3)] cannot be justified by appeal to such evidence.
>
> (c) [(3)] cannot be justified any other way.
>
> (d) [(3)] may be false.

In responding to this argument, Wright accepts (a) and (b), but questions (c) — which calls (d) into question. Wright notes that (c) would be falsified if "it could be reasonable to accept [(3)] *without reason*; that is without evidence" (450). And if(f) such acceptance is reasonable one has *non-evidential* warrant for, or epistemic *entitlement* to, (3). For Wright, in (1985), it can be reasonable to accept (3) without evidence *because* (3) (and similar 'cornerstones' — see Wittgenstein (1969: 341–43)) lies outside the domain of truth-evaluability: (3) is, for Wright, not up for grabs as either true or false — it is *beyond doubt*.[10]

Wright now (2004: 167, n. 2) remarks, however:

> The major strategic contrast with the present proposal is in how such warrant is conceived. In [1985] I proposed that [(3)] might be regarded as defective in factual content and that accepting [it] might accordingly be freed from the requirements of evidence that I took to be characteristic of the factual. In the present discussion non-factuality is not assigned a role in making a case that rational acceptance need not be evidence-based.

It's one thing to say that non-factuality isn't assigned a role in making a case that rational acceptance of (3) needn't be evidence-based, and

---

9 I thus highlight Wright's *Humean*, rather than *Cartesian*, pattern of sceptical argument.

10 Wright, following Wittgenstein, also refers to cornerstones as 'hinge propositions', but I bracket this since talk of propositions is not easy to square with non-truth-evaluability. Finally, for an interesting view that Wright's and Wittgenstein's conceptions of hinge propositions come apart, see Pritchard (2005a: 204–05).

another to say that (3) is no longer to be regarded as non-factual. Wright here commits to the former (justificatory) claim, but makes no commitment to the latter (semantic) claim. The claims are distinct, and we can forbear from ascribing the latter claim to Wright, while respecting his shift with regard to the former.

Entitlement to accept a proposition P, for Wright (2004: 175), is *unearned*: I may have it "even though I can point to no cognitive accomplishment in my life, whether empirical or *a priori*, inferential or non-inferential, whose upshot could reasonably be contended to be that I had come to know P, or had succeeded in getting evidence justifying P". It's in this context that Wright introduces the notion of 'mere acceptance' of (3), as distinct from a more full-blooded acceptance, involving *belief*:[11]

> We may propose the notion of acceptance of [(3)] as a more general attitude than belief, including belief as a sub-case, which comes apart from belief in cases where one is warranted in acting on the assumption that P or taking it for granted that P or trusting that P for reasons that do not bear on the likely truth of P. Of course one may — sometimes irrationally — also believe P on such occasions, in the sense implicit in a conviction that one knows that P. Successful sceptical arguments may then embarrass such convictions [...] Such scepticism may prove to carry no challenge, nevertheless, to the corresponding *acceptances* and [...] warrant to accept — rather than to believe — cornerstone[s] may be enough to block the sceptical paradoxes that attend arguments to the effect that there is no such thing as getting evidence to believe them. (2004: 177)

Wright recognises a burden to delimit the scope of what we have non-evidential warrant to accept: "This is a good result [...] only if it is selective — only if the entitlements generated turn out to be cornerstones of our actual ways of thinking about and investigating the world and do not extend to (what we would regard as) all manner of bizarre and irrational prejudices." (2004: 195)

1.3 We've now considered the standard view of the (MOORE)-transmit problem. We can go further and consider how to *answer* it. A dogmatist answer has been proposed by Davies (2004: 238–43). Davies

---

11 Pryor (2004: 355–56) ignores this aspect of Wright's epistemology "to keep our discussion manageable". Unfortunately, without more, manageability is here achieved at the cost of distortion.

(now) claims that there is (or can be) warrant transmission in (MOORE)-reasoning, while conceding that something (still) *seems* wrong with (MOORE)-reasoning. But, if warrant transmission *in abstracto* isn't the problem, what is?

Davies suggests (2004: 240–41):

> [T]here is a kind of epistemic project whose conduct is conditioned by suppositional doubt, namely, the project of *settling the question* whether a particular proposition is true [...] Imagine that I undertake the project of settling the question whether or not there is an external world as ordinarily conceived [...] by deploying the warrants I have for believing the premises of Moore's argument. I begin the project by regarding the question of the truth of the conclusion of Moore's argument as open *pro tem*. So my conduct of the question-settling project is conditioned by the initial supposition that Moore's conclusion is, or may very well be, false[12] [...] [T]hen I could not rationally regard my experience as constituting a warrant for believing [(1)]. In short, I cannot settle the question whether or not [3] is true [...] by deploying the epistemic warrant I have for believing [(1) and (2)].[13]

This answer to the (MOORE)-transmit problem delimits the epistemic situations in which (MOORE)-reasoning transmits warrant. If Wright faces the (MOORE)-transmit problem, it seems he can't avail himself of this answer. Davies's answer to the (MOORE)-transmit problem rests on *suppositionally doubting* (3). But (3)'s status as a cornerstone, for Wright, precludes *its truth* being doubted — suppositionally or otherwise. (3) isn't — on pain of irrationality — eligible for doubt; it's to be unquestioningly accepted. Put differently: according to the 'cornerstones' conception of (3) in (MOORE)-reasoning, there's no question-settling project that can even be attempted. So, for Wright, the problem with (MOORE)-reasoning cannot, it seems, be that the

---

12   Davies adds elsewhere (2009: 369): "[A] fuller treatment of the project of settling the question would have to allow for the case where I begin by supposing that *it is as likely as not that Q is false*". So *principled* or *mandated agnosticism* (see Wright 2007) about Q — in which one assigns a credence of 0.5 to both Q and its negation — might seem to be a form of suppositional doubt about Q (cf. Chapter Three, n. 9).

13   Pryor (2004, 2012) suggests the problem with (MOORE)-reasoning is not epistemic, but rather *dialectical*.

argument cannot be deployed in settling the question whether or not (3) is true — for there's no such project.[14]

This is my (tentative and separable) stronger claim: not only does Wright face the (MOORE)-transmit problem; he faces it in a particularly debilitating way. I consider this stronger claim in section 3. First I need to demonstrate — *contra* the standard view — that Wright indeed faces the (MOORE)-transmit problem.

2. The Standard View Contested

2.1 Wright's analysis of (MOORE)-reasoning[15] *seems* internally consistent. But there's a wrinkle. Stephen Schiffer (Wright 2004: 177, n. 8) has argued that Wright faces what Wright himself terms the *leaching* problem:

> How exactly does [my analysis] promise to shore up the possibility of justified belief in [(1)]? We are proposing to concede, after all, that we may indeed have no (evidentially) *justified belief* in [(3)] — that maybe we can point to no cognitive accomplishment of which the effect is a reason to take it that [(3) is] more likely to be true than not — but countering that we may nevertheless be rationally entitled to accept [(3)]. But if standard closure principles govern justified belief, then the counter comes too late to do any good. Standard closure principles will have it that justified belief in [(3)] will be a necessary condition for justified belief in anything one knows to entail it. To surrender the former will therefore be to surrender justified belief in [(1)] [...] Maybe an entitlement to accept them nonetheless can be salvaged. But the idea was to use entitlement to save justification, not to replace it. (Wright 2004: 177–78)

---

14 Wright and Wittgenstein differ here, in that for the latter, but not the former, doubt about cornerstones is *not meaningful* (and hence is *not rationally possible*). For Wright, doubts about cornerstones *are* meaningful (and can be responded to by showing that they rest on a mistaken conception of warrant for cornerstones). But for such doubts to be meaningful is not yet for them to be rationally possible. More on this later, in Section 3.

15 Wright's (2007: secs. II and IV) is a general strategy to deal with *"justificational triads"* resembling (MOORE) whose subject-matter include "other minds, the laws of nature, the future, and the substantial past" (all of which can be "called into (Humean) sceptical doubt").

In short: if justified belief is closed under known entailment, and if in addition, as on Wright's view, we *cannot* justifiably believe (3), then — problematically — we *cannot* justifiably believe (1).

2.2 The leaching problem is a nice one. And Wright has a nice answer thereto:

> [I]t cannot be that evidentially justified belief is closed under (known/justifiably believed) entailment [...] But if we let 'warrant' disjunctively cover both evidential justification *and* entitlement, it can still be that warrant, inclusively so understood, obeys closure principles suitable to do justice to our strong conviction that 'justification' — pre-theoretically understood — should do so. (2004: 178)

In sum: we can preserve justified belief in (1) without it following that we justifiably believe (3). This involves abandoning the closure of evidentially justified belief under known/justifiably believed entailment. But, according to Wright, "[t]hat is not so remarkable once one notices that evidential relations themselves are not so closed" (178) — indeed Wright takes this to be the "minimal lesson" of Dretske's (1970) 'zebra' example. Closure is maintained, however, for Wright's inclusive 'disjunctive' notion of warrant (cf. principle *(WC)* introduced at 0.2): evidential warrant for (1), given (2) is known/justifiably believed, entails some kind of warrant — evidential or otherwise — for (3). And, for Wright, there's merely non-evidential warrant for, or entitlement to, (3).

The leaching problem originated as a *closure-based* problem for Wright. I want to use Wright's response thereto to generate the *transmission-based* (MOORE)-transmit problem for Wright. In brief, Wright's response to the leaching problem introduces a disjunctive notion of warrant; and reflection on that disjunctive notion of warrant prompts consideration of (non-)transmission principles specific to the *evidential* disjunct (see 2.6–2.9 *infra*). Consider (abstracting, for now, from these specific (non-)transmission principles): in virtue of an entitlement to (3) I can justifiably believe (1). The conditional premise in (MOORE) is knowable *a priori*. So I can believe that. And there is a simple inferential route to (3). So it seems I'd do well, epistemically speaking, to believe (3). This prompts the question: if we start out with an entitlement to (3), and then engage in (MOORE)-reasoning, should we, resultantly, come to *justifiably believe* (3)?[16] I think the answer is 'yes'. I'll argue (*contra* Wright) that *evidential* warrant does transmit in (MOORE)-reasoning for Wright. The resultant justified belief in (3) means Wright faces the (MOORE)-transmit problem. In essence, the point here is that there is transmission failure when there is epistemic circularity; but, I'll argue, there is no circularity in (MOORE)-reasoning involving specifically *evidential* warrant.

2.3   Let's fix rules of engagement with Wright. What am I granting Wright? First, his (non-)transmission of warrant theses (see 0.2); second, his notion of positive entitlement (see 0.3); third, his (putatively epistemic) notion of non-evidential warrant (see 1.2); and, finally, his (stipulated) disjunctive notion of warrant and its associated closure principle (see 2.2).[17]

2.4   What am I *not* granting Wright? First, I leave the question whether evidentially justified belief is closed under known/justifiably believed entailment open *pro tem* (see 2.2).[18] Here this is cashed out in terms of whether there is an entailment from evidentially justified belief in (1) — assuming knowledge/justified belief in (2) — to evidentially justified belief in (3).

Second, recall Wright takes (3) to be non-factual (see 1.2). So, for Wright, the question: if we start out with an entitlement to (3), and then engage in (MOORE)-reasoning, should we come to *justifiably believe* (3)?, is a closed one. Even if — *pace* Wright — (MOORE)-reasoning transmits (evidential) warrant, there's a sense in which, for Wright, one still shouldn't — indeed *couldn't* — come to justifiably believe (3). But to grant Wright this at the outset would be to foreclose the *possibility* of warrant transmission in (MOORE)-reasoning for Wright. We must, rather — in order not to foreclose this possibility — find a way to make

---

16   Cf. Davies (2004: 222–23) who describes such reasoning as *epistemic alchemy*.
17   See also my third response to Wright at 2.5 *infra* for a further concession to Wright.
18   I also leave open *pro tem* whether "evidential relations themselves are [...] so closed" (Wright 2004: 178). There is a complication here. In Wright's *presentation* of the leaching problem, he talks of closure under 'known' entailment. Then, in his *response* to the leaching problem, he puts 'known/justifiably believed' in brackets when considering the entailment. Finally, in a footnote (178: n. 9), he appears to be focusing on a closure principle where the entailment needn't be known or justifiably believed. Throughout, I focus on the most plausible such principles in which the entailment is known/justifiably believed (cf. n. 28 *infra*).

it possible to come to justifiably believe (3) by (MOORE)-reasoning while respecting as much of Wright's analysis of (MOORE)-reasoning as possible. Here are three non-conditional routes to achieving this:

(A) Leave it an open question whether (3) is non-factual.

(B) Grant that (3) is non-factual, but allow that one can come to justifiably believe (3) by (MOORE)-reasoning.

(C) Deny that (3) is non-factual, and allow that one has an entitlement to (but not justified belief in) (3) prior to (MOORE)-reasoning.

2.5 Each of these three strategies is worthy of extensive discussion and each faces possible objections. In brief, however: (A) has the merit of *not denying* that (3) is non-factual, but is vulnerable to the objection of not properly engaging with Wright, for whom (3)'s status as non-factual is seemingly *not* an open question. (B) respects Wright's claim about (3)'s non-factuality, but, by allowing a justified belief in (3) to be generated by (MOORE)-reasoning, it threatens inconsistency. (C), meanwhile, promises to generate more questions than it answers: if (3) is — *pace* Wright — *factual*, on what epistemic basis could we have an entitlement to (3)?[19] I thus assume merely the following conditional, which I take to be the barest commitment we must make:

(D) Even if (3) is non-factual this doesn't automatically rule out the possibility of coming to justifiably believe (3) by (MOORE)-reasoning.

That is, (3) may (or may not) be non-factual, but, if it is, this doesn't preclude coming to justifiably believe (3) by (MOORE)-reasoning. By endorsing (D) we can postpone the question of which of (A)-(C) is to be endorsed and proceed to engage with Wright. A corollary of the minimal nature of (D) is that it allows engagement with positive entitlement theorists other than Wright, who may share Wright's notion

---

19 See Wright (2004: 205, 2008: 506, n. 3) for inchoate answers *not committed to* (3)'s non-factuality.

of entitlement yet *not hold* that (3) is non-factual (cf. n. 8 *supra*). Our focus, though, remains on Wright.[20]

Suppose, however, perhaps predictably, Wright refuses to accept (D). Four (related) responses are in order. First, consider the following remarks of Kent Bach (online manuscript):

> There are many everyday *beliefs* and *statements*[21] *that are not true or false, or at least not straightforwardly true or false* (to borrow a phrase from Field [1994]). There are many common one-place predicates, such as 'large', 'poisonous', 'tasty', 'interesting', 'disgusting', and 'illegal', which do not express one-place properties but which we often use as if they do. *We use them in ordinary subject-predicate sentences to make statements and thereby express beliefs.* Although we say 'Fido is large' to mean that Fido is large for a dog, 'That mushroom is poisonous' to mean that it is poisonous to humans (we certainly do not mean that it is poisonous to all creatures), and 'Anchovies are tasty' to mean that they are tasty to oneself, *these utterances, taken strictly and literally, are neither true or false.* They are true or false only relative to something, something that these utterances do not make explicit (there are many sorts of relativity, e.g., category-, argument place-, location-, time-, reference frame-, and norm-relativity). They would be straightforwardly true only if that something were made explicit. (My emphases added)

Bach's remarks detail a substantive position in the philosophy of language, and I concede that there is no clear analogy between the statements Bach considers and statements involving cornerstones.[22]

---

20 It must be conceded that, if Wright holds to various (Wittgensteinian) aspects of his (1985) view, then he is not open to the (MOORE)-transmit problem. But it is far from clear that Wright does now hold to all those aspects. (D), then, can be viewed as a minimal claim offered as a starting point for engagement with a Wright-like character who does not hold to all those aspects of his (1985) view (cf. also (MOORE-EW) and (EW), introduced later at 2.9, for further minimal claims with a similar function).

21 Bach uses the asterisks "to leave it open whether *statements* and *beliefs* in a given area really are true or false and qualify as genuine statements and beliefs". So it is noteworthy that the asterisks are removed when Bach next uses 'statements' and 'beliefs', in the second italicised portion of this passage.

22 On a natural reading, Bach's point is that utterances of these sentences are not literally true or false, yet these utterances express thoughts or beliefs that are true or false. The sentences, even as uttered on a particular occasion, are not literally true or false because they do not specify something that is crucial for truth evaluation. Yet we use the sentences to express propositions that are true or false, propositions to which we adopt attitudes such as belief or doubt — and to which we adopt these attitudes sometimes with, but sometimes without, justification or warrant. So

Nonetheless, Bach's remarks reveal there is *conceptual space* (at least) for justified beliefs in the realm of the non-factual; and such conceptual space is all that is required for a defense of (D). Second, we noted at 1.2 that, for Wright, non-factuality is *no longer* assigned a justificatory role in making a case that rational acceptance of (3) need not be evidence-based. Given this downplaying of the justificatory role of (3)'s non-factuality it might seem dubious for Wright to then give it the devastating role of automatically ruling out the possibility of coming to justifiably believe (3) by (MOORE)-reasoning. Third, we can grant Wright, consistently with endorsing (D), that one cannot come to justifiably believe (3) *simply by redeploying one's non-evidential warrant for (3)*:[23] (D)'s consequent only speaks of not automatically ruling out coming to justifiably believe (3) *by (MOORE)-reasoning*. Finally, a different component of (D)'s minimal nature can be emphasised: its consequent only speaks of not automatically ruling out *the possibility of* coming to justifiably believe (3) by (MOORE)-reasoning. Endorsing (D) leaves open *not ultimately* coming to justifiably believe (3) by (MOORE)-reasoning. In sum, rejection of (D) does not seem dialectically advisable for Wright (recall, also, how much of Wright's analysis of (MOORE)-reasoning we granted him at 2.3). Nonetheless, should Wright resolutely refuse to accept (D) our focus would shift to an engagement with positive entitlement theorists other than Wright, who may share Wright's notion of entitlement yet *not hold* that (3) is non-factual (again: cf. n. 8 *supra*).

2.6 Recall, by (α) and (β) (see 0.2), and operating with Wright's disjunctive notion of warrant, warrant fails to transmit, for Wright, in (MOORE)-reasoning: one needs antecedent (non-evidential) warrant for (3) in order for one's visual experience to provide warrant for (1).

While Wright operates with a disjunctive notion of warrant, we need to separate the disjuncts again for our analysis of (MOORE)-reasoning. To see why (MOORE)-reasoning *does* transmit warrant for

---

Bach's point depends on the distinction between sentences (or utterances thereof), on the one hand, and propositions (or attitudes towards propositions), on the other hand. It seems clear, however — our concession — that neither Wright's nor Wittgenstein's notion of 'non-factual' relates to sentences that are neither true nor false being used to express propositions or thoughts that are true or false.

23 Cf. Wright (2004: 176). To allow for non-evidential warrant to *believe* (3) would complicate things considerably.

Wright, we need to set out two more specific, plausible accounts of (non-)transmission of warrant, catering for (non-)transmission of *evidential* warrant. Consider, initially:

(γ) Non-transmission of *evidential* warrant

Evidential epistemic warrant is not transmitted from the premises of a valid argument to its conclusion if the putative evidential support offered for one of the premises is conditional on its being antecedently and independently reasonable to evidentially accept the conclusion.

Theses (α) and (γ) are independent theses: (MOORE)-reasoning *fails to transmit* warrant by (α), yet *doesn't fail to transmit* warrant by (γ). So there is non-transmission of (disjunctive) warrant, but there *isn't* non-transmission of evidential warrant, in (MOORE)-reasoning. In other words, thesis (α) is met, while thesis (γ) is not.[24]

2.7 So the names of the theses can mislead, for satisfaction of (α) doesn't, as the names might suggest, entail satisfaction of (γ). How counterintuitive a result is it that (MOORE)-reasoning fails to transmit (disjunctive) warrant but doesn't fail to transmit evidential warrant? Warrant is a positive epistemic relation a subject can have to a proposition. Is it not therefore contradictory to say — as it might *seem* I want to — that (MOORE)-reasoning fails to provide one with a positive epistemic relation (disjunctively construed) to (3), but doesn't fail to provide one with a proper subset of that positive epistemic relation to (3)?[25]

We should recognise that, while (MOORE)-reasoning doesn't fail to transmit evidential warrant by (γ), nor does it transmit evidential warrant by (β). If the matter were left there, this would be an unhappy

---

24 It cannot be that thesis (γ) is met while thesis (α) is not: (simplifying) if it must be antecedently and independently reasonable to evidentially accept the conclusion, it must be antecedently and independently reasonable to accept the conclusion. And so theses (α) and (γ) are not *both-ways* independent.

25 Recall, transmission failure is the result of circularity. There is circularity of inclusive (disjunctive) warrant, but there is no circularity of evidential warrant. There is, I shall show, not first-time inclusive warrant for (3); but there is first-time *evidential* warrant for (3).

result. But we can construct a more specific, plausible condition for the transmission of evidential warrant (similar in form to (β)):

(δ) Transmission of *evidential* warrant

A valid argument transmits evidential warrant if to have warrant for its premises (including evidential warrant for at least one of its premises) and then to recognise its validity is to acquire — perhaps for the first time — an evidential warrant to accept the conclusion.

Now we have the result that (MOORE)-reasoning both doesn't suffer from non-transmission of evidential warrant by (γ), and does transmit evidential warrant by (δ). This is perfectly compatible with (MOORE)-reasoning suffering from non-transmission of (disjunctive) warrant by (α) and failing to transmit (disjunctive) warrant by (β).

2.8 Here's the dialectical position. We've four *prima facie* plausible theses of (non)transmission of warrant: (α), (β), (γ), and (δ). By (α) and (β) (jointly) there's non-transmission of (disjunctive) warrant; by (γ) and (δ) (jointly) there's transmission of evidential warrant. (Wright can't just elect to use (α) and (β), rather than (γ) and (δ). I'm putting all four forward as plausible theses. It's up to Wright to show those theses disfavourable to him to be implausible.) But what is counterintuitive about this? Sure, it is counterintuitive if reasoning with an argument can provide evidential warrant for its conclusion but no (disjunctive) warrant for its conclusion. To allow this is to allow a contradiction, akin to: x is a married man but not a man. But this isn't the result these four theses deliver. If a subject has evidential warrant for an argument's conclusion it follows he has (disjunctive) warrant for that self-same conclusion. No work to which these four theses can be put places this result in jeopardy. The only thing the four theses mandate is that evidential warrant will, while (disjunctive) warrant will not, transmit in (MOORE)-reasoning. Specifically, one's warrant for having hands — a visual experience as of having hands — *will transmit* insofar as it's (quite naturally) treated as evidential warrant, but will *fail to transmit* insofar as it's treated as (disjunctive) warrant. Maybe that's a little puzzling; but it's not contradictory.

2.9 To emphasise: evidential warrant doesn't fail to transmit by (γ) as the putative support offered for one of (MOORE)'s premises is only conditional on its being antecedently and independently reasonable to *non-evidentially* accept (MOORE)'s conclusion. This seems right. Why should having an antecedent *non-evidential* warrant to accept (3) preclude *evidential* warrant for (1) transmitting across the conditional to generate — crucially, *for the first time* — *evidential* warrant for, and justified belief in, (3)? A principle on which one might base an objection is:

(γ*) Non-transmission of *evidential* warrant

Evidential epistemic warrant is not transmitted from the premises of a valid argument to its conclusion if the putative support offered for one of the premises is conditional on its being antecedently and independently reasonable to accept — evidentially or non-evidentially — the conclusion.[26]

But (γ*) is implausible. Consider Wright operating with (γ*) when analysing (MOORE)-reasoning. He'd point out that having non-evidential warrant to accept (3) is a precondition for one's visual experience evidentially warranting (1). Fine. But (MOORE)-reasoning generates *for the first time* (Wright's phrase) a *justified belief* in (3). The only thing presupposed is the reasonableness of a *mere acceptance* of — that is, a non-belief in — (3). So it's unclear why the putative generation of a justified belief in (3) *for the first time* should suffer from non-transmission of evidential warrant.

My opposition to (γ*) is anchored by:

(MOORE-EW) One's having non-evidential warrant for (3) is no bar to one's acquiring evidential warrant for (3) in virtue of competent inference from (1), for which one has evidential warrant.

---

26 (γ*)'s twin *transmission* principle reads:

(δ*) Transmission of *evidential* warrant

A valid argument transmits evidential warrant if to have warrant for its premises (including evidential warrant for at least one of its premises) and then to recognise its validity is to acquire — perhaps for the first time — a warrant (disjunctively-construed) to accept the conclusion.

Note the confined scope of *(MOORE-EW)*. Perhaps its moral is extendable, *mutatis mutandis*, to reasoning by means of a more general class of arguments. One might, then, attempt to anchor *(MOORE-EW)* by:

> *(EW)* One's having non-evidential warrant for the conclusion of a valid argument is no bar to one's acquiring evidential warrant for that conclusion in virtue of competent inference from premises,[27] for (some of) which one has evidential warrant.

But, given our focus is on (MOORE)-reasoning, I commit only to *(MOORE-EW)*.

2.10 As a final dialectical point, suppose I'm taken to have failed to make out my case for the implausibility of (γ^*). As we're now separating the disjuncts of disjunctive warrant, we'd have two *prima facie* plausible (sufficient) theses for non-transmission of evidential warrant, (γ) and (γ^*), the former mandating (in conjunction with (δ)) transmission of evidential warrant, the latter mandating non-transmission of evidential warrant. This would be a puzzling state of play; but such a state of play is more troubling for Wright than for me. The onus is on Wright to show (γ) to be *implausible*. And so long as (γ) (and its positive cousin, (δ)) is plausible — notwithstanding (γ^*), *arguendo*, is *prima facie* plausible too — Wright faces the (MOORE)-transmit problem.

2.11 In sum: (γ) is not satisfied. There's no non-transmission of evidential warrant: by starting off with non-evidential warrant for (3), and then engaging in (MOORE)-reasoning, one generates — *for the first time* — an *evidential* warrant to accept the conclusion, (3). In other words, (δ) is satisfied.

This is what Wright must say (cf. n. 20 *supra*). He'll recoil from saying this: (3) is non-factual, and we shouldn't be in the business of generating justified beliefs in (3). Nevertheless, evidential warrant transmits for Wright, and justified belief in the existence of an external world has been delivered via a visual experience and a simple *a priori* inference.[28]

---

27 Of course, the number of 'premises' may be one: the relevant argument may be single-premise (cf. n. 2 *supra*).

28 So we finally oppose Wright's view that: (MOORE) is a locus for a counterexample to evidentially justified belief being closed under known/justifiably believed entailment (in part) *for the reason that we cannot justifiably believe (3)*. Consistently with this, we

The standard view has it that the (MOORE)-transmit problem targets only the dogmatist, but, with a more refined view of (non-)transmission of warrant, we can see it targets Wright too.

3. The Potentially Devastating Nature of the (MOORE)-Transmit Problem

3.1 Let's take stock of the dialectical situation: the dogmatist says that (MOORE)-reasoning transmits warrant — it can provide a first-time warrant to justifiably believe (3). So the dogmatist faces the (MOORE)-transmit problem. On the standard view, Wright doesn't face that problem because he says that (MOORE)-reasoning doesn't transmit warrant; rather it's an example of transmission failure. But I've shown Wright can, and should, allow that, beginning from an unearned warrant to trust in (3), (MOORE)-reasoning provides a route to a first-time earned warrant (based on perception plus inference) to believe (3) — provided, that is, we operate with assumption (D) (see 2.5). So Wright (too) faces a version of the (MOORE)-transmit problem.

3.2 One response — Pryor's — to the (MOORE)-transmit problem on behalf of the dogmatist is to say that (MOORE)-reasoning seems wrong because it's dialectically unconvincing. As Wright is committed to the idea that (MOORE)-reasoning suffers from a genuinely epistemic defect — *viz.* transmission failure — Wright cannot locate its defectiveness merely in its dialectical unconvincingness.

On Davies's (2004) view, (MOORE)-reasoning suffers not merely from dialectical unconvincingness; it also suffers from a kind of epistemic limitation. (MOORE)-reasoning cannot be deployed in the service of a particular kind of epistemic project that he calls settling the question. Can Wright say something along the same lines? Earlier I suggested not. Recall, Davies accepts there need be no transmission failure in (MOORE)-reasoning, but argues that, in circumstances in which one suppositionally doubts (3), warrant no longer transmits: one's visual experience won't provide a *rationally deployable* warrant

---

may ultimately wish to join Wright in rejecting this (doxastic) closure principle. We also finally oppose Wright's view that (MOORE) is a locus for a counterexample to "evidential relations themselves [being] so closed" (cf. n. 18 *supra*).

for (1) or (3). But, given Wright's 'cornerstones' conception of (3) in (MOORE)-reasoning, Wright isn't in a position, on pain of irrationality, *to doubt (3)'s truth* — suppositionally or otherwise. The question-settling project is conditioned by suppositional doubt, but Wright cannot allow that (3) is subject to doubt — not even to suppositional doubt. Wright (1985: 470) *does* say: "[Cornerstones] may, in a different context, take on a more purely hypothetical role; and [...] our confidence in them, in such a context, may be defeasible by empirical or theoretical considerations". I am not sure which contexts Wright has in mind, but while the *inputs* to the question-settling project can be "purely hypothetical" — in (MOORE)-reasoning I suppose, *just for the purposes of the project*, that (3) is false — its *outputs* — *settling questions* — are clearly not.[29]

For Wright, then, there's seemingly unfettered transmission of evidential warrant in (MOORE)-reasoning — a curious result. Let's briefly consider three responses to this peculiar outcome. The first two are possible responses from Wright; the third is a possible response from a hypothetical positive entitlement epistemologist.[30]

3.3 Response 1. To summarise the dialectic: (i) we outlined Wright's view that (3) is non-factual and so isn't eligible to be justifiably believed; (ii) we saw that (MOORE)-reasoning does, for Wright, transmit evidential warrant, and that, *despite* Wright's views about (3)'s non-factuality, Wright ends up with a justified belief in (3); and finally (iii) we observed that, *because of* Wright's 'cornerstones' conception of (3) in (MOORE)-reasoning (which, for Wright, entails (3)'s non-factuality), he's not able to doubt (3) — suppositionally or otherwise. Wright might seize on steps (ii) and (iii). He might contend that, in step (ii), I compromised one of his key semantic claims about cornerstones like (3) — *viz.* that they're non-factual — by pinning a justified belief in (3) on him. But then in step (iii), he might contend, I inconsistently relied on that self-same semantic claim by denying him the possibility of doubting (3).

---

29 If Wright were to adopt the view that cornerstones are no longer to be regarded as non-factual, room for (suppositional) doubt *might* open up. But insofar as cornerstones are still *presuppositional* in our various cognitive projects, it's not clear how such doubt could be explained.

30 These responses are, concededly, only given summary treatment here, and merit more detailed consideration. The claim of this final section is, though, as we've already noted, tentative and separable.

To answer this (and the third) response we need to have recourse to theses (A), (B), and (C) (see 2.4). In light of this response, (B) seems optimal. To adopt either (A) or (C) would disable us from taking step (iii) — doubt about (3) would then be possible. Only with (B) in hand can we consistently take both steps (ii) and (iii).

3.4   Response 2 (to step (iii)). Wittgenstein remarks: "Doubting and non-doubting behaviour. There is a first only if there is a second." (1969: 354) Drawing on this, Wright might claim: In step (ii) you lumbered me with a justified belief in (3); (only) once you've done that, I'm now in a position to doubt (3).[31] Having anticipated this possible reply I leave it to Wright to speak for himself.

3.5   Response 3. The claim that Wright cannot avail himself of Davies's answer to the (MOORE)-transmit problem relies on Wright's view about (3)'s non-factuality. So we might, to concretise things, consider a positive entitlement theorist employing Wright's notion of entitlement yet adopting (C) (cf. n. 8 *supra*). Such an epistemologist would be able to adopt Davies's answer to the (MOORE)-transmit problem — he would not be precluded from doubting (3). But adoption of (C) seems unmotivated, given entitlement is a putatively *epistemic* notion: when (3) is *ex hypothesi factual*, don't epistemic bases for accepting (3) require evidence, whether empirical or *a priori* (cf. n. 19 *supra*)?

3.6   There may be other ways for Wright to answer the (MOORE)-transmit problem.[32] But in the absence of any developed suggestions, there's a potentially devastating problem here. This is what I described earlier (1.3) as 'my (tentative and separable) stronger claim'. We might view the problem in the form of a dilemma. Limb 1: maintain *both* the non-factuality of (3) *and* (3)'s ineligibility for justified belief. However, we've seen (MOORE)-reasoning generates a justified belief in (3) while respecting as much of Wright's analysis of (MOORE)-reasoning as possible. Limb 2: allow (3)'s eligibility for justified belief (whether by

---

31   Strictly, to make this claim, the final sentence of Wittgenstein's must be: there is a second only if there is a first.
32   A (undeveloped) candidate: for the dogmatist, (MOORE)-reasoning provides a route to a wholly new warrant to believe (3). But for Wright it only provides an earned warrant to believe something that one already had an unearned warrant to trust.

denying the non-factuality of (3) or not), but maintain one *can only* assess (MOORE)-reasoning by means of theses (like) (α) and (β) (and (γ*) and (δ*)), and *not-possibly-additionally* (γ) and (δ). But there's no argument for such a strong modal claim.

4. Conclusion

4.1 We began with the question: what, if anything, is wrong with (MOORE)-reasoning? We've seen that one reason, according to the standard view, for favouring Wright's answer over the dogmatist's doesn't stand up to scrutiny: the (MOORE)-transmit problem is Wright's problem as much as the dogmatist's. In fact we can go further, though in a provisional spirit: the problem is, seemingly, Wright's in a peculiarly devastating fashion. So much for the standard view.

2. First Reflections on the Problem of Easy Knowledge

Continuing with the pattern of objection to dogmatism, immediate justification, and basic knowledge, I examine, and ultimately reject, Zalabardo's (2005) radical response to Cohen's (2002, 2005) problem of easy knowledge. Along the way, I discuss warrant, inference, and transmission in some detail.

0.1 Stewart Cohen (2002, 2005) considers a case in which his son wants a red table for his room. Cohen and his son go to the furniture store. Cohen's son is concerned that the table his father is considering purchasing, which appears red, may in fact be white with red lights shining on it. Cohen (2005: 418) responds with the following reasoning:

(WARRANT FOR 1) The table looks red.

(EK)

(1) The table is red.

(2) If the table is red, then it is not white with red lights shining on it.

(3) The table is not white with red lights shining on it.

(The (EK) argument is what was earlier — in the Introduction — called the (TABLE) argument.) If one reasons thus, say one's engaged in *(EK)-reasoning*. Cohen finds such a response to his son's concern unsatisfactory. Intuitively, believing (1) on the basis of the experience described in (WARRANT FOR 1), and then reasoning one's way to (3), is not a way of coming to know — finding out, confirming — that (3) is true. It is *too easy*.

0.2   Structurally similar reasoning delivers (knowledge of)[1] the falsity of sceptical hypotheses concerning the external world, testimony, other minds etc. Consider the testimony case:

(WARRANT FOR 1) Danny tells me he has a red table in his office.

(1) Danny has a red table in his office.

(2) If Danny has a red table in his office, then it is not the case that Danny has no red table but told me that he does have.

(3) It is not the case that Danny has no red table but told me that he does have.

Here, the intuition is that believing (1) on the basis of Danny's testimony, and then reasoning one's way to (3), is not a way of coming to know that (3) is true — it is not a way of confirming that Danny told the truth, and not a way of ruling out the possibility that he spoke falsely. It is too easy. The unsatisfactoriness, therefore, threatens to generalise.

0.3   (EK)-reasoning in outline: In each of our two examples (and in other examples with the same structure), the *immediate transition* from the experience or evidence described in (WARRANT FOR 1) to knowledge of (1) involves reliance on a potential source of knowledge — visual perception or being told by Danny. The transition would apparently be blocked by acceptance of:

KR   A potential knowledge source K can yield knowledge for S, only if S knows K is reliable.[2] (Cohen 2002: 309)

---

1   I use this parenthetical device again in Chapter Three: it signals that the key issue up for debate is whether such knowledge is indeed delivered.

2   Assume that the fact that a knowledge source is reliable does not guarantee that the knowledge source *always* delivers truths. So, to accept KR, know K is reliable, and then to engage in (EK)-reasoning is to learn something new, *viz*.: K is not misleading *on this particular occasion*. How counterintuitive this is (if at all), I leave to the reader. I also bracket problems concerning the individuation of knowledge sources. Finally, I read Cohen to take KR to make knowledge of the reliability of a source merely a *corequisite*, and not — more strongly — a *prerequisite*, for having knowledge by means of that source. For further exploration of this distinction, cf. Sosa (2009) and Van Cleve (2011).

But rejection of KR is not, by itself, sufficient to underwrite the transition, because the mere possibility of cases in which some source delivers knowledge prior to my knowing that the source is reliable does not entail that the present case is one such. Moreover, rejection of KR leaves open that there are other necessary conditions on a knowledge source yielding knowledge — conditions which may not be met. Cohen (2002: 310) calls knowledge delivered "prior to one's knowing that the source is reliable" *basic knowledge*. Many epistemologists — including Alston, Dretske, Ginet, Goldman, Klein, Nozick, Pollock, Pryor, and Sosa — reject KR, for various reasons, and with various qualifications. (For Cohen and KR, see n. 4.) Such epistemologists allow for the possibility of basic knowledge. The problem is that basic knowledge of (1) seems to lead to *too-easy* knowledge of (3). The conditional premise (2) is knowable *a priori*. If I know (1) and (2) then, given a plausible knowledge-closure principle,[3] I can seemingly come to know (3) by (EK)-reasoning. Thus (EK)-reasoning transforms *basic* knowledge of an everyday proposition about the colour of a table into *easy* knowledge of the falsity of a sceptical hypothesis. The generation of easy knowledge "suggests that we were wrong to think we had the basic knowledge in the first place" (Cohen 2002: 311). Thus the *problem* of easy knowledge.[4]

0.4 Cohen is convinced that (EK)-reasoning is an unsatisfactory response to his son:

> [I]t seems very implausible to say I could in this way come to know that I'm not seeing a white table illuminated by red lights. Note that on this view, my inductive evidence against the possibility that there are red lights shining on the table turns out to be irrelevant to my knowing that

---

3 Say: If S knows p and S knows p entails q, then S knows (or at least is in a position to know) q. Knowledge-closure principles have been denied by Dretske (1970, 1971, 2005) and Nozick (1981). This denial hasn't proven popular, however (see Hawthorne 2005). (Knowledge-closure is discussed in detail in Chapters Six and Seven.)

4 *Cohen's* response to the problem (2002, 2005) involves distinguishing between *animal* and *reflective* knowledge (cf. Sosa 2007, 2009). KR is rejected when considering animal knowledge, but so is deductive closure (cf. 1.7 *infra*). When considering reflective knowledge, meanwhile, KR is accepted. Either way: no problem of easy knowledge. Cohen (2002: sec. VI, 322), more positively, appeals to a *holism* on which "[g]radually, as we acquire more and more sensory evidence, thereby accumulating a relatively large and coherent set of beliefs, those beliefs, including the belief that our cognitive faculties (perception, memory, reasoning) are reliable become knowledge".

the table is not white with red lights shining on it. This is surely a strange result. (Cohen 2002: 313)

We'll follow Cohen by talking of the *unsatisfactoriness* of (EK)-reasoning, but such talk involves no suggestion that the reasoning is somehow invalid. Nor are we committed to denying many plausible knowledge-closure principles (cf. n. 3 *supra*). It is a further — so-called *bootstrapping* — question whether S is in a *position to know*, in some way, that K is reliable. Instead, all we mean is that a subject is *epistemically criticisable* in attempting to *acquire* knowledge of (3) — to find out or to confirm that (3) is true — *by means of (EK)-reasoning*.

1. Zalabardo's Response

1.1   I want to sketch (one strand of)[5] José Zalabardo's (2005) original and heterodox response to the problem of easy knowledge. By consideration of Zalabardo's response we can gain insight into the nature of *warrant*, *inference*, and *transmission (of warrant)*.

1.2   Before reconstructing Zalabardo's argument, let's take note of two key principles (or: schemata) operative therein (where 'S' is a placeholder for a subject, and 'p' and 'q' for propositions):

Closure: If p has warrant for S,[6] and S knows that p entails q, then q has warrant for S. (36)

Transmission: If p entails q and S knows that p,[7] then inferring q from p[8] would enable S to obtain warrant for q. (39)

---

5   Another strand — Zalabardo's starting point — focuses on bootstrapping.
6   My note: 'p has warrant for S' is equivalent to 'S has warrant for p'.
7   My note: (1) Could we, without loss, weaken the antecedent of *Transmission* by replacing 'S knows that p' with 'p has warrant for S'? Or indeed, weaker still, saying *nothing* about S's epistemic position *vis-a-vis* p? (Suppose S has no warrant for p, but has warrant for a proposition in the neighbourhood of p, p'. Could S infer q from p and thereby obtain p'-warrant for q?) Perhaps. I suspect Zalabardo wants to sidestep issues over inferring from unknown premises. (2) As hinted at already, *Transmission* is somewhat strange on account of the antecedent not *explicitly* mentioning warrant (yet that is what is supposed to be transmitted).
8   The inference of q from p must, I take it, be deductive — though the deduction need not consist of a formally valid argument — and performed competently (cf. Hawthorne 2004: 34–35).

When I talk generically I'll use lower-case 'closure' and 'transmission'. *Closure* and *Transmission* are valid schemata just in case — iff — they have no false instances; invalid otherwise.[9] Thus we can talk of the truth or falsity of an instance of the schema *Closure*. The schema will be instantiated to a particular subject and a particular set of propositions. For brevity, and somewhat loosely, we can talk of an instance of *Closure in an argument*. And we can talk of the truth or falsity of an instance of *Transmission* in a particular *piece of reasoning* with an argument.[10] Say there is *Transmission* (of warrant) — warrant *Transmits* — just in case, the instance of the schema *Transmission*, in a particular piece of reasoning, has a true antecedent and a true consequent. (So this is equivalent to an instance of *Transmission*'s non-vacuous truth.) And say there is not *Transmission* (of warrant) just in case, in a particular piece of reasoning, *Transmission* has either a false antecedent or a true antecedent and a false consequent. (So this is equivalent, respectively, to either an instance of *Transmission*'s vacuous truth or its falsity.) And say finally there is *Transmission* failure — or non-*Transmission* — just in case, in a particular piece of reasoning, *Transmission* has a true antecedent and a false consequent. (So this is equivalent to an instance of *Transmission*'s falsity.) So, that there is not *Transmission* does not entail *Transmission* failure; the converse entailment, however, holds.

1.3   We might reconstruct Zalabardo's response to the problem of easy knowledge as follows:

---

9   Note that Zalabardo is not endorsing *Transmission*'s — cf. *Closure*'s — *validity*, given he allows for instances of transmission *failure*. Thus, to give a complete account of transmission, it would seem that Zalabardo must either reformulate Transmission to render it valid (e.g. for him, as we'll see, making '*S has no warrant for q prior to inference*' a condition of the antecedent), or supplement *Transmission* with a *trouser-wearing*, putatively *valid* (sufficient) condition for transmission *failure*.

10 *Transmission* is an indicative conditional whose consequent is a subjunctive conditional. In evaluating *Transmission* in a particular piece of reasoning with an argument we assume the truth of the antecedent of that subjunctive conditional — we assume, that is, the *performance* of an inference. In what follows we are investigating the (temporal) preconditions on inference.

(ZALABARDO)

(A) The problem of easy knowledge presupposes *Transmission* of warrant in (EK)-reasoning.

(B) *Transmission* of warrant in (EK)-reasoning presupposes the falsity of an instance of *Closure* in (EK).

(C) But *Closure* is valid, and thus has no false instances.

(D) So, from (B) and (C): There is no *Transmission* of warrant in (EK)-reasoning.

(E) So, from (A) and (D): There is no problem of easy knowledge.

The argument is clearly valid. If it is to be resisted, one or other of its premises must be shown to be false.

1.4   Argument (A)-(E) needs unpacking. We need to cash out Zalabardo's closure and transmission principles. Zalabardo remarks (39):

> [T]ransmission is different from, and independent of, Closure. Transmission postulates a sufficient condition for an inference to have the power to furnish the subject with warrant for its conclusion. Closure, by contrast, imposes a constraint on an admissible combination of warrant attributions to a subject: that for all propositions p, q and every subject S, if we ascribe to S knowledge that p entails q, we should not ascribe to her warrant for p without also ascribing to her warrant for q. (footnote omitted)

Note that *Transmission* is posed as a *sufficient* (and not *necessary*) condition. Thus it is left open that other transmission principles are operative.[11] A result of this is that the fact that there is not *Transmission* in a piece of reasoning does not entail that that piece of reasoning does not transmit warrant. And nor does the fact that there is *Transmission* failure in reasoning entail that that reasoning suffers transmission failure.

1.5   For Zalabardo, "when p is true and S believes that p, S will know that p just in case p has warrant for S" (33). In other words, 'warrant' operates as a placeholder for whatever is required, in addition to

---

11   Often, though, proponents of sufficient transmission conditions (tacitly) take them to be *lone* sufficient conditions.

a true belief, to constitute knowledge (see Plantinga 1993).[12] Let's locate this usage of 'warrant' with respect to two prominent types of warrant — *propositional* and *doxastic*. A subject, S, has propositional warrant for a proposition, p, iff it is epistemically appropriate for S to believe p (notwithstanding S may not in fact believe p) (see Goldman 1979). (I leave open whether a thinker could have propositional warrant to believe a proposition p even though the thinker had never even conceptualised the proposition, p.) And if this is the case, one can talk of S having warrant *to* believe p (or warrant *for* (believing) p).[13] Meanwhile, S has doxastic warrant for p iff S has propositional warrant for p and S believes p *on the basis of*[14] his propositional warrant for p. If this is the case, one can talk of S having a warrant*ed* belief in p.

How does Zalabardo's (Plantingan) notion of warrant fit into this taxonomy? First, it's *not-merely-propositional*, as there is nothing in the definition of propositional warrant which guarantees — as Zalabardo's warrant does — that adding it to a true belief gets one knowledge. For one thing, one's having propositional warrant leaves open that one's true belief is not *based on* the propositional warrant: the mere availability of a warrant, even availability to the thinker in question, is not sufficient, when added to a true belief, for knowledge. Additionally, it's *not doxastic*, as it's left open that Zalabardo's warrant is in place for a proposition absent that proposition being believed. So Zalabardo's (Plantingan) warrant occupies a middle ground of being *not-merely-propositional* but *not doxastic* either.[15]

1.6 Insofar as Zalabardo's notion of warrant is not the notion of warranted belief — doxastic warrant — consider Nicholas Silins's (2005: 75–77) claim that debates over transmission of warrant oughtn't to be

---

12 So the possibility of *Gettierisation* is stipulated away. I don't question *Closure*'s validity in this chapter, though it is psychologically questionable on account of this usage of 'warrant'. Principles like *Closure*, operating with this Plantingan, *Gettier-proof* notion of warrant, have not received much scrutiny.
13 The *propositional* reading of the 'warrant for believing' locution is not, it seems, in line with Silins (2005: 74), but is in line with Pryor (2001: 104) and others.
14 The *basing relation* is left undeveloped here (see Korcz 2006).
15 The basing relation presents a bit of a problem for Zalabardo's (Plantingan) approach. If true belief plus warrant equals knowledge, then warrant needs to include basing. But it is not easy to see how warrant that includes basing could be present in the absence of belief.

conducted in terms of the notion of warrant to believe — propositional warrant (cf. also Tucker (2010)):

> [I]t is too demanding to define transmission of warrant in terms of acquisition of [propositional] warrant [...] To see this, note that many cases of transmission of [propositional] warrant [...] would be *automatic*. For example, if you believe on the basis of some warrant that Moby Dick is a whale (and you know that all whales are mammals), then you have [propositional] warrant [...] that Moby Dick is a mammal regardless of whether you have inferred the conclusion or not. Moreover, you cannot acquire [propositional] warrant [...] that Moby Dick is a mammal by reasoning from the proposition that Moby Dick is a whale. Rather than provide you with new evidence to believe that Moby Dick is a mammal, the inference would instead allow you to base a belief on evidence you already had to believe the conclusion. The upshot is that, if we define transmission of warrant so as to require the acquisition of [propositional] warrant [...], many legitimate pieces of reasoning will then suffer from failure of transmission of warrant. For example your inference that Moby Dick is a mammal from the proposition that Moby Dick is a whale will fail to transmit warrant. But such a verdict is far too harsh. After all, you can acquire [doxastic] warrant [...] [for] the conclusion through the inference, that is, you can come to believe the conclusion on the *basis* of a warrant through the inference.

Closure of propositional warrant under known entailment (*CPW*) requires that, if a thinker has some warrant or other to believe p and knows that p entails q, then that thinker has some warrant or other to believe q. As a conceptual point, *CPW* does not impose any constraints on the nature of the warrant to believe q. It does not say, for example, that the warrant to believe q should be partly constituted out of the warrant to believe p. For example, suppose that (contrary to fact) it were a metaphysical necessity that, for each thinker x, if x is situated in such a way that a warrant to believe p (Moby Dick is a whale) becomes available to x and x knows that p entails q, then x is visited by *the oracle* and is told on the highest epistemic authority that q, thereby being provided with a warrant to believe q (Moby Dick is a mammal). That would be sufficient for the metaphysically necessary satisfaction of *CPW* in this case. But the foregoing is not what Silins describes as *automatic transmission* of propositional warrant. The warrant to believe q that Silins says one has automatically, if one has a warrant to believe p and knows that p entails q, has the following property: if a thinker were to base his belief on the propositional warrant that is automatically 'transmitted' then that thinker would be basing his belief q in part on the propositional warrant to believe p (and in part on the warrant to take the step of inference from p to q). In contrast, if the thinker in our strange story were to base his belief on the propositional warrant to believe q that makes *CPW* come out true (that is, were to base his belief on the word of the oracle),[16] then that thinker would not be basing his belief q in part on the propositional warrant to believe p. In our strange story, a thinker who bases his belief that Moby Dick is a mammal on the word of the oracle is basing his belief on a warrant that is *epistemically independent* from, and not *epistemically posterior* to, the warrant to believe that Moby Dick is a whale. In contrast, the warrant to believe that Moby Dick is a mammal, which is (according to Silins) automatically available to a thinker who has a warrant to believe that Moby Dick is a whale and who knows that all whales are mammals, is *epistemically dependent* on, and epistemically posterior to, the warrant to believe that Moby Dick is a whale.

If Silins were right that having a warrant to believe p and knowing that p entails q (and being a competent thinker, perhaps) adds up to having a warrant to believe q,[17] then this fact would guarantee *CPW* (for competent thinkers). But, conversely, *CPW* does not guarantee that Silins is right. Again, if Silins were right, he might call the principle that he would be right about: transmission of propositional warrant under known entailment (for competent thinkers) — *TPW*. *TPW* might even be *exceptionless*: that is, there might be *no failures* of *TPW*. If there were no failures of this kind of transmission of warrant, then we might infer that this kind of transmission of warrant was not exactly what was under discussion in debates over failures of warrant transmission.[18]

---

16   Perhaps it can be shown that an epistemically ideal thinker would never base his belief q on the warrant made available by the oracle; but neither *Transmission* nor *Closure* says anything about epistemically ideal thinkers.

17   Admittedly, Silins just talks of "many cases" of *automatic transmission*, but I take it that our stipulation here that our thinker *knows* that p entails q (and is competent, perhaps) is sufficient to commit Silins to this claim.

18   Suppose the exceptionless principle of transmission of propositional warrant *does* require that the thinker should *actually take* the step of inference (competently). We would still say that, in that case, this was not what people had in mind in discussion of transmission *failure*.

In sum, and returning to the excerpted passage, Silins imagines that friends of transmission failure might say that transmission of propositional warrant across known entailment *(TPW)* is too easy. It does not really require anything of the thinker (other than perhaps that the thinker should be competent). Silins then imagines that friends of transmission failure might try to make transmission more demanding on the thinker. Perhaps — new proposal — warrant transmission should be a matter of the thinker acquiring a new warrant (that is, a new propositional warrant) by carrying out a particular bit of reasoning. Silins's point in response to this suggestion is that, if a warrant to believe q is automatically available to a thinker who has a warrant to believe p and knows that p entails q, then nothing that the thinker can do (whether carrying out some reasoning or anything else) can make that very same warrant to believe q *newly available* to the thinker. Before the thinker did anything, the warrant to believe q was already automatically available. So, following the new proposal, there would be too much transmission failure. Of course, the thinker could do something to make a different warrant to believe q newly available. The thinker could, for example, go and visit the oracle. But making a different warrant newly available — a warrant that is epistemically independent from the warrant to believe p — would not be warrant transmission. Overall, Silin's point seems to be that, if warrant transmission is defined wholly in terms of propositional warrant — warrant *to* believe — then there will either be no transmission failure or else too much. I leave explicit discussion of Silins here, but the points raised will be relevant in what follows.

1.7 So, returning to *(ZALABARDO)* itself: whence premise (A)?

(A) The problem of easy knowledge presupposes *Transmission* of warrant in (EK)-reasoning.

The problem of easy knowledge is the problem of *(EK)-reasoning* providing knowledge that the table is not white with red lights shining on it. It's *not* the problem of *possessing* knowledge that the table is not white with red lights shining on it. Most philosophers can agree that one could obtain and use inductive evidence against the possibility that there are red lights shining on the table to come to know this proposition. Indeed closer visual scrutiny of the table and its environs could rule out this local sceptical hypothesis. So, as only *Transmission* — and not, crucially, *Closure* — poses a requirement on *how* knowledge that the table is not white with red lights shining on it *is acquired, it* is the principle directly germane to the problem of easy knowledge.

Note premise (A) is not in conflict with the following remark from Cohen (2005: 418): "Since I know [(2)] *a priori*, then given [deductive closure], I can come to know [(3)], on the basis of [(1)] and [(2)]." Cohen here locates the problem of easy knowledge as a problem centred on *closure*, rather than *transmission* (cf. Klein 2004: 165). But this is an apparent — rather than a genuine — conflict with Zalabardo because Cohen operates with a closure principle that is distinct from Zalabardo's. Cohen's closure principle is "DC: If S knows P and S competently deduces Q from P, then S knows Q"[19] — a principle, crucially, requiring an *act of inference*. Thus, the difference in location of the problem of easy knowledge does not reflect a deep disagreement between Zalabardo and Cohen.

1.8 Whence premise (B) (cf. (38–39)) — the main load-bearing component in Zalabardo's argument?

(B) *Transmission* of warrant in (EK)-reasoning presupposes the falsity of an instance of *Closure* in (EK).

Closure, assuming I have warrant for (1) and know (2), mandates I have some warrant or other to believe (3)[20] — the warrant to believe (3) might be epistemically antecedent to, epistemically posterior to (dependent on), or epistemically independent from the thinker's warrant to believe (1). (More on this later.) *Closure* does not commit on the origins of that warrant. Suppose it is a warrant to believe (3) that does not depend on my actually carrying out the inference from (1) and (2) to (3). It might be a propositional warrant automatically transmitted from (1), warrant from the oracle, or an *a priori* default warrant. Now suppose I engage in (EK)-reasoning and perform an (EK)-inference. Zalabardo maintains (as would Silins) that, assuming *Closure* — which guarantees

---

19 It is a good exercise to probe the difference between closure principles, such as Cohen's, which require an act of inference, and transmission principles.
20 I here gloss Zalabardo's warrant as 'warrant to believe' (though we've seen it has properties additional to those had by propositional warrant — see 1.5 *supra*).

that I have warrant to believe (3) regardless of whether I engage in (EK)-reasoning — there's no sense in which I can — as warrant *Transmission* requires — *obtain* warrant to believe (3) by engaging in (EK)-reasoning. I cannot newly enter the condition of having a warrant to believe (3) because, *ex hypothesi*, I am *already* in that condition; I already have such a propositional warrant.[21]

Premise (B) has, seemingly, been vindicated: *Transmission* of warrant in (EK)-reasoning presupposes the falsity of an instance of *Closure* in (EK).[22] But, before proceeding further with *(ZALABARDO)*, we must pause to reflect on *precisely how* Zalabardo vindicates premise (B) — in particular, drawing on our work in the Introduction, we must spell out the implicitly *temporal* nature of Zalabardo's operative transmission principle.

1.9 It's clear that 'obtain' is bearing great weight in *Transmission*, and thus in vindicating premise (B): to *obtain* warrant for (3) it's necessary that one not already have warrant for (3). As a purely conceptual matter, this is questionable: consider cases in which S already has warrant for (3) but this is epistemically *independent* from S's warrant for (1), say from an alternative knowledge source (cf. Silins 2005: 83–84). Why should that conceptually preclude S from *obtaining additional warrant* for (3)?

So, if we were being uncharitable to Zalabardo we might straightaway conclude that premise (B) is false. To avoid such uncharitability, it's plain we need to draw out the implicitly temporal nature of *Transmission*. It must be taken to read instead: 'obtain warrant for q *for the first time'* or '*for the first time*, enter the state of having warrant for q'. (Hereinafter read this into *Transmission*.) We now straightforwardly have a vindication of

---

21 There is one sense in which, for Zalabardo, you could obtain warrant to believe a proposition for which you already have warrant: when you come into a new relation to the proposition that would make you have warrant to believe the proposition if your original source of warrant wasn't there. (EK)-reasoning (and like reasoning), though, doesn't satisfy this condition, since, if the original source of warrant to believe (3) wasn't there, by *Closure* you wouldn't have warrant to believe (1).

22 Thus the unorthodoxy of Zalabardo's response: the received wisdom seems to be that, put crudely, transmission entails closure but that closure does not entail transmission. Wright (1985, 1991, 2003, 2004), for example, always makes the point that transmission *failure* is consistent with closure. But, for Zalabardo, put crudely, *Transmission* entails *Closure*'s falsity *in (EK)-reasoning* (and so *Closure* entails *Transmission*'s falsity *in (EK)-reasoning*). More on this, and on Zalabardo on the relationship between *Transmission* and *Closure in general*, in section 2.

premise (B): *Closure* would ensure that S would already have warrant to believe (3), even before engaging in the inference.

Now inferences take place in time. That much is clear. What's less clear is how relevant *temporal* — as opposed to *epistemic* — antecedence is to any plausible transmission principle. I want to claim epistemic antecedence (and dependence) is the key to transmission questions. Here is my strategy: I want to draw out the different analysis of (EK) which arises when we switch from Zalabardo's *Transmission* to a plausible transmission principle, framed instead in terms of epistemic dependence, which I'll call *Epistemic Transmission*.[23] Then in section 2 I'll vindicate my preference for a focus on epistemic antecedence by demonstrating a principle to which *Transmission*, but not *Epistemic Transmission*, is committed.[24] This principle is 2.4's (~K-ENT). And I come to show that endorsement of (~K-ENT) is associated with serious costs.

Consider, then (modelled on Zalabardo's *Transmission*):

Epistemic Transmission: if p entails q, S knows that p, S infers q from p, *and S's warrant for p isn't epistemically dependent on S's warrant for q*, then S thereby obtains warrant for q.[25]

In *Epistemic Transmission*, there is warrant transmission — not epistemic circularity and not transmission failure — even if S has some warrant or other for q before inferring q from p. *Epistemic Transmission mandates* warrant transmission in (EK)-reasoning unless warrant for (1) epistemically depends on warrant for (3).[26] And this is all just to say that *Epistemic Transmission* doesn't endorse premise (B) (with *Epistemic Transmission* replacing *Transmission* therein).

---

23 The points will generalise: from (EK) to other arguments, and from *Epistemic Transmission* to other plausible such transmission principles. Of course, Zalabardo's *Transmission* is an epistemic principle — framed in terms of warrant and knowledge. So the contrast here is with Zalabardo's focus on *temporal antecedence*.

24 This commitment arises on the assumption of *Closure* — an assumption Zalabardo, my interlocutor, makes.

25 I don't suggest this is an *optimal* such principle; rather the aim — served by modelling it on Zalabardo's principle — is merely for contrast.

26 *Modulo* the other conditions in its antecedent being met. Thus, unlike Zalabardo's principle, this principle has a shot at being valid (cf. n. 9 *supra*).

1.10   Returning to *(ZALABARDO)* itself, (D) and (E) are straightforward deductive consequences of (B) and (C) ((C) is an unargued assumption which I grant for the purposes of the present discussion), and (A) and (D), respectively. Nevertheless, there is more to be said about premise (B).

2. Exploring Premise (B) Further: Upshots of Zalabardo's Response

2.1   Recall premise (B):

> (B) *Transmission* of warrant in (EK)-reasoning presupposes the falsity of an instance of *Closure* in (EK).

Why is Zalabardo committed to premise (B) rather than only to some weaker principle? Why, for example, does *Transmission* of warrant in (EK)-reasoning presuppose the *falsity* — and not just the *false-false vacuous truth* (i.e. false antecedent-false consequent) — of an instance of *Closure* in (EK)? Put differently: isn't there *Transmission* of warrant in (EK)-reasoning when an instance of *Closure* is false-false vacuously true — and not false — in (EK)?

For the reader's ease, let me, at this juncture, repeat Zalabardo's operative principles:

> *Closure*: If p has warrant for S, and S knows that p entails q, then q has warrant for S. (36)

> *Transmission*: If p entails q and S knows that p, then inferring q from p would enable S to obtain warrant for q. (39)

If *Closure*'s antecedent is stipulated to be false then either (i) p fails to have warrant for S or (ii) S fails to know that p entails q (or both). If (i), then *Transmission*'s antecedent is, by stipulation, false (as if p fails to have warrant for S, it follows that S fails to know that p). We've thereby stipulated that there is not *Transmission* in (EK)-reasoning when an instance of *Closure* is false-false vacuously true in (EK). So option (i) gets us nowhere. What if — option (ii) — one doesn't, *prior to* performing a competent inference, antecedently know the entailment which licenses that inference. We might, moreover, suppose that one can come to know that p entails q *as a result of* competent inference (more on this later).

At base, however: suppose one's antecedently failing to know that p entails q is no bar to competently inferring q from p. If this is so, then it's not that *Transmission* in (EK)-reasoning presupposes the falsity of an instance of *Closure* in (EK); it just presupposes its falsity or false-false vacuous truth.

But it should be clear that this challenge to premise (B) — *viz.* pointing to the possibility of *Closure* being false-false vacuously true — simply isn't open *in dealing with the problem of easy knowledge*. As the problem of easy knowledge is set up, one, by stipulation, *knows* the premises of (EK) — *viz.* (1), and (2) (the *relevant entailment*) — *prior to* an act of inference.²⁷ When facing the problem of easy knowledge, the antecedent of *Closure* is true in (EK): *Closure*, in (EK), can't be false-false vacuously true. So Zalabardo is indeed committed to premise (B) (and not to some weakened variant thereof).

2.2 We made Zalabardo's argument as strong as possible by making premise (B) as weak as possible: it only makes claims about (EK), and reasoning therewith. But *Closure* and *Transmission* are general principles. Consider, then:

---

27 Two related points. First, what do I mean by 'knowing (or having warrant for) the relevant entailment' — a locution which features prominently in the remainder of this chapter? (2) is a conditional expressing an entailment relation. Thus, to know (2) is to know the relevant entailment relation expressed by (2). And we can refer to the proposition expressed by (2) as the *relevant entailment proposition*. Importantly, such knowledge does not entail that one knows that: [(1) and (2)] entail (3) (and so on). Second, and relatedly, the set-up for (EK) does *not*, however, require that: one knows that premise (1) and premise (2) together entail conclusion (3). It follows from this (I leave the proof to the reader) that a revised premise (B), operating instead with the following plausible two-premise versions of *Transmission* and *Closure*, would, without more, be false:

Two-premise Transmission: If p1 and p2 together entail q, and if S knows that p1 and S knows that p2, then *(competently) inferring q from p1 and p2* would enable S to obtain a warrant to believe q.

Two-premise Closure: If S has a warrant to believe p1, and S has a warrant to believe p2, and *S knows that p1 and p2 together entail q*, then S has a warrant to believe q.

The moral for Zalabardo is: don't construct the argument with these two-premise principles.

(GENERALISED B) *Transmission* of warrant presupposes the invalidity of *Closure*.

Glossing (GENERALISED B): in order for *any* competent inference to enable one to obtain warrant for the inferred proposition, *Closure* must have at least one false instance — in particular, it must have a false instance in the particular argument in which one is performing the inference. Is Zalabardo committed to (GENERALISED B)?

2.3 The answer is 'no'. But seeing why he *isn't* so committed leads us to a further principle to which Zalabardo *is* committed. Commitment to that further principle reveals some interesting upshots of his response. Let's back up a little. Note that we can reformulate (EK) — indeed some, although not Cohen, have done so — thus:

(WARRANT FOR 1*) The table looks red.

(EK*) (1*) The table is red.

    So:

    (2*) The table is not white with red lights shining on it.

That is, we can suppress the conditional in (EK). (EK*)-reasoning is analogous to the commonly discussed *a priori* deduction of 'Something is coloured' from 'Something is red'. And there are many more such deductions. Consider, then, the following two (single-inference) argument schemata (and assume p entails q):

(MP) (1) p   (MP*) (1*) p

      (2) If p then q   So:

      (3) So: q   (2*) q

We want to allow that competent (deductive) inferences need not consist of formally valid arguments: the *a priori* consequences of a claim can be drawn out without one's reasoning being formally valid. And it would be mistaken to insist that ostensible (MP*)-reasoning is enthymematic.[28] In sum, abstracting from the problem of easy knowledge, we want to allow for a subject competently inferring q from p while failing to know that p entails q.

Standardly, however, in order for a proposition to function as a premise for a subject, it must be warrantedly believed or known by that subject.[29] Thus (MP) — but not (MP*) — has a requirement that a propounder of an instance of schema (MP) have, at least, a warranted belief in the relevant conditional and, *ex hypothesi*, the relevant entailment. It follows, *modulo* our assumptions concerning warrant (see 1.5 *supra*), and p entailing q, that (MP) — but not (MP*) — has a requirement that a propounder of an instance of schema (MP) *know* the relevant entailment (though (MP*) is, of course, compatible with such knowledge).[30]

2.4 So it turns out Zalabardo isn't committed to (GENERALISED B):[31] *Transmission* of warrant is compatible with the false-false vacuous truth of *Closure* just in case the relevant entailment is not known by the reasoner *prior to* an act of inference. In other words, Zalabardo's *Closure* and *Transmission* principles — which interact in premise (B) — commit him to the following principle:

---

28 Wright (2007: sections II and IV) presents a series of "*justificational triads*" concluding with the falsity of sceptical hypotheses concerning the external world, testimony, other minds etc., which share (MP*)'s property of not being formally valid.

29 Hawthorne and Stanley (2008) argue a premise must be known by a subject engaging in *practical* reasoning, and note that such a requirement also seems plausible in the domain of *theoretical* reasoning. If Hawthorne and Stanley are right on this latter claim, my conclusion that a propounder of an instance of schema (MP) must *know* the relevant entailment can be reached directly.

30 Even in (MP) the three propositions — premises (1) and (2) and conclusion (3) — do not tell the whole story. There is also a rule of inference. In (MP*) there is also a rule of inference — not a logical rule of inference, but still a rule of (proper or non-logical) inference that is a priori valid. There is no evident requirement, however, that the thinker should have formulated as a proposition, and should have a warrant to believe, the relevant rule of inference (in the case of (MP), the rule *modus ponens*). All we assume is that the thinker in question is a competent reasoner.

31 This is a good thing. Given Zalabardo assumes the validity of *Closure*, if premise (B) were to have generalised in this way, Zalabardo would have been in the unenviable position of ruling out *Transmission* of warrant *tout court*.

(~K-ENT) Warrant *Transmits* in reasoning, only if[32] the reasoner does not know the relevant entailment proposition prior to an act of inference.

Why so? Because, according to *Closure*, it's only if our propounder fails to know the relevant entailment *prior to* an act of inference that the propounder can fail to have warrant already for the argument's conclusion.[33] By contrast, *Epistemic Transmission* isn't committed to (~K-ENT) (with *Epistemically Transmits* replacing *Transmits* therein): even if our propounder knows the entailment, and thus has a warrant for the conclusion prior to inference, warrant *Epistemically Transmits* provided warrant for the premise(s) does not epistemically depend on warrant for the conclusion.

Now let us note two interesting upshots of (~K-ENT) — upshots of ascending importance. First, consider a rough continuum within the set of single-inference arguments (our focus), ranging from *simple* to *complex* inferences: the more complex an inference, the more readily foreseeable it is that a subject may fail to know the relevant entailment *prior to* an act of inference. By (~K-ENT), the more complex the relevant entailment, the more likely it is that reasoning employing that entailment *Transmits* warrant for the propounder. For some, this would seem, if anything, to get things the wrong way round. For Zalabardo, however, this is perfectly intuitive: the more complex the entailment, the more likely it is that inferential reasoning will provide you with something you don't already have.

Second, and more importantly, let us focus on some interesting specific cases of what (~K-ENT) *permits* by way of warrant *Transmission*. (~K-ENT) permits *Transmission* of warrant in reasoning with arguments — of the form either (MP)[34] or (MP*) — in which one comes

---

32   Not 'if': there is not, for Zalabardo, *Transmission* in reasoning if the reasoner has an *a priori* default warrant for the conclusion (though any such cases are bracketed here).

33   And, of course, a propounder can fail to meet this necessary condition — can know the relevant entailment *prior to* an act of inference — whether the argument with which he reasons is constituted in the form (MP) or (MP*).

34   Thus, on this view, (EK)-reasoning as understood with respect to the problem of easy knowledge, in which one knows the relevant entailment *prior to* an act of inference, is but one form of (MP)-reasoning.

to know the relevant entailment *in the act of*[35] competent inference. (~K-ENT) permits *Transmission* of warrant in reasoning with arguments of the form (MP*) — but not (MP) — in which one comes to know the relevant entailment *as a result of* competent inference.[36] Why this difference between (MP)-reasoning and (MP*)-reasoning when one comes to know the relevant entailment *as a result of* competent inference? Because we are positing the performance of a competent inference *prior to* knowledge of the relevant entailment — a posit forbidden by constituting an argument in the form (MP).

Thus we can conclude that the *only circumstances* in which (MP)-reasoning *Transmits* warrant are those in which one comes to know the relevant entailment *in the act of* competent inference. For some, this would seem unduly restrictive. Be that as it may, given the fundamentality of (MP)-reasoning, and given the only circumstances in which it *Transmits* warrant are those in which the act of competent inference and the acquisition of knowledge of the relevant entailment are *simultaneous*, one would like to hear more about the nature of this form of inference. It is not merely — as with certain instances of (MP*)-reasoning — that one comes to know the relevant entailment *as a result of* competent inference: this is an interesting feature of certain inferences, but we have a rough idea of how such a performance — or series of performances — can (causally) lead to such knowledge. The process of drawing an inference — or series of such inferences — can make it appropriate, after completion of the process, to ascribe knowledge of the relevant entailment to the reasoner. By contrast, instances of (MP)-reasoning which *Transmit* warrant have a quite exceptional, and underexplored, feature: one comes to know the relevant entailment *in the act of* — simultaneously with — competent inference. Put differently: coming to know the relevant entailment is, in some sense, *constitutive* of this type of inference. This putative feature of certain inferences

---

35 A key issue here, relevant to our simple/complex inference distinction, will be individuating acts of inference. When do they start? When do they end? When is warrant obtained? A defender of (~K-ENT) owes us an answer to these questions (cf. 2.5 *infra*).

36 (~K-ENT) permits warrant *Transmission* in reasoning with arguments of the form (MP*) — but not (MP) — in which one does not come to know the relevant entailment *at all*.

warrants further scrutiny.[37] In sum, given (~K-ENT) is a presupposition of premise (B), should (~K-ENT) prove to be unsustainable, so too will be Zalabardo's response to the problem of easy knowledge.

2.5   Is, then, (~K-ENT) unsustainable? I have no principled objection to the possibility of any of the foregoing types of inference permitted by (~K-ENT).[38] Thus, I have no straightforward objection to (~K-ENT) to the effect that it permits inferences which ought not to be permitted. Let me, instead, gesture at a more cautious objection to (~K-ENT) to the effect that its defenders have an explanatory burden which they have yet to discharge. The explanatory burden arises given two assumptions. First, assume it is a *desideratum* on any theoretical account such as Zalabardo's that it be able — given adequate information — to accurately *classify* or *characterise* the form of argument involved in as many *successful inferences*,[39] of those to which it *speaks*, as possible — here, whether (MP) or (MP*). Second, assume that many successful inferences involve the form of argument (MP). I take each of these assumptions to be relatively uncontroversial.

Now, on the back of these assumptions, let us make two particular suppositions in advance of outlining the explanatory burden faced by a defender of (~K-ENT): first, suppose that a reasoner does not know the relevant entailment *prior to* an act of inference. Second, suppose that the inference in question is performed competently. Now, whether the form of argument involved in this inference is (MP) or (MP*) (in part) depends on whether our reasoner comes to know the relevant entailment *in the act of — simultaneously with* — competent inference.

---

37   To switch emphasis: This putative feature of certain instances of coming to know an entailment warrants further scrutiny.

38   While, as far as I am aware, none of the foregoing types of inference permitted by (~K-ENT) has received detailed discussion in the literature, none is straightforwardly unintuitive. I do not attempt to go beyond the basic adumbration of the foregoing types of inference permitted by (~K-ENT) provided in 2.4 (an adumbration which, saliently, does not provide an account of what it is to know an entailment); indeed, given the shape of my coming objection to (~K-ENT) — which takes the form of an explanatory challenge for defenders of (~K-ENT) — it would be unwise of me to do so.

39   I will stipulate that a successful inference just is a competent inference plus whatever additional constraints, if any, are required in order for the inference in question to furnish the subject with warrant for that which is inferred. For Zalabardo, thus, (~K-ENT) would be such an additional constraint. Thus, what counts as a successful inference, in this sense, will vary depending on the theoretical account in question.

If he so comes to know, we have a candidate case of (MP)-reasoning (though also a candidate case of (MP*)-reasoning).[40] And if he fails to so come to know, we have a case of (MP*)-reasoning (and *not* also a candidate case of (MP)-reasoning).[41]

Now, here is our explanatory challenge: defenders of (~K-ENT) must offer clear, prospective *individuation conditions* for the type of inference in which one comes to know the relevant entailment *in the act of* — simultaneously with — competent inference. We can call these *knowledge-constitutive inferences*. And we can call those inferences in which one comes to know the relevant entailment *as a result of* competent inference, *knowledge-resulting inferences*. In particular, then, such individuation conditions must enable us to distinguish between knowledge-constitutive and knowledge-resulting inferences.

We can dramatise the urgency of this challenge by contrasting two inferences — one knowledge-constitutive and one knowledge-resulting (yet suppose the two inferences are otherwise identical, in advance of determining the form of argument involved therein). We can stipulate that the knowledge-resulting inference is one in which, as a matter of fact, the reasoner acquires knowledge of the relevant entailment a millisecond (or less) after completing the inference (cf. n. 35 supra). The point is that in the absence of clear, prospective individuation conditions for knowledge-constitutive inferences it is unclear how — even given adequate information about how, independently of whether known, the relevant entailment features in the reasoner's reasoning process etc. (cf. n. 40) — we can distinguish between these two inferences.[42] Without

---

40 (MP*)-reasoning is, I take it, compatible with such knowledge. (At any rate, in advance of further information on the nature of such inferences we must assume this to be the case.) I take it that further information about how such knowledge features in the reasoner's psychology — how, independently of whether known, the relevant entailment features in his reasoning process — will determine whether the argument involved in this inference is (MP) or (MP*). Note that such facts about a reasoner's psychology *alone* cannot determine the form of argument involved; it is such facts *in combination with* whether, and when, the reasoner knows the relevant entailment.
41 To fail to make our supposition that the inference is performed competently, both the foregoing cases may be cases of non-successful — *failed* — reasoning (cf. n. 39 *supra*).
42 Why not, instead, begin at the other end with a search for clear, prospective individuation conditions for *knowledge-resulting* inferences? To my mind this would not be a fruitful way to proceed (though defenders of (~K-ENT) are free to adopt this strategy if they so wish). First, I take it that *knowledge-resulting* inferences are

such conditions we can, in this and like cases, have no idea whether the form of argument involved in the inferences in question is (MP) or (MP*). And it follows, given (~K-ENT), that we can have no idea when a successful piece of (MP)-reasoning has taken place.[43]

In sum, in advance of defenders of (~K-ENT), like Zalabardo, discharging this explanatory burden, we can enter a provisional verdict: (~K-ENT) is, without more, unsustainable, and so too, without more, is Zalabardo's response to the problem of easy knowledge.

---

a motley group of inferences, with potentially little conceptually to unite any two such inferences. Second, and relatedly, I do not see how, even assuming some such set of individuation conditions could be reached, such conditions could help us distinguish between the two inferences in our dramatisation.

43 Doesn't this explanatory challenge arise *regardless of (~K-ENT)'s truth-value*? Yes — but with less urgency *if (~K-ENT) is false*. The challenge is less urgent because if (and only if) (~K-ENT) is false, it's no longer the case that the only circumstances in which (MP)-reasoning furnishes the subject with warrant for its conclusion are *knowledge-constitutive* inferences. That is, if (and only if) (~K-ENT) is false, cases in which the relevant entailment is known *prior to* an act of inference can serve as quotidian cases in which the inference in question is successful — furnishes the subject with warrant for that which is inferred (cf. n. 40 *supra*). Given adequate information, we can accurately classify or characterise the form of argument involved in such cases on a case by case basis (cf. n. 38 *supra*). Clearly, in such circumstances the need to provide clear, prospective individuation conditions for *knowledge-constitutive* inferences is less urgent (cf. our two assumptions made two paragraphs ago in the main text).

3. The Problem of Easy Knowledge: Towards a Solution

I develop my own solution to the problem of easy knowledge, criticising and improving on a proposal by Davies (2004). My solution is available to the dogmatist. Thus, so far, the prospects look good for a defense of dogmatism, immediate justification, and basic knowledge against the pattern of objection.

0.1   In Chapter Two, I introduced Stewart Cohen's (2002, 2005) problem of easy knowledge (in sections 0.1–0.4 of that chapter), and then offered an extended commentary on José Zalabardo's response to the problem. In this chapter, I take some steps towards a solution to the problem of easy knowledge.

1. Responses to (EK)-reasoning

1.1   One could accept KR (and thereby face a version of *the problem of the criterion*):[1]

> KR   A potential knowledge source K can yield knowledge for S, only if S knows K is reliable. (Cohen 2002: 309)

This principle would block basic knowledge, and so the problem of generating easy knowledge from basic knowledge by (EK)-reasoning wouldn't arise. But I want to consider responses to the problem of easy

---

[1] See Cohen (2002: 309–10) on the problem of the criterion.

knowledge which don't accept KR² (and thereby *avoid* the problem of the criterion). My focus is on a response which can be attributed to Martin Davies (2004, 2009). Davies's response is promising, but my claim is that it is *incomplete*. In section 2 I introduce Cohen's important modification of his original case. And in section 3 I identify, and make a positive move to remedy, the incompleteness of Davies's response. First, though, I need to delineate Davies's response.

1.2 Some preliminaries: first, Davies (2004: 229–31) endorses — at least for the sake of the argument — James Pryor's (2000: 519–20) *dogmatist* epistemology, which licenses an immediate, though defeasible, transition from the experience described in (WARRANT FOR 1) to basic knowledge of (1). To the extent that Davies is a dogmatist we can conclude he doesn't accept KR.

Second, Davies distinguishes between two epistemic projects: the epistemic project of *deciding what to believe*, and the epistemic project of *settling a question*.³ Here is Davies (2009: 361) on the epistemic project of deciding what to believe (call it the *D-project*):

> If you review some of your beliefs, $P_1,..., P_n$, and notice a valid argument from those premisses to Q then you should⁴ adopt the belief Q or, if other considerations argue against Q, then you should reconsider your beliefs $P_1,..., P_n$.

Note a feature of this project: it's deciding what to believe, Q, *on the basis of* noticing a valid argument from a set of premises, $P_1,...,P_n$, to Q. The type of D-project of particular interest here is reasoning with an argument to come to *know* its conclusion.⁵

And here is Davies (2009: 364–65) on the epistemic project of settling a question (call it the *S-project*):

---

2   And, indeed, don't accept WR: A potential knowledge source K can yield knowledge for S, only if S has warrant to accept that K is reliable.
3   This *epistemological* distinction parallels, respectively, Frank Jackson's (1987: ch.6) *dialectical* distinction between the *teasing out* and the *convincing* purposes of arguing.
4   '[M]ay' is preferable to avoid the project mandating the adoption of countless time-consuming and pointless beliefs.
5   Although Davies (2009: 363) does not speak explicitly about knowledge (in connection with either of his two epistemic projects), but only about "three progressively less demanding norms for the project of deciding what to believe".

The project of settling the question whether or not Q is true [...] begin[s] by taking the question to be open *pro tempore* [...] I *suppose*, for the purposes of the question-settling project, that I have reasons to think that Q is, or may very well be, false. This suppositional doubt then governs my conduct of the project.⁶

Suppose that I have a warranted belief P and that my project is to deploy my warrant to believe P, and my appreciation of the valid argument from P to Q, in order to settle the question whether or not Q is true in favour of the positive. My conduct of the question-settling project is governed by suppositional doubt about Q. In some cases, my suppositional doubt about Q may prevent me from rationally availing myself of my warrant to believe P *within the project that is governed by that suppositional doubt*. In such cases, although I do have a warrant to believe P and there is an obviously valid argument from P to Q, I cannot deploy that warrant to settle the question in favour of Q.⁷

Note, as before, that undertaking an S-project doesn't threaten many plausible knowledge-closure principles: while an (EK)-reasoner has warrant for (1), it's left open that he has warrant for (3) *other than by means of (EK)-reasoning within the scope of suppositional doubt*.⁸ The type of S-project of particular interest here is reasoning with an argument to come to *know* its conclusion.

1.3 So, by Davies's lights, when one undertakes a D-project in (EK)-reasoning a subject can put together antecedent warranted beliefs in

---

6   Davies also adds elsewhere (2009: 369): "[A] fuller treatment of the project of settling the question would have to allow for the case where I begin by supposing that *it is as likely as not that Q is false*". This suggests that *principled* or *mandated agnosticism* (see Wright 2007) about Q — in which one assigns a credence of 0.5 to both Q and its negation — is, for Davies, a form of suppositional doubt about Q, but caution is in order. It may be that a Bayesian will describe a state of open-mindedness as a state in which probability 0.5 is assigned to a proposition and its negation. Those may also be the probabilities that are suppositionally assigned in suppositional doubt, but the fact that the Bayesian assigns the same probabilities in these two conditions does not show that the two conditions are epistemically equivalent. (In any case, it's clear that Davies would not want to say that mere open-mindedness makes it impossible to make rational use of one's warrant for (1) in the project of deciding what to believe.)
7   The extension of the S-project to multi-premise arguments is straightforward.
8   It will usually be that the thinker has a warrant to believe (3). But the project of settling the question is more demanding than the project of deciding what to believe and the set-up of the more demanding project may prevent the thinker from rationally deploying his warrant to believe (1) within the scope of the demanding project.

(1) and (2) to come to know (3). But when one undertakes an S-project in (EK)-reasoning one suppositionally doubts (3). Now (WARRANT FOR 1) cannot be rationally deployed to settle the question in favour of (3). Thus no warrant for, and so no knowledge of, (3) is acquired by (EK)-reasoning within the S-project.[9] Davies offers a like diagnosis of reasoning with Moore's 'Proof' of (knowledge of)[10] the existence of an external world.[11]

2. Cohen's Modified Case

2.1 Cohen (2005: 420) considers a modification of his original case — a case designed to "eliminate entirely any dialectical context" from (EK)-reasoning:

> Suppose my son is not worried about the possibility that the table is deceptively illuminated. He accepts that I know that the table is red and not white with red lights shining on it. He is just curious about *how* I know it. I respond in just the same way. "Oh that's easy. It looks red, so it is red, so it is not white with red lights shining on it." By my lights there is something unsatisfactory about my response.

---

9   Though Davies does not explicitly say this in his 2009 paper (cf. n. 5 *supra*), his earlier discussion of the problem of *armchair knowledge* (2000, 2003) suggests this way of speaking. (In terms of warrant: the thinker does have a warrant to believe (3) and may well have a warranted belief in (3). But the warrant to believe (1) cannot be (re-)deployed within the context of suppositional doubt in order to settle the question whether or not (3) is true.) Given the distinction between two epistemic projects, it seems he should say that, if the thinker undertakes the more demanding project then he cannot arrive at knowledge of (3), but that he can arrive at knowledge of the *very same proposition* ((3)) by undertaking the less demanding project (cf. *epistemic contextualism* — see Rysiew 2007). This sounds a bit paradoxical, however. It may be we tend to run together two standards for knowledge — the standard of doing well in deciding what to believe and the standard of doing well in settling the question. Perhaps we tend to impose the more demanding standard — unless there is no possibility of meeting that standard, in which case we might shift to the less demanding standard. More on this later.

10 I use this parenthetical device throughout to signal that the key issue up for debate is whether such knowledge is indeed delivered.

11 Davies (2009) uses notions of *defeat* and *transmission failure* to explain how suppositional doubt can limit the rational deployment of warrant (in (EK)-reasoning, with respect to *both (1) and (3)*). Rather than explore this explanation further, I leave the *explanandum* intuitive, with (EK)-reasoning and Moore's 'Proof' serving as putative exemplars thereof.

Two responses are available. First, one might dispute Cohen's intuition about this case. Maybe Cohen has been misled by considering a case in which, even though a dialectical context has been eliminated, there are still *two parties* involved — two parties, we can assume, sharing background assumptions. Perhaps the involvement of two parties — Cohen and his son — has misled Cohen into finding something unsatisfactory about a genuinely satisfactory response. That is, maybe Cohen has unconsciously imported differing background assumptions onto the parties in the case; such an importation rendering a satisfactory response ostensibly unsatisfactory. This first response would be hasty. I share Cohen's intuition about the unsatisfactoriness of the father's response in the modified case, but reliance on bare intuitions is philosophically unsatisfying. So I want — the second response — to give a philosophically satisfying account of this intuition.[12] Doing this will reveal the incompleteness of Davies's response to the problem of easy knowledge.

(Perhaps, though, we can, even at this stage, do slightly better than reliance on a bare intuition. It seems that the question, 'How do you know?" is rather different from the question, 'Why do you believe?'. One natural answer to the second question is: (a) I believe that the table is red; so, on that basis, (b) I believe that the table is not white; and so (c) I believe that the table is not both white and lit with red lights. If I do well in believing (a) then it seems that I also do well in believing (c). Dogmatism says that there is no epistemic circularity here. On one view, the intuitions about 'know' owe something to an intuition about sensitivity — a condition explored in Chapter Seven. However, I try to show that that latter intuition seems to be limited in some way. Sometimes sensitivity is unachievable in principle. In sum: the 'How do you know?' question seems more demanding, more challenging.)

2.2 By eliminating the dialectical context, Cohen removes any possibility of the dialectical phenomenon of *begging the question* entering the picture. Cohen's son is prepared to grant Cohen that he does indeed know (3) and wants to be told how Cohen achieved the feat of coming

---

[12] This is the first of several points in this chapter where, concededly, I use a *contestable* intuition (here: Cohen's) as a stimulus to providing a theoretical underpinning thereof.

to know (3). What Cohen's case illustrates is that we find the answer intuitively inadequate if all it does is to spell out how Cohen did well in the D-project. This suggests that the son's request calls for, but does not receive, an account of how Cohen settled the question whether or not (3) is true. So it's not that eliminating the dialectical context removes the S-project from consideration, leaving only the D-project. Rather, the son's question, 'How do you know?' — cf. 'How did you find out?', 'How could you tell?', 'How did you rule out relevant alternatives to (3)?' — asks for an account of Cohen's conduct of the S-project. The son wants to know what evidence Cohen was able rationally to deploy in the context of a project that began by his suppositionally regarding the question whether or not (3) is true as a genuinely open one. And the son is unsatisfied by an account merely of Cohen's conduct of the D-project.

3. Identifying and Remedying the Incompleteness of Davies's Response

3.1 Consider the following variant on (EK), (EK*):

(WARRANT FOR 1) The table looks red.

(EK*)

(1) The table is red.

(2) If the table is red, then I'm not a BIV[13] being deceived into falsely believing the table is red.

(3) I'm not a BIV being deceived into falsely believing the table is red.

This is just (EK) but with a different consequent in (2) and, resultantly, a different conclusion. And (EK*), predictably, can be explained in much the same way as (EK): we have a piece of basic knowledge, a bridging conditional that is knowable *a priori*, and an anti-sceptical

---

13 BIV = Brain-in-a-Vat, being fed pseudo-perceptual-experiences (by an evil scientist). One's being a BIV is compatible with there *being* an external world — just not with one coming *to know* (any features) thereof. I leave open that a BIV can engage in competent intellectual functioning, cf. Wright (1991: 104).

conclusion. What's the purpose of setting out (EK*), and considering (EK) and (EK*) side-by-side? The problem of easy knowledge, recall, is that particular arguments (beginning from a premise of which we have basic knowledge) seem to offer a 'too-easy' route to knowledge of a conclusion. But (EK) and (EK*) elicit very different intuitions about the legitimacy of the argument as a route to knowledge: (EK*)-reasoning seems much less unsatisfactory as a route to knowledge of its conclusion than (EK)-reasoning. However, both (EK)-reasoning and (EK*)-reasoning do well by the standards of the D-project and neither does well by the standards of the S-project.[14] On these two projects, (EK)-reasoning and (EK*)-reasoning are matched. Given that the only theoretical considerations on which Davies can draw in determining whether a thinker knows a conclusion is whether that thinker does well in the D- and S-projects, if the question is whether to say that a thinker knows the conclusions of (EK) and (EK*), then Davies apparently has to (counterintuitively) give the same answer for this pair of examples matched on their performances in the D- and S-projects. Thus the incompleteness of Davies's response.[15]

3.2 Now consider the following intuition of Cohen's (2002: 313):

> I think [(EK*)-reasoning] may look plausible only because it is obscure in general how we know global sceptical alternatives do not obtain, e.g., how we know we're not brains-in-a-vat. And insofar as we are inclined to say we do know such things, this can seem like a reasonable hypothesis about how we know.
>
> But the problem is that we cannot limit the knowledge we acquire in this way to denying global sceptical alternatives [...] Presumably, I cannot know that it's not the case that the table is white but illuminated by red lights, on the basis of the table's looking red.

---

14 Davies (2009) has two notions of transmission failure — one for each of the D- and S-projects — which, if met, result in a failure of transmission of epistemic warrant from premises to conclusion. Reasoning fails to do well in the relevant epistemic project iff that project's transmission failure condition is met.

15 I've raised an 'incompleteness' problem for Davies. But, additionally, it *seems* (at least some) *epistemic contextualist* and *subject-sensitive invariantist* responses will inherit such a problem. On these analyses, so long as — as, suppose (cf. Lewis 1996), in Cohen's modified case — the possibility that the table is deceptively illuminated is *not raised*, there is no way of diagnosing anything unsatisfactory about responding with (EK)-reasoning. I leave open how other analyses of knowledge will handle Cohen's modified case.

As before, two responses are available: we might reject Cohen's intuition or we might try to give a philosophical underpinning to it. As before, I prefer the second response. Cohen admits to an intuition that (EK*)-reasoning is less unsatisfactory than (EK)-reasoning, although the two examples have the same structure ("the knowledge we acquire *in this way* [...]" (my emphasis)). He seems to conjecture that the difference is that the conclusion of (EK*) denies a global sceptical hypothesis, while the conclusion of (EK) denies a more local sceptical hypothesis. He also enters a conjecture about why this difference should make a difference; namely, that "it is obscure" how we know global sceptical hypotheses to be false. I take it that the reason that this "is obscure" is that, in general, it is not plausible that we know they are false on account of sensory or perceptual evidence that *counts against them*. So, if we want to say that we do know that they are false then maybe "[(EK*)-reasoning] can seem like a reasonable hypothesis about how we know". So, is the global/local distinction important here? Is the global/local distinction what's driving Cohen's intuition?

Where (EK*) and (EK) differ, then, is in (EK*) concluding with the falsity of a *global* sceptical hypothesis, whereas (EK) merely concludes with the falsity of a *local* sceptical hypothesis. The truth of a global sceptical hypothesis is incompatible with our knowing — but not necessarily with the truth of — *any* of the things we ordinarily take ourselves to be able to know by means of sense perception. The truth of a local sceptical hypothesis is incompatible with our knowing — but not necessarily with the truth of — a proper *subset* of the things we ordinarily take ourselves to be able to know by means of sense perception. Local sceptical hypotheses come in varying degrees of strength. The conclusion of (EK), for example, is the falsity of a fairly weak local sceptical hypothesis.[16]

---

16 For interesting remarks on conditions on being a sceptical hypothesis, see Beebe (2010).

3.3 Let's now stipulate the following argument template:

(EK)-style argument: A valid argument with a first premise establishing a piece of basic knowledge, a second conditional premise knowable *a priori*, and a conclusion — reachable by a *modus ponens* inference — delivering (knowledge of) the falsity of a sceptical hypothesis (global or local).[17]

Notably, Moore's 'Proof' is an (EK)-style argument. Call reasoning with an (EK)-style argument *(EK)-style reasoning*. While such arguments and reasoning are my focus from here on, my final proposal purports to have application to knowledge and reasoning *in general* (within the scope of our two epistemic projects).

Moreover, let us stipulate that the three instances of (EK)-style arguments encountered thus far — *viz*. (EK), Moore's 'Proof', and (EK*) — are *central cases* of (EK)-style arguments in the following sense: each has a first premise establishing a piece of basic knowledge of *an everyday proposition which is not the negation of a sceptical hypothesis*. 'Everyday proposition' is not a perfectly precise term; moreover nor is 'sceptical hypothesis' — cf. n. 16. However, 'I have hands' and 'The table is red' serve as clear exemplars of everyday propositions which are not the negations of sceptical hypotheses. It is a characteristic of central cases of (EK)-style reasoning (but not *only* of such central cases) that they do badly in the S-project.

Finally, we can stipulate that (EK)-style arguments which are not central cases thereof — by virtue of *not* having a first premise establishing a piece of basic knowledge of an everyday proposition that is not the negation of a sceptical hypothesis — are *peripheral cases*. I think that this central/peripheral distinction is an important and natural one to draw. Indeed it captures the differing degrees of attention lavished by contemporary epistemologists on the two types of (EK)-style arguments, and on reasoning therewith. And, though we'll encounter peripheral

---

17 Wright (2007: sections II and IV) presents a series of *"justificational triads"* which — with a little modification — can be fitted into my (EK)-style argument template, concluding with the falsity of sceptical hypotheses concerning the external world, testimony, other minds etc. In Wright's triads the conditional does not function as a premise. My final proposal can go through operating with Wright's formulations.

cases in what follows (see nn. 24–25 *infra*), our focus — following contemporary epistemologists — will be on central cases.

Now let's ask the following two questions:

(Local Necessary?) Is the delivery of (knowledge of) the falsity of a (merely) local — and not global — sceptical hypothesis in (EK)-style-reasoning *necessary* to generate intuitions of unsatisfactoriness *to (roughly) the level generated by (EK)-reasoning* (even in a non-dialectical context)?

(Local Sufficient?) Is the delivery of (knowledge of) the falsity of a (merely) local — and not global — sceptical hypothesis in (EK)-style-reasoning *sufficient* to generate intuitions of unsatisfactoriness *to (roughly) the level generated by (EK)-reasoning* (even in a non-dialectical context)?[18]

(A key point is that, compatibly with a piece of reasoning *not* generating intuitions of unsatisfactoriness to (roughly) the level generated by (EK)-reasoning, something could still *seem* — and *be* — unsatisfactory about a piece of reasoning in question. Indeed my coming analysis of (EK*)-reasoning, and, by analogy, (MOORE)-reasoning, bears out this compatibility. (EK*)-reasoning is less unsatisfactory than (EK)-reasoning, yet suffers from an epistemic limitation: it cannot be used in the epistemic project of settling the question. Albeit this limitation, I'll claim, is *not* such as to preclude knowledge.) It turns out that the answer to both questions is: 'no'. We'll discover this by means of two thought experiments. This will support the proposal that the global/local distinction *isn't* driving Cohen's intuition. In fact the two thought experiments lead us to the real distinction — a distinction cross-cutting the global/local distinction — that drives Cohen's intuition.[19]

---

18 I omit the parenthetical 'even in a non-dialectical context' from here on in, simply to keep things less cumbersome. Our focus, though, is on *both* dialectical and non-dialectical contexts.

19 Cohen (2002: 313) hints at the real distinction to which my thought experiments lead. I therefore take any disagreement with Cohen to be one of emphasis rather than substance.

3.4 *Thought experiment one — why the answer to (Local Necessary?) is 'no'.* We need a piece of (EK)-style-reasoning which seems as unsatisfactory as (EK)-reasoning, but which delivers (knowledge of) the falsity of a global — and not (merely) local — sceptical hypothesis. To get this we need to draw the following distinction:

> *Weak* BIV: One is a *Weak* BIV iff one is a BIV with the availability of knowledge-conferring evidence that one is a BIV.

> *Strong* BIV: One is a *Strong* BIV iff one is a BIV with no availability of knowledge-conferring evidence that one is a BIV.[20]

So Weak BIV and Strong BIV exhaustively and exclusively partition the set of BIVs. What might be some examples of evidence that one is a BIV? Pryor (2000: 537–38) suggests the following:

> [A] ticker tape appears at the bottom of your visual field with the words: "You are a brain in a vat..."

> [S]tatistical evidence, such as evidence that 7 out of 10 subjects are brains in vats, or evidence that you are a brain in a vat 7 mornings out of 10.

Pryor introduces these examples as cases of positive evidence that one *is* a BIV, which thus form evidence potentially undermining any warrant one might have that one *is not* a BIV. Pryor (537–38) categorises the ticker tape example as a case of "positive empirical evidence" that one is a BIV (and doesn't explicitly categorise the statistical evidence example). I take the ticker tape — and the statistical evidence — example as a case of *pseudo-perceptual* evidence. Finally, why is one's being a Weak BIV a *global* — and not merely *local* — sceptical hypothesis? Because a Weak BIV *cannot* — as local sceptical hypotheses permit — come to know *anything* by means of *sense perception*. That which it can come to know — that it *is* a BIV — is not, *ex hypothesi*, knowable by sense perception. BIVs have no such faculties; they're limited to *pseudo-perception*.

With this distinction drawn, and examples explained, we can construct our argument:

---

20   Cf. Cohen's (1999: 69) 'Brain-in-a-vat*'.

(WARRANT FOR 1) The table looks red.

(Local Necessary? No)

(1) The table is red.

(2) If the table is red, then I'm not a Weak BIV being deceived into falsely believing the table is red.

(3) I'm not a Weak BIV being deceived into falsely believing the table is red.

Why does such (EK)-style reasoning dictate that the answer to *(Local Necessary?)* is 'no'? As with — and to the level of — (EK), something is unsatisfactory with coming to know that one is not such a Weak BIV in such a manner. But *(Local Necessary? No)* has delivered a conclusion — unlike as with (EK) — falsifying a *global* sceptical hypothesis. Could the characteristic shared by *(Local Necessary? No)* and (EK) that explains our like dissatisfaction with reasoning therewith be the following: that there is *(ex hypothesi) other reliable evidence available* — other, that is, than evidence acquired by (EK)-style reasoning — for coming to know their conclusions?[21]

With respect to *(Local Necessary? No)* such evidence would be the *absence* of ticker-tapes, statistical evidence etc. informing you that you *are* a Weak BIV.[22] What background knowledge a subject must have to exploit such evidence is something I don't explore. Just assume that whatever background knowledge is required, our subject has it. I'm supposing our subject could, at a certain point, engage in the following non-(EK)-style *modus tollens* reasoning:

(Weak BIV)

(1) If I am a Weak BIV, then I will have received evidence that I am a Weak BIV by now.

(2) I haven't received evidence that I'm a Weak BIV.

(3) I'm not a Weak BIV.

---

21   It's a presupposition of the *availability of other reliable evidence* that the relevant subject is *able to recognise and exploit* such evidence as evidence for the hypothesis in question (cf. n. 30 *infra*).
22   Cf. Cohen (1999: 69).

Note that (3) leaves open that one *is* a Strong BIV. Now suppose, as a result of (Weak BIV)-reasoning, our subject acquires reliable evidence for (3). (This supposition is not uncontroversial: in general, it is not clear how much weight in favour of Not-Weak-BIV is provided by the *absence* of evidence *for* Weak BIV.) Our subject can then deploy such evidence to come to know, by non-(EK)-style reasoning, the conclusion of *(Local Necessary? No)*.[23] Such evidence can be evidence directly for the conclusion of *(Local Necessary? No)*, and thus deployment of it needn't proceed by way of (EK)-style reasoning.[24] Before — as I shall — conclusively answering affirmatively to the question whether the *availability of other reliable evidence* is the key to explaining our intuitions, let's press on to thought experiment two and our negative answer to *(Local Sufficient?)*.

3.5 *Thought experiment two — why the answer to (Local Sufficient?) is 'no'.* We need a piece of (EK)-style reasoning which doesn't seem as unsatisfactory as (EK)-reasoning, but which delivers (knowledge of) the falsity of a (merely) local sceptical hypothesis. We need (EK) again, but with an accompanying stipulation:

---

23 I concede, given that a global sceptical hypothesis undermines all *perceptual* warrants, that (Weak BIV)-reasoning (which presupposes some form of externalism about perceptual evidence) is not clear-cut. I think my final proposal may go through without *reliance on* (Weak BIV)-reasoning, however (i.e. with reliance instead on the coming thought experiment two).

24 Two related points. (1) Of course, there *is* inference involved in *obtaining* the evidence, viz. (Weak BIV)-reasoning. The 'directness' point (here and, *mutatis mutandis*, later in the chapter) is simply that once this evidence is obtained, no further inference — and certainly not (EK)-style reasoning — *need* be involved: a non-inferential transition can instead occur. (2) *Needn't* so proceed; but *can*. Consider:

(WARRANT FOR 1) (Weak BIV)-reasoning, concluding with reliable evidence for its conclusion.

(1) I'm not a Weak BIV

(2) If I'm not a Weak BIV, then I'm not a Weak BIV being deceived into falsely believing the table is red.

(3) I'm not a Weak BIV being deceived into falsely believing the table is red.

In principle this is a live candidate for being a case of (EK)-style reasoning. Indeed, let us grant that (1) is a piece of basic knowledge (bracketing the difficult question of identifying the operative knowledge source). We can note that, not only is (1) *not* an everyday proposition, but, moreover, it *is* the falsity of a sceptical hypothesis. It is thus a peripheral case of (EK)-style reasoning. Notably, reasoning with this argument — unlike central cases of (EK)-style reasoning — does well in the S-project. And this is so because (WARRANT FOR 1) can be evidence directly for (3).

(WARRANT FOR 1) The table looks red.

(Local Sufficient? No)

(1) The table is red.

(2) If the table is red, then it is not white with red lights shining on it.

(3) The table is not white with red lights shining on it.

Accompanying stipulation: Unlike with (EK), there's no other (inductive) knowledge-conferring evidence available against the possibility that there are red lights shining on the table.

Such — *ex hypothesi* proscribed — (inductive) evidence could be perceptual, memorial, or testimonial. Such evidence can be evidence directly for the conclusion of *(Local Sufficient? No)*, and thus deployment of it needn't proceed by way of (EK)-style reasoning.[25] (Note that this is merely a thought experiment designed to prise apart conceptually the real distinction driving Cohen's intuition from the (cross-cutting) global/local distinction. There is thus no need to demonstrate that the accompanying stipulation is commonly true. Indeed, as a matter of fact, it will commonly be false. We are countenancing a scenario in which there is no other way of gaining evidence one way or the other about red lights, other than following through the (EK)-reasoning. One thing

---

25 *Needn't* so proceed; but *can*. Consider:

(WARRANT FOR 1) Inductive evidence that there aren't red lights shining on the table.
(1) There aren't red lights shining on the table.
(2) If there aren't red light shining on the table, then the table is not white with red lights shining on it.
(3) The table is not white with red lights shining on it.

Again (cf. n. 24), in principle this is a live candidate for being a case of (EK)-style reasoning. Indeed, let us grant that (1) is a piece of basic *inductive* knowledge. This time, however (cf. n. 24), we can note that, while (1) *is*, plausibly, an everyday proposition, it is *also* the negation of a sceptical hypothesis. It is thus a peripheral case of (EK)-style reasoning. Notably, reasoning with this argument — unlike central cases of (EK)-style reasoning — does well in the S-project. And this is so because (WARRANT FOR 1) can be evidence directly for (3).

is clear, however: in order to keep the sceptical hypothesis relevantly local, the scenario cannot be one in which an evil demon is going to prevent our discovery of the red lights by providing experiences as of there not being red lights.)

So, why does *(Local Sufficient? No)*-reasoning dictate that the answer to *(Local Sufficient?)* is 'no'? As with (EK*), *(Local Sufficient? No)*-reasoning has *not* generated intuitions of unsatisfactoriness to the level generated by (EK)-reasoning. But, in contrast with (EK*), it's delivered (knowledge of) the falsity of a (merely) local sceptical hypothesis. I suggest the characteristic shared by *(Local Sufficient? No)* and (EK*), which explains our similar level of satisfaction with reasoning therewith, is that there's *(ex hypothesi) no other reliable evidence available* — other, that is, than evidence acquired by (EK)-style reasoning — for coming to know, respectively, that there aren't red lights shining on the table, and that I'm not a BIV.[26] Consider the following dilemma apropos of *(Local Sufficient? No)*: Either one doesn't know the conclusion at all — in which case (local) scepticism is true — or, in the absence of alternative satisfactory routes to knowledge of (3), one does know the conclusion by means of (EK)-style reasoning such as *(Local Sufficient? No)*-reasoning. Given we — I assume — don't want to cave in to scepticism by taking the first horn, we must — however reluctantly — grasp the second horn. (As the accompanying stipulation will commonly be false, circumstances in which one would *need* to employ *(Local Sufficient? No)*-reasoning in order to acquire knowledge of (3) will be vanishingly small. But the moral to be drawn from this thought experiment is *not* that *(Local Sufficient? No)*-reasoning is a vital form of anti-sceptical reasoning. We are simply using this thought experiment to try to identify the *correct basis* on which (EK*)-reasoning — a (putatively) vital form of anti-sceptical reasoning — is less unsatisfactory than (EK)-reasoning.)

Quite apart from the question whether the two thought experiments are ultimately dialectically effective, there seems to be something intuitive about the main idea. On the whole — and especially when we are doing science, for example — we prefer evidence that retains its

---

26   There is, however, a salient difference between *(Local Sufficient? No)* and (EK*) in this regard: in the former, such evidence is stipulated to be *de facto* unavailable, whereas in the latter, such evidence is *in principle* unavailable. Considering further possible implications of this difference is a good exercise.

evidential status even if we begin by doubting the hypothesis that the evidence is supposed to support. We are not keen to allow that evidence that lacks this property provides a route to knowledge, if evidence that has the property is available. But if we do well doxastically in a case where there is no possibility of evidence with the preferred property, then we are inclined to allow that this might be sufficient for knowledge. (We might also think that there is a distinction to be made between knowledge that meets the additional condition and knowledge that does not, because it cannot, meet it.)

3.6   In sum: there is something to be said for the idea that doing well in the D-project yields knowledge. But there is also something to be said for the idea that knowledge requires doing well in the S-project. When someone does not do well in the S-project — say, in (EK), by not being able to settle the question whether (3) is true — it is natural to say that he has not come to know (3), because there is a higher standard that the person could meet. This generates conflicting pressures on our use of 'knows', since there are some cases where one does well in the (less demanding) D-project, but not in the (more demanding) S-project.[27] One of those pressures is towards saying that knowledge requires doing well, not only in the D-project but also in the S-project. So, when Cohen's son asks: 'How do you know?', he is (usually) looking for an answer to the question how Cohen did well in the S-project. That is, how did Cohen deploy evidence to settle the question whether (3) is true?[28] The answer that Cohen gives his son in the case of (EK) is unsatisfying. It says nothing, for example, about evidence that shifts the balance of probability in favour of proposition (1), 'The table is red', and against

---

[27] There may be additional conflicting tendencies generated by the S-project itself. Consider a case — say (EK) — in which the thinker did well in deciding to believe (1) and also in settling the question whether (1), but is not able to settle the question whether, say, (3): On the one hand, the thinker did settle the question whether (1) was true, so we might say that he did come to know that (1) is true (even by the demanding standard of doing well in the S-project). On the other hand, a plausible closure principle, plus the fact that the thinker is unable to settle the question whether (3) is true, may add up to a reason for saying that he does not know (by the demanding standard of doing well in the S-project) that (1) is true after all. So there may be conflict *between* the two standards and there may be additional conflicts *within* the use of the more demanding standard.

[28] This would have to be evidence that one could rationally deploy even while suppositionally regarding the question as open *pro tem*.

the sceptical hypothesis ~(3). But now we see that this is equally true in the case of (EK*). Yet, in this case, it is less clear that the account is unsatisfying, and it is less clear that we want to conclude that Cohen really does not know.

What all this suggests is that there is pressure towards saying that knowledge requires doing well in the S-project except in cases where it is *not possible* to use evidence — *no other reliable evidence is available* — to settle the question whether the proposition in question is true or not.[29] The foregoing, and related, modals are left uninterpreted.[30, 31] Perhaps the pressure towards saying that knowledge requires doing well in the S-project reduces as the operative notion of possibility (and availability) becomes more difficult to meet (and vice-versa). In the case of (EK) it *is possible* to use evidence — *other reliable evidence is available* — to settle the question whether or not (3) is true: deploying inductive evidence, for example (though not the evidence of a table looking red).[32] So, in the case of (EK), Cohen has failed to measure up to a standard that he could have measured up to — doing well in the project of settling the question whether or not (3) is true. The question-settling warrant provided by the evidence described in (WARRANT FOR 1) cannot be redeployed as a

---

29   Quotidian extensions of knowledge by competent deduction or inference — in which there is often other reliable evidence available for the conclusion — are correctly permitted: such deductions or inferences do well in the S-project.

30   Clearly, in one sense — the sense that such uninterpretedness leaves some degree of indeterminacy about application of my proposal — this is regrettable (cf. n. 21 *supra*). However, in another sense, such uninterpretedness is welcome. My proposal, though abstract, is still assessable. And there is a sense in which it can be considered a merit of an abstract proposal such as this that it can be assessed independently from, and in advance of, committing on how to interpret the modals in question. Finally, we can note that in the case of (EK*), *however these modals are cashed out*, there *is no (reliable) evidence (available)* to settle the question whether or not (3) is true.

31   Relatedly, it is possible — though I have not done so here — explicitly to prise apart two notions in the area of 'evidence (un)availability': (1) there *is a kind of evidence* such that, if one were to experience it, then one would have some support for X; (2) there *is a kind of investigation that one can undertake*, which has some prospect of uncovering evidence that would provide some support for X. It may be that ~(1) is a more natural understanding of 'unavailability' when considering the Weak/Strong BIV distinction and ~(2) is more natural when considering 'red-table' cases. Be that as it may, I'm confident my proposal — perhaps, once the two notions are explicitly prised apart, provided we do not flit unreflectively between them — survives such an observation.

32   The evidence described in (WARRANT FOR 1) does, however, normally count as settling the question whether the table is red or blue, for example.

question-settling warrant for (3), but other evidence, we've noted, *could* have been used in an S-project for (3). In the case of (EK*), in contrast, Cohen has failed to measure up to a standard that he *could not* have measured up to. It is not just that the evidence described in (WARRANT FOR 1) cannot be redeployed to settle the question whether or not (3) is true. There is *no evidence* that could be deployed to settle that question. Both (EK)-reasoning and (EK*)-reasoning count as examples of doing badly in the S-project.[33] But in the case of (EK*), this failure does not exert as much pressure towards saying that the reasoning is not a route to knowledge.[34]

---

33 By dint of suffering transmission failure. Davies (2009) uses two notions of transmission failure. The kind of transmission failure that he discerns in easy knowledge arguments is not, however, the kind that is closely related to epistemic circularity. (On a dogmatist conception of the situation, there is, of course, no epistemic circularity in these examples.)

34 Objection: consider the following kind of (direct) inference: The table is red; therefore, either I am not a BIV being deceived into falsely believing that the table is red, or there is not a zebra standing behind me right now. This disjunction is presumably one that a subject could come to know by other reliable means (by knowing the second disjunct via, say, perception or testimony). Given this, my proposal, given such reasoning does badly in the S-project, thereby classifies such reasoning as defective. But — objection — the reasoning is, intuitively, not clearly defective. Reply: we explain this intuition by noting that the conclusion can be reached non-defectively in two discrete steps: I (step 1) infer the first disjunct by satisfactory (EK*)-reasoning; I then (step 2) reach the conclusion by disjunction introduction.

4. Evidence and Transmission Failure

Against the claim that the impression that there are instances of transmission failure is the product of a flawed conception of evidence, I argue that transmission failure (conceived as related to epistemic circularity) is possible on most plausible accounts of evidence. The importance of this (exploratory) chapter is primarily theoretical, rather than dialectical.

0.1 Consider the following argument:

(MOORE)

(1) I have hands.

(2) If I have hands an external world exists.

(3) An external world exists.

Our focus in this chapter is on (MOORE), but points will generalise to (reasoning by means of) arguments with a similar structure (e.g. (TABLE)/(EK)). (MOORE) is clearly valid and its premises are true. Yet, to many, reasoning by means of this argument — which we are calling *(MOORE)-reasoning* — seems defective. On one view (e.g. Wright's), it is an example of *transmission failure*. In section 2 we'll come to precisify this concept. For now let's make do with a very rough first pass at transmission failure. Philosophers locating the defectiveness of (MOORE)-reasoning in transmission failure, typically take (MOORE)-reasoning to suffer from a form of *epistemic circularity*: it's only if one already has warrant for (3), that one can have a warrant for (1). If (MOORE)-reasoning suffers from transmission failure in this way, we can say that propounding the argument cannot offer one a new route to a warranted belief in its conclusion.

0.2   What's one's warrant to believe (1)? Put differently: what's one's evidence for (1)? (Suppose the conditional premise (2) is knowable *a priori*.) These questions are badly formed. There are various different warrants one might have for (1). Lots of things could be one's evidence for (1). Suppose I'm sitting blindfolded, unable to see my hands, and Edna whispers gently in my ear: 'You have hands'. Edna's utterance — on one plausible view — counts as good testimonial evidence for me that I have hands. That's one form of evidence I might have for (1), and there are many others.

Let's focus, though, on visual-perceptual evidence that I have hands, and specifically the *mere having* of a visual experience *as of* having hands — the having of which is compatible with my failing to have hands.[1] (Indeed, unless we focus on a particular form of evidence it will be indeterminate whether transmission failure occurs.) With this assumption about the nature of my evidence for (1), the idea that (MOORE)-reasoning involves epistemic circularity has some initial plausibility. For, it might be said, it's only if I antecedently and independently have a warrant for (3) that an experience as of having hands constitutes a warrant for (1). If, by contrast, I had good reason to think that (3) was false and that I was a handless brain-in-a-vat (BIV) with experiences that were being generated by an evil scientist, then merely having a visual experience as of having hands would not be such good evidence for (1). (But, whether or not you think that you are a BIV, it can be maintained that an experience as of having hands raises

---

1   An experience *as of* x is an experience representing x, the having of which is compatible with ~x (and, indeed, compatible with x). This may need to be finessed, depending on one's view on object-dependent experience, to the following: an experience *as of* x is an experience representing x, *and the having of an experience with the same conscious character* is compatible with ~x (and, indeed, compatible with x). Finally, note that even when we settle on a specific possible warrant for (1), the questions may still be alleged to be badly formed on account of the notion of evidence not having been explicitly introduced (e.g. the Bayesian might ask is evidence *simply* a proposition on which credences can be updated by conditionalisation?).

the probability of (1) [I have hands — rather than flippers, or bloody stumps] and also of (1)′ [I am a BIV and the evil scientist is producing an experience as of having hands — rather than producing an experience as of having flippers or as of having bloody stumps].)

If (MOORE)-reasoning does involve epistemic circularity, then following through the reasoning could not provide a new route to a warranted belief in (3). Even if one were to allow that it would provide a *new*, gratuitously circuitous, *route*, still it would not be a way of arriving, *for the first time* (cf. Wright 2002: 333), at a position in which one had a warrant to believe (3). (Recall, in Chapter One I showed that, even if it would not be a way of arriving, for the first time, at a position in which one had some warrant or other to believe (3), it could still be a way of arriving, for the first time, at a position in which one had a (partly) perceptual warrant to believe (3).)

0.3   Some philosophers — *viz*. Timothy Williamson (2000: ch.9), John Hawthorne (2004: 34, n. 86),[2] and Nicholas Silins (2005)[3] — (can be taken to) claim that there are *no* genuine instances of transmission failure, provided we operate with the right *account of the sources of warrant-or-evidence*[4] *for future reasoning*.[5] This novel terminology requires some preliminary exposition. As to sources of warrant-or-evidence, pre-theoretically, or before commitment to any particular theory, warrant or evidence can come in myriad forms: blood and DNA samples,

---

2   "I find most alleged examples of [transmission failure] unconvincing."
3   But cf. Silins (2007: 128, n. 27) for an evolution in his views. These three philosophers — *viz*. Williamson, Hawthorne, and Silins — say very different things of relevance to the issues presently under consideration; moreover, they do not always explicitly mention such issues when saying things of relevance thereto (hence my hedging device of 'can be taken to' in the main text). For example, here are two distinct, but closely related claims (and it is not always clear which is best ascribed to these philosophers): (1) there are no genuine instances of transmission failure (full stop); (2) it can seem as if there are cases of transmission failure, but when you look more closely you will see that these seemings are the product of a flawed view about sources of warrant-or-evidence for future reasoning.
4   Cf. Klein's (1995) notion of 'sources of justification'.
5   We can certainly grant to these epistemologists that there is *an* exceptionless notion of what we might call warrant transmission. We would then say that when *other epistemologists* talk about there being instances of transmission failure, this suggests that they are using a more demanding notion of warrant transmission than the exceptionless notion. And one possible more demanding requirement — our focus — would be to exclude epistemic circularity.

hearsay, facts, states of affairs, objects etc. Our principal focus, though, will be on two particular possible sources of warrant-or-evidence: an experience and a premise (i.e. a proposition).[6] As to future reasoning, we may take inference to be our paradigm case thereof (as contrasted, for example, with coming to know that from which one infers).[7] My aim in this chapter is to (begin to) clear the way for instances of transmission failure *regardless of* the account of the sources of warrant-or-evidence for future reasoning with which one operates. My aim is not to claim there *are in fact* genuine instances of transmission failure; merely to render it *possible* on *all* — or most — plausible accounts of the sources of warrant-or-evidence for future reasoning.[8]

0.4 Silins (2005: 84–89) claims instances of transmission failure only arise on a particular — putatively flawed — account of the sources of warrant-or-evidence for future reasoning.[9] Call this *Silins's claim*. Here's a key commitment of this account. (Silins is going to reject the commitment and reject the account of which it is a commitment. It may help to keep (MOORE) in mind when reading this passage.):

> [Y]ou might know a certain premise, or indeed be absolutely certain that the premise is true, yet still not possess the premise as a warrant for a conclusion you have competently deduced from the premise. On this view, if your inference provides you with any warrant for believing[10]

---

6 Regarding experience: cf. Conee and Feldman (2008), for whom all *ultimate* evidence is experiental. Regarding premises: some readers may find it hard to think of a premise in an argument as *warrant-or-evidence*. My parenthetical reference to a proposition may make it less hard. Regardless, I ask for patience on the part of the reader, and trust the idea will be clearer by the chapter's end.

7 And so 'future' is not the temporal notion where the contrast is with 'past' and 'present' reasoning. Instead, in our paradigm case, we suppose a reasoner knows a proposition and ask what sources of warrant-or-evidence such a reasoner has at his disposal should he go on (*in the future; subsequently*) to perform an inference. Finally, our focus in this chapter is on future *deductive* reasoning.

8 And, indeed, on *all* — or most — plausible *conceptions of evidential warrant* (a term explained in 1.1 *infra*).

9 I call the account *fallibilism* — (explained in 1.2 *infra*). Strictly it is an account of the sources of warrant-or-evidence for future reasoning *and a conception of evidential warrant*. Silins's claim receives a sharpening later (see n. 37 *infra*), but this version will do in the meantime. Finally, I take it this claim can be fairly ascribed to Silins. Nonetheless, should he resist it, the claim itself is worth independent exploration.

10 For Silins (2005: 74), "when [he] say[s] that someone's warrant *for believing* that p is that w…[he] means that the person believes that p, and that the person believes that p on the basis of the relevant [warrant, w]". (And so Silins appears to use 'warrant

the conclusion at all, the warrant provided is the prior warrant for which you believe the premise. Thus even if you know that p, or are absolutely certain that p, it is still not the case that your warrant for believing the conclusion is that p. (Silins 2005: 88)

Sticking with (MOORE), suppose, as before, my warrant to believe (1) is my having an experience *as of* having hands. Nonetheless, suppose I can come to know, on the basis of this warrant, that I have hands. Suppose also, that I know (1), and am certain that (1) is true. Finally suppose I competently deduce — using the conditional, (2) — (3) from (1). Silins now cuts in that, on this (to-be-rejected) account of the sources of warrant-or-evidence for future reasoning, if my inference provides me with any warrant to believe (3) at all, the warrant provided is my experience as of having hands. Crucially, Silins points out, on this account, even though I know that I have hands, and am certain that I have hands, it's not the case that I can use the fact that I have hands as a source of warrant-or-evidence *for future reasoning*. Specifically, I can't use *the premise* that I have hands — a premise, note, whose truth is *incompatible with* my being in an idealistic world — as a source of warrant-or-evidence to believe there to be an external world. Rather, on this account, all I can use is *my experience* as of having hands, combined with inference — an experience, note, the having of which is *not incompatible with* my being in an idealistic world.[11]

Silins's claim that instances of transmission failure arise only on one (to-be-rejected) account is resisted in this chapter. One cannot confine the possibility of transmission failure to this one account of the sources of warrant-or-evidence for future reasoning. So, at least, I shall argue.

---

for believing' for doxastic, rather than propositional, warrant.) I do not take this to be orthodox usage, but we can grant it for present purposes without harm.

11 Silins pins this account on Wright (2002) and Davies (2003). It might be worth quickly pointing out what else a philosopher operating with this account *can* do (all assuming he meets the epistemic standards for knowing (1)). First, he can competently deduce (3) and come to believe (3) on that basis: he can allow that, in the exceptionless sense of what we might call warrant transmission (cf. n. 5 *supra*), the experiential warrant for (1) is transmitted to (3). Second, if such a philosopher is a *dogmatist* (see Pryor 2000), he can allow that, even in a more demanding sense of warrant transmission that excludes epistemic circularity, the experiential warrant for (1) is transmitted to (3). Finally — whether dogmatist of not — he can allow that, if asked why he believes (3), he can legitimately reply: well, I have hands — I know that much — and (3) follows from what I know.

1. Conceptions of Evidential Warrant and Accounts of Sources of Warrant-or-Evidence for Future Reasoning

1.1 Consider (where, throughout, 'S' is a placeholder for a subject and 'p' for a proposition):

Fallibilism: S can know p when S's evidence for p is compatible with $\sim p$.

Infallibilism: S cannot know p when S's evidence for p is compatible with $\sim p$.

Focusing on (MOORE), fallibilists can suppose my *having an experience as of having hands* is — or can be — (part of) my way of coming to know that I have hands.[12] Infallibilists, by contrast, typically suppose my *seeing that I have hands* is my way of coming to know that I have hands, where my seeing that I have hands is incompatible with my not having hands.[13] Think of fallibilism and infallibilism as particular *conceptions of evidential warrant*: they're particular views of what it takes for a piece of evidence to warrant a belief in a proposition for a subject such that that subject can acquire knowledge. A philosopher's conception of evidential warrant is typically associated with a particular account of the sources of warrant-or-evidence for future reasoning. A fallibilist typically takes an *experience* as of having hands as his source of warrant-or-evidence for future reasoning (and indeed sometimes, perhaps often, for (1) itself). An infallibilist typically takes (knowledge of) *(1) itself* — a *premise* — as his source of warrant-or-evidence for future reasoning (and indeed sometimes, perhaps often, as his source of warrant-or-evidence for (1) itself).

---

12 Such fallibilists will be dogmatists. All dogmatists are fallibilists; but not all fallibilists are dogmatists. For non-dogmatist fallibilists (e.g. Wright) we must rely on the parenthetical 'part of': this experience is supplemented with my having an unearned warrant to accept/trust/believe that I am not a BIV etc.

13 Cf. McDowell (1982, 1986, 2008), a *fact disjunctivist*, and Williamson (2000: ch.1) for whom seeing that p entails knowing that p. Note that a fallibilist may also, for example, allow that sometimes, perhaps often, we see that p — that is, we *enjoy* evidence incompatible with $\sim p$.

1.2 Philosophers who've explored the *possibility* of transmission failure in (MOORE)-reasoning (and in like arguments) — *viz.* Martin Davies (2004, 2009), James Pryor (2004), and Crispin Wright (1985, 2002) — operate with a fallibilist conception of evidential warrant. Let's — exhaustively and exclusively — partition fallibilism as follows:

Fallibilism—: S can know p when S's evidence for p is compatible with ~p, and when S knows p, p itself is not part of S's evidence-base for future reasoning.[14]

Fallibilism+: S can know p when S's evidence for p is compatible with ~p, and when S knows p, p itself is part of S's evidence-base for future reasoning.

These theses are constructed by combining a conception of evidential warrant (first conjunct: fallibilism) with an account of the sources of warrant-or-evidence for future reasoning (second conjunct: 'evidence-base for future reasoning').[15] Precisely what the second conjunct of fallibilism— forbids is a subtle matter (cf. n. 11 *supra*). I take it, somewhat suggestively, to be the following: the fallibilist— denies that a known premise, p, can *itself* be *used* in future reasoning, but this leaves open that future reasoning *from* a known premise, p, can lead to, for example, further knowledge.[16] Fallibilists are typically fallibilists—;[17] but nothing in fallibilism rules out being a fallibilist+.

---

14 Note that this leaves open that, though p itself is *not* part of S's evidence base *for future reasoning*, it *is* part of S's evidence base *for knowing p*.

15 A note about the *exhaustivity* of these two theses: I take it that p either *necessarily is* or *necessarily is not* part of S's evidence base for future reasoning. Consistently with this, contingent matters could be in play rendering p, though part of S's evidence base for future reasoning, *not exploitable* (e.g. on account of epistemic circularity). (Alternatively, one might recast the second conjunct of fallibilism— as 'p itself *necessarily* is not part of S's evidence base for future reasoning' and the second conjunct of fallibilism+ as 'p itself is *or can be* part of S's evidence base for future reasoning'.)

16 Where 'used' is, perhaps, elliptical shorthand for 'used *as a source of warrant-or-evidence*'. And where 'future reasoning *from* a known premise' is, perhaps, elliptical shorthand for 'future reasoning *from warrant for* a known premise'. Finally, such a fallibilist can allow that, if the premise, p, is not known, perhaps because it is not true, then reasoning from p to a conclusion may be above reproach and yet will not normally lead to knowledge.

17 E.g. Fred Dretske, notwithstanding that he's classifiable as an infallibilist on a different way — present in the literature — of carving things up. Finally, I take it that dogmatists can be either fallibilists— or fallibilists+.

1.3   Now consider:

> *Infallibilism+*: S cannot know *p* when S's evidence for *p* is compatible with ~*p*, and when S knows *p*, *p* itself is part of S's evidence-base for future reasoning.[18]

As with our previous two theses, this thesis is constructed by combining a conception of evidential warrant (first conjunct: infallibilism) with an account of the sources of warrant-or-evidence for future reasoning (second conjunct: 'evidence-base for future reasoning'). To conclude: how do the fallibilist+ and infallibilist+ differ? Each, after all, allows *p itself* into one's evidence-base for future reasoning. Two features distinguish them. First, most obviously, they operate with different conceptions of evidential warrant: for the former — but not the latter — one can know *p* when one's evidence for *p* is compatible with ~*p*. Second, and less obviously, the latter's allowance of *p* itself into one's evidence-base *may well not be confined* to future reasoning (*p* itself, on versions of this view, is part of one's evidence-base *for knowing p*), while the former's allowance *may well be* so confined (on versions of this view) — cf. nn. 13 and 14 *supra*. In part because our chief focus in this chapter is on *future* reasoning, and in part because we only seek to secure the *possibility* — rather than genuine instances — of transmission failure, neither difference, though important, turns out to be fundamental for our purposes.[19]

We now have a (novel) taxonomy of conceptions of evidential warrant and accounts of the sources of warrant-or-evidence for future

---

18   There is close to being merely *logical space* for *infallibilism*— (*modulo* 'evidence base' being used in the way I describe). At any rate, it's difficult to discern the motivation for such a thesis. Given this, in the main text I quickly revert to simply talking of infallibilists.

19   Many issues I've opened up in this section require more detailed treatment. For example: What does it take — knowledge? warrant(ed belief)? truth? — for a proposition to be included in one's evidence? Is (possession of) propositional evidence for *p* compatible with ~*p*? On some views your evidence will include the proposition that *p* when you know *p*, but you could have had that evidence even if you warrantedly, yet falsely, believed that *p*. Moreover, my discussion of the presented theses has proceeded in hedged terms with, for example, 'often', 'typically', and 'may well' in place of 'necessarily' at many junctures (here and in what follows). I don't see that this is avoidable, however.

reasoning to hand. Now let's try to precisify the concept of transmission failure and locate it within this taxonomy.

2. Transmission Failure and (In)fallibilism

2.1 Consider this (sufficient) condition for non-transmission:

(NT) Non-transmission of warrant

Epistemic warrant is not transmitted from the premises of a valid argument to its conclusion if the putative support offered for one of the premises is conditional on its being antecedently and independently reasonable to accept the conclusion. (Davies 2004: 221)

Let's spell out *one* view of how (MOORE)-reasoning *might* suffer from transmission failure. Let's take the fallibilist—. Suppose the fallibilist— claims (cf. Wright 1985, 2002, 2004) that:

(AW) In order for one's visual experience as of having hands to act as warrant for (1) one must, antecedently, have warrant for (3).[20]

If *(AW)* is true, one's warrant for (1) will depend on an antecedent warrant for (3). So (MOORE)-reasoning will suffer from epistemic circularity and *(NT)* will be triggered. Suppose that one *in fact has* antecedent warrant for (3), so that one's visual experience does count as warrant for (1). Then, according to *(NT)*, the warrant for (1) that is constituted by one's experience as of having hands is not transmitted across the conditional — (2) — to serve as warrant for (3).[21]

---

20 Rejection of *(AW)* is a defining feature of dogmatism. In this section we focus on fallibilists not flatly rejecting *(AW)*: that is, fallibilists allowing that (MOORE)-reasoning might involve epistemic circularity, and so might suffer from transmission failure. Indeed given the chapter's overall focus is not to claim there *are in fact* genuine instances of transmission failure, but merely to render it *possible* on *all*, or most, plausible accounts of the sources of warrant-or-evidence for future reasoning, we do not definitively adjudicate on *(AW)* (or its cognate, *(AW*)* — see 3.2 *infra*) at all in this chapter.

21 This failure of transmission is, trivially, not a failure of transmission in the exceptionless sense (cf. n. 5 *supra*). It is failure of transmission in the more demanding sense that requires that there not be epistemic circularity. And it seems that this remains the situation even if we regard the warrant for (1) as being *constituted* by *both* the experience as of having hands *and* the antecedent warrant for (3).

2.2 What about our fallibilist+ (cf. Silins 2005)? Consider him debating with our fallibilist−, and arguing thus: if you, fallibilist−, are allowing, as a good fallibilist should, that I can come to know p notwithstanding my evidence for p is compatible with ~p, and allowing that I do indeed come to know (1) on the basis of such *non-entailing* evidence, why are you preventing me from using *(1) itself* as evidence in my future reasoning? (I leave open whether the non-entailing evidence for (1) is just the experience, or is additionally the antecedent warrant for (3).) If you were a sceptic about our knowledge of quotidian propositions, I'd vehemently disagree with you, being a good fallibilist myself, but I could at least make sense of your prohibition on my use of (1) as evidence in future reasoning: I couldn't so use (1) as I wouldn't, *ex hypothesi*, know (1). But given, as we can happily agree as fallibilists, I know (1), your exclusion of *it — that premise —* from my evidence-base for future reasoning is unmotivated.[22]

Our fallibilist+ makes a good case. So let's grant him, *pro tem*, victory over his fallibilist− foe. Our fallibilist+ may have won this particular battle, but not yet the war. Fallibilist− is a dogged soul. Suppose he accepts defeat over the inclusion of *(1) itself* in one's evidence-base for future reasoning, but then marshals *(AW)* and claims that fallibilist+'s *(MOORE)*-reasoning thereby suffers transmission failure.

If, however, fallibilism+ is true, it's no longer clear that *(AW)* leads to *(MOORE)*-reasoning suffering (complete)[23] transmission failure. Why not? After all, isn't it still the case, thanks to *(AW)*, that *(NT)* is triggered? Recall, *(NT)* distinguishes between premises (which are propositions

---

22 Both of these fallibilists should agree that, provided that one knows (1), one will do well to believe (3), since it follows from (1) by a palpably valid inference (cf. n. 11 *supra*). (Of course, if one gets good evidence against (3), then the palpably valid inference may have to be run in the opposite direction.) But, because of possible epistemic circularity, there is more to be said about why one does well to believe (3). The argument via (1) and (2) appears to involve a detour and, in order to understand one's warrant to believe (3) after the inference, one needs to articulate the nature of the antecedent warrant — that is, one's warrant to believe (3) even before the inference.

23 As will become clear, here (and in what follows), when I talk of 'complete' transmission failure I am bracketing any exceptionless notion of warrant transmission (cf. n. 5 *supra*) and focusing on a more demanding notion. If there is, in this sense, 'complete' transmission failure, it means *all*, and not just *some*, of one's sources of warrant-or-evidence for future reasoning fail to transmit. I explicitly expand what I call the *standard* account of *warrant* in 3.2 *infra*.

like (1), in the (MOORE) example) and support for premises (which is an experience as of having hands, in the (MOORE) example). *(NT)* talks about a valid argument, and the only valid argument in view is from (1) via (2) to (3).

The wrinkle, though, is that it's no longer clear that *(NT)* is *applicable, given the truth of fallibilism+*. This is because of *(NT)*'s mere talk — when it comes to matters of transmission — of "support [...] for one of the premises", and not, additionally, talk of *premises themselves*.[24] *(NT)* seems, *pace* fallibilism+, to preclude *(1) itself* from counting amongst one's evidence-base for future reasoning. In other words, *(NT)* doesn't seem to capture adequately the account of the sources of warrant-or-evidence for future reasoning with which a fallibilist+ operates. Take this to be what I'm driving at in suggesting *(NT)* isn't *applicable* to fallibilism+ (and, *mutatis mutandis*, in subsequent uses of 'applicable'). Put differently: the non-transmission of one's *warrant for (1)* — which, by *(NT)*, is one's *support for* (1) — leaves open that *(1) itself* (which one *ex hypothesi* knows) transmits across the conditional ((2)) — perhaps, better, to account for the optionality of (2): across the relevant *inference* — to provide warrant for (3). In sum, I think, for all we've said, our fallibilist+ has won another (interim) battle.

Might it be objected that, if *(1) itself* is here being considered as a warrant that might be transmitted across the valid argument from (1) to (3), then presumably *(1) itself, qua* warrant, starts out as a warrant for (1), and is then transmitted to (3)? But, continues the objector, *qua* warrant for (1), *(1) itself* is not a fallibilist warrant but an infallibilist warrant. Such an objection misunderstands things. We noted before (cf. n. 13) that fallibilism— is compatible with the premise itself being part of one's evidence-base for *knowing the premise* (it just precluded the premise from forming part of one's evidence-base for *future reasoning*); *a fortiori* this is so for fallibilism+ (which has no such preclusion with respect to future reasoning). Fallibilism, abstracting from its species, is only a claim about what *can*, not what *must*, be the case when coming to know a proposition.

2.3   Before responding to our fallibilist+, let's tie together the fallibilist+ and the infallibilist (i.e. the infallibilist+, cf. n. 18 *supra*). To be sure each

---

24   This is evidence that philosophers operating with *(NT)* are (closet) fallibilists—.

philosopher, both the fallibilist+ and the infallibilist, operates with a different conception of evidential warrant. However, for the purposes of *this* transmission failure debate, this difference is less important than one's account of the sources of warrant-or-evidence for future reasoning.[25] Of *more* importance, then, is whether or not, when a subject comes to know (1) (or a like proposition), *(1) itself* becomes part of that subject's evidence-base for future reasoning. Their response unites the fallibilist+ and the infallibilist: it does. We thus must alter standard taxonomies. Typically, in debates pertaining to evidence, fallibilists and infallibilists are taken to be the two camps ripe for comparison.[26] However, in this transmission failure debate, it's best to group fallibilists— in one corner (by dint of their *refusal to allow* (1)-type propositions into one's evidence-base for future reasoning), and fallibilists+ and infallibilists together in the other corner (by dint of their *allowing* (1)-type propositions into one's evidence-base for future reasoning). To be clear, the fallibilist— does allow that (1)-type propositions are *premises* in future reasoning, in the sense that conclusions can be (competently) deduced from them; the prohibition is simply that (1)-type propositions can't be *sources of warrant-or-evidence* for said conclusions. We thus might hope that a good response, in the case at hand, to the fallibilist+ will also count as a good response to the infallibilist.

3. Modifying (NT) (and other germane theses)

3.1 The challenge is to see if we can construct a motivated (sufficient) condition for non-transmission of warrant which, unlike *(NT)*, is applicable to fallibilism+ and infallibilism, and which, if the condition is satisfied, precludes (1) itself from transmitting across the conditional

---

25 Our excursus into conceptions of evidential warrant was still useful. First, standard taxonomies foreground conceptions of evidential warrant: so this excursus helps locate our taxonomy in relation to standard ones. Second, while there are no entailments in play from one's conception of evidential warrant to one's account of the sources of warrant-or-evidence for future reasoning (or conversely), we might think that the former helps explain the latter.

26 Or a divide is effected between forms of *internalism* (typically associated with fallibilism) and *externalism* (typically associated with infallibilism). Effecting such a divide will not serve present purposes.

((2)) to provide warrant for (3).²⁷ A natural first response to putting the challenge this way would be to ask: what does it mean for *(1) itself* to fail to transmit across the conditional ((2)) to provide warrant for (3)? After all, (MOORE) is an instance of *modus ponens*. Let's assume a plausible knowledge-closure principle, say: If S knows p and S knows p entails q, then S knows (or at least is in a position to know) q. Given this (and given (2) is knowable *a priori*), if I know (1), I know (or am *in a position to know*) (3). What room is there for a motivated principle — a modification of *(NT)* — granting this, yet allowing that (1) itself can fail to transmit across the conditional ((2)) to provide warrant for (3)?

3.2   First, let's distinguish between a closure question and a transmission question. The germane closure question asks: is it possible to know (1), know that (1) entails (3), yet not be in a position to know (3)? The germane transmission question asks: is it possible to know (1), know that (1) entails (3), yet not *thereby* — that is, in virtue of knowing (1) and recognising the entailment from (1) to (3) — be in a position to know (3)? Or, putting the transmission question differently: is it possible to know (1), know that (1) entails (3), yet not be in a *first time* position to know (3)? Let's answer the closure question 'no' (closure is exceptionless), yet remain agnostic about the transmission question.²⁸ I take it that, even answering the closure question 'no', conceptual room is left open to deny that (1) itself transmits.

Second, let's expand what I'll call the *standard* account of *warrant*. Standardly, one's warrant is one's warrant *for this or that proposition*, and does not include *the proposition itself*; but we're not bound by standard usage. Indeed we're currently granting the fallibilist+ and infallibilist their claims that premise (1) becomes part of one's evidence-base for future reasoning, once one knows (1). We might therefore modify *(NT)*

---

27 The notion of non-transmission of warrant in play here is still based on epistemic circularity. Ideally this condition would also be applicable to *fallibilists*—. But this seems unrealistic. Nonetheless, a *desideratum* of parsimony (*viz. ceteris paribus*, construct as few theses as possible) operates in what follows.

28 For philosophers answering the closure question: 'yes', cf. Dretske (1970, 1971, 2005a, 2005b), Nozick (1981), and Heller (1999). For remarks on how one's operative account of the sources of warrant-or-evidence for future reasoning affects one's answer to the closure question, see Klein (1995).

by making explicit that warrant includes any known premises.[29] Here's a first pass:

(NT*) Non-transmission of warrant

Epistemic warrant — where warrant includes any known premises — is not transmitted from the premises of a valid argument to its conclusion if the putative support offered for one of the premises — or knowledge of any of the premises themselves — is conditional on its being antecedently and independently reasonable to accept the conclusion.[30]

Recall that, to show that (MOORE)-reasoning suffers transmission failure by *(NT)*, our fallibilist— marshalled thesis *(AW)*. And we can construct a thesis paralleling *(AW)* (call it *(AW*)*) which makes room for (complete) transmission failure in (MOORE)-reasoning by *(NT*)*:

(AW*) In order for one's warrant for (1), where warrant includes any known premises, to so act as warrant, one must, antecedently, have warrant for (3).

If *(AW*)* is true, and (as a central case) if one *in fact has* antecedent warrant for (3), (MOORE)-reasoning suffers transmission failure by *(NT*)*. Is the pair of theses *(NT*)* and *(AW*)* motivated?[31]

4. Motivating our Modifications

4.1 Let's start with *(AW*)*. As with *(AW)*, I don't want to marshal arguments purporting to secure *(AW*)*'s truth. Instead, I simply want to

---

29 'Warrant' is hereinafter used in this broad sense unless indicated otherwise.
30 Objection: if knowledge of a premise is conditional on antecedent warrant for the conclusion then this will be because epistemic warrant for the premise is conditional on antecedent warrant for the conclusion. It is therefore unclear why we need to introduce *(NT*)*. Reply: insofar as this objector is adopting my expanded account of warrant, I agree with the premise but not the conclusion. Only *(NT*)* allows us to make explicit the pivotal relation of epistemic antecedence between a *(known) premise* and a *standard warrant* (see sections 4 and 5 *infra*). Finally, insofar as warrant now includes known premises, it also *a fortiori* includes doxastically justified premises (cf. Tucker (2010), sections 2.1 and 3.1).
31 My focus in this section (and those to come) is on *known* premises. What happens when, say, the premise is false but warrantedly believed (cf. n. 19 *supra*)? I bracket this question, but see, *inter alia*, Klein (2008: 25–61).

present a way of formulating or expressing a defense of these (modified) theses. Recall, our overall strategy is not to secure *genuine instances* of transmission failure; it's merely to render it *possible*, on *all* — or most — plausible accounts of the sources of warrant-or-evidence for future reasoning. So, how might one go about expressing a defense of *(AW*)*? Let's approach this question indirectly. We'll first consider how one might express a defense of *(AW)* and see if that helps us in discerning a way to express a defense of *(AW*)*. Recall *(AW)*:

(AW) In order for one's visual experience as of having hands to act as warrant for (1) one must, antecedently, have warrant for (3).

One (likely) way of formulating or expressing a defense of this thesis would be by making use of notions contained within an account of a relation of *epistemic antecedence* (or *priority*):

(EA) One's warrant for accepting p is antecedent to one's warrant for accepting q iff one's reasons for accepting p do not *presuppose or rest on* one's reasons for accepting q.[32]

Someone defending *(AW)* would likely claim that one's visual experience acting as warrant for (1) presupposes, or rests on, one's reasons for accepting an external world exists. We don't need to *agree* with that bald statement offered in defense of *(AW)*. Indeed we here offer no reasons for *(AW)*'s (or *(AW*)*'s) truth. We just need to understand the claim so formulated or expressed.[33]

---

32 Cf. Pryor (2000: 525). Should the left-hand-side of *(EA)* strictly be: it's not the case that one's warrant for accepting q is epistemically antecedent (or prior) to one's warrant for accepting p? Couldn't the right-hand-side be satisfied and one's warrant for p be epistemically *neither-prior-to-nor-posterior-to* one's warrant for q? Finally, note that we can also, I take it, say: one's warrant for $p1$ is antecedent to one's warrant for $p2$ iff one's warrant for $p2$ is *dependent* on one's warrant for $p1$ and one's warrant for $p1$ is *not dependent* on one's warrant for $p2$.

33 Two related points. First, to see (EA)'s relevance to (AW), it is best to revert to n. 32's left-hand-side: if warrant for (1) presupposes or rests on one's warrant for (3), then it follows from (EA) that one's warrant for accepting (3) is epistemically antecedent (or prior) to one's warrant for accepting (1). Second, we need not find this notion of one reason presupposing or resting on another perfectly perspicuous; it's left intuitive.

4.2 That's *(AW)*. Now what about *(AW*)*? We might formulate or express a defense of *(AW*)* by making use of notions contained within an account of the following relation of epistemic antecedence:

> *(EA*)* One's warrant for accepting *p* is antecedent to one's warrant for accepting *q* — where warrant includes any known premises — iff one's reasons for accepting *p* do not *presuppose or rest on* one's reasons for accepting *q* — where one's reasons include any known premises.

We're supposing, recall, that *(1) itself* — which we *ex hypothesi* know — is part of our evidence-base for future reasoning. (We're leaving open whether or not *(1) itself* is part of our warrant for accepting (1). If it is, one might argue that my experience as of having hands *isn't* also part of my warrant for accepting (1), because *(1) itself* is an entailing (logically sufficient) warrant for (1), and so (1) does not need any additional support from the experience. Be this as it may, our chief focus is on one's evidence-base *for future reasoning*, and, as we'll come to see, this argument will not carry over to future reasoning in a straightforward manner.) In assessing (MOORE)-reasoning armed with notions from *(EA*)*, we're (in part) asking: does my knowing that (1) presuppose or rest on my reasons for accepting (3)?

Let's make an assumption — an assumption favourable to fallibilists+ in particular. To understand why we're making this assumption we need to understand a claim some (prominent) infallibilists make. Some infallibilists claim that *all and only* what one knows is one's evidence (see Williamson 2000: ch.9). So for this type of infallibilist our supposition that (1) itself is *part of* one's evidence-base for future reasoning, and that one's evidence-base for future reasoning *includes* (1) itself, is a slightly misleading supposition: for them, (knowledge of) (1) itself *exhaustively constitutes* one's evidence-base for future reasoning (prior to an act of inferring (3)).[34] Any pragmatic implication that there must or may be

---

[34] An infallibilist *might* claim that one's evidence for (1) consists of knowledge of (1) *and knowledge* of one's having an experience as of having hands. If he does so, the points I make in relation to the fallibilist+ here can be marshalled, *mutatis mutandis*, with respect to this infallibilist. But this is — for good reason — currently an unpopular way to be an infallibilist, so I'll ignore it in what follows. An infallibilist will typically only claim that one's evidence for (1) consists of knowledge of one's

more to one's evidence-base for future reasoning than (1) itself should be cancelled. (We can call this the *pragmatic implication objection*, with the cancellation operating as a reply thereto.) I hereby cancel any such implication by explicitly noting that 'part' does not mean 'proper part', and 'includes' does not mean there need be any more evidence. For our fallibilist+, meanwhile, *all* that one knows is in one's evidence-base for future reasoning, but not *only* what one knows: one still, in addition to (knowledge of) (1) itself, has one's visual experience as of having hands as part of one's evidence-base for future reasoning. This, at least, is one plausible way of carving up evidence for a fallibilist+.[35]

What's the purpose of this detour? Recall, the strategy is to explore using notions from *(EA*)* to formulate or express a defense of *(AW*)*, and to claim that *(AW*)* opens up the possibility of transmission failure for fallibilists+ and infallibilists by *(NT*)*. Given this, we don't want the fallibilist+[36] to be inexorably lumbered with (complete) transmission failure in (MOORE)-reasoning because *part of his warrant for (1)*, the part he shares with the fallibilist−, *viz.* a visual experience as of having hands, fails to transmit to (3).[37] To allow for this would be to slur over the important difference between the fallibilist− and the fallibilist+. To preclude this from happening, we make our assumption, *viz. some of one's warrant can fail to transmit in an argument without all of one's warrant failing to transmit*.[38] Maybe this assumption seems too

---

having an experience as of having hands in the *bad case* — that is, when ~(1) — but our principal focus in this chapter is not on bad cases.

35 There's logical space for a fallibilist+ to claim that his knowledge that (1) *trumps* or *wipes out* any non-entailing evidence he has for (1). But I find this a peculiar way of carving things up. To complete the picture, for our fallibilist− neither all that one knows, nor only what one knows, is in one's evidence base for future reasoning.

36 Or the infallibilist (cf. n. 34), but the fallibilist+ is the philosopher driving our present concern.

37 Recall that the fallibilists+ allows that when S knows p, p itself is part of S's evidence base for future reasoning. It is thus not a flawed account of the sources of warrant- or-evidence for future reasoning by the lights of Silins's claim (cf. 0.4 *supra*). It should, however, be clear that we would not have answered Silins's claim by showing that the warrant the fallibilist+ can share with the fallibilist− may fail to transmit. To make the dialectic clearer we may wish to sharpen Silins's claim thus: instances of *complete* transmission failure only arise on a particular, and putatively flawed, account of the sources of warrant-or-evidence for future reasoning (cf. n. 23 *supra*).

38 *Mutatis mutandis* for *reasons*: some of one's reasons for (1) may presuppose or rest on one's reasons for (3) without other of one's reasons for (1) presupposing or resting on one's reasons for (3).

obvious to need stating. But note that, without this assumption, if we suppose that *(AW*)*'s truth can be secured (perhaps with use of notions from *(EA*)*), this inevitably leads to a fallibilist+ being committed to (MOORE)-reasoning suffering transmission failure by *(NT*)*. That's because our trio of theses, *(EA*)*, *(AW*)*, and *(NT*)*, don't themselves discriminate between different warrants one might have for (1) (and for (3)). Given the two types of warrant on which we're focusing, *viz.* an experience and a premise, are lumped together, if one type fails to transmit in (MOORE)-reasoning (*viz.* the experience) *(NT*)* is sufficiently coarse-grained (a bad thing) that it delivers the result that (MOORE)-reasoning suffers from transmission failure, period. (We can call this the *coarse-grained objection*, with the ensuing deflection operating as a reply thereto.) This is an unwelcome result: our modified (transmission failure) theses — *(EA*)*, *(AW*)*, and *(NT*)* — should be able to discriminate on the basis of the salient differences between the fallibilist— and the fallibilist+. We need theses which *leave room*, in line with our assumption, for one type of warrant to *fail to transmit* in (MOORE)-reasoning (e.g. here, the experience), and another type of warrant *to transmit* (e.g. here, the premise). Rather than further refining, and complicating, our modified theses *themselves*, I leave the task of avoiding the foregoing unwelcome result to *sensitive application* of the modified theses.

(Let's pause briefly to think back to Chapter One. If one adopts Wright's view (which Silins would locate as fallibilism— in the present taxonomy), then (MOORE)-reasoning does not put one into a position of having warrant for (3) for the first time, but it does, I argued in Chapter One, put one into the position of having perceptual warrant for (3) for the first time. The antecedent warrant for (3) does not transmit, because one already had that warrant; but the perceptual warrant provided by the experience as of having hands (given the antecedent warrant for (3)) does transmit. Is this the opposite of what I am now saying in Chapter Four? No. Here I am simply *countenancing* the experience failing to transmit, compatibly with which the premise *could* transmit. In engaging with Silins, that was the apposite compatibility relation to consider. Whether the foregoing possibility actually obtains will depend on what the correct (non-)transmission theses decree (which, in turn, I've argued here, will depend on what relations of epistemic antecedence obtain). In Chapter One I made an attempt, given certain background assumptions, at sketching some plausible (non-)transmission theses on which antecedent warrant does not, but perceptual warrant does, transmit.)

4.3 Let's take stock. We might reconstruct the foregoing dialectic thus: we set out fallibilism—. We then set up three theses, *(EA)*, *(AW)*, and *(NT)*, which seemed motivated, and captured adequately the fallibilist—'s account of the sources of warrant-or-evidence (for future reasoning). We used notions from *(EA)* to descry one way to express a defense of *(AW)*. We then noted that, assuming *(AW)* and fallibilism—, we had transmission failure in (MOORE)-reasoning by *(NT)*. Fine. We then noted that it wasn't clear the account of the sources of warrant-or-evidence (for future reasoning) presupposed by these three theses was the same account with which fallibilists+ and infallibilists operate. Next we set up three modified theses, *(EA*)*, *(AW*)*, and *(NT*)*, to see if we could construct a motivated transmission failure thesis that operated with an account of the sources of warrant-or-evidence for future reasoning that was friendly to fallibilists+ and infallibilists. But while our three modified theses operated with a (disjunctive) account of the sources of warrant-or-evidence (for future reasoning) not unacceptable to fallibilists+ and infallibilists, they were vulnerable to two objections from the two camps: a *pragmatic implication* objection (from infallibilists, which we cancelled) and a *coarse-grained* objection (from fallibilists+, which we deflected).

In sum, our original three theses, *(EA)*, *(AW)*, and *(NT)*, are serviceable for analysis of fallibilism— (but not fallibilism+ and infallibilism). Our three modified theses, *(EA*)*, *(AW*)*, and *(NT*)*, are serviceable for analysis of fallibilism+ and infallibilism (but not fallibilism—). We therefore have two sets of three theses, which jointly cover all, or most, plausible accounts of the sources of warrant-or-evidence (for future reasoning).

5. Might Introducing (EA*) be More Difficult than Introducing (EA)?

5.1 There may be especial problems involved with introducing our *modified* theses. Let's focus on a putative problem arising over introducing *(EA*)* (which doesn't arise when introducing *(EA)*). How exactly can *a premise*, a source of warrant-or-evidence for future reasoning by fallibilism+ and infallibilism, fail to transmit? I accept this explanatory challenge. Consider a fallibilist+ or infallibilist debating with a proponent of our modified theses, and reasoning thus: I can partially understand *support for* a premise — say, an experience — failing to transmit across entailments or inferences. I've heard talk of an *abstract space of warrants* and I can see that some warrants might be *epistemically antecedent* to others in that abstract space of warrants. So if I'm trying, without begging the question, to engage the external world sceptic, I can see that my warrant for (1) could fail to be epistemically antecedent to my warrant for (3). However, I can't make sense of relations of epistemic antecedence between a *premise* ((1)) and a *warrant* for a conclusion ((3)). The former is a proposition I, *ex hypothesi*, know; the latter is warrant for a proposition I fail to know prior to inference. To talk of a relation of epistemic antecedence between a premise and warrant for a premise is close to a category error: it's introducing an epistemic relation between two radically different things. While, for example, knowledge is an epistemic relation between a (knowing) *subject* and a *proposition* (at a time) — two very different *relata* if ever there were — there's something distinctively problematic about introducing a relation of *epistemic antecedence* between two *relata* of radically different kinds. To introduce a relation of epistemic antecedence, don't the *relata* have to be of the same kind?[39] This, I take it, is a forceful objection that could be made by a fallibilist+ or infallibilist to *(EA*)*, and any resultant use of *(NT*)* via *(AW*)*.[40]

---

39 Cross-categorial relations are routinely posited in philosophy. An example from metaphysics: the truthmaker relation has been posited between a (non-propositional) truthmaker and a (true) proposition (see Armstrong 2004). So the objection in the main text is a specific objection focused on the relation of epistemic antecedence.

40 A trio of theses such as these is *a* (prominent) way to argue for transmission failure; it may not be the *only* such way (cf. 2.1 *supra*).

5.2 We must distinguish between *a premise* and *knowledge of* a premise. Once we do so the objection dissolves. So far I've played fast and loose with what form evidence for future reasoning takes (better: how we should describe such evidence) for a fallibilist+ or infallibilist. I've switched between *(1) itself* and *knowledge of* (1). I take it these are, for our purposes, two different descriptions of the same piece of evidence given we suppose I know (1). We can note that epistemologists who operate with the former description take (1) itself to be in one's evidence-base for future reasoning *because* one (*ex hypothesi*) knows (1). I propose we describe (part of) the fallibilist+'s and the infallibilist's evidence-base (source of warrant-or-evidence) for future reasoning as *knowledge of* (1) (rather than as *(1) itself*).[41] Once this is done there's no especial problem about seeing how a relation of epistemic antecedence might hold. We simply ask: does my knowing (1) presuppose or rest on my warrant for (3)? To be sure, different epistemologists will give different answers to this question, but that's no slur on its intelligibility: indeed, it counts in its favour.[42] A caveat: to require that the fallibilist+ and infallibilist describe this evidence in this way in this transmission failure debate, isn't to require that he *always* so describes his warrant. Nor, relatedly, is it to say that the alternative description of the evidence is deficient.

In sum, one might have difficulty with the intelligibility of notions of epistemic antecedence or epistemic dependence, period. But I've shown there's no especial problem of applying the notion of epistemic antecedence to a fallibilist+'s and an infallibilist's account of the sources of warrant-or-evidence for future reasoning. Put differently: if one hasn't a problem with *(EA)*, then one shouldn't have a problem with *(EA*)*.

---

[41] Why, then, did I play fast and loose with my description of the evidence? First, I want to leave open (cf. n. 19 *supra*) that something short of knowledge of a proposition can suffice for a proposition to be in one's evidence base for future reasoning. Second, I want to keep vivid, with Silins, the thought that, upon competent inference from a known premise, *the premise itself* can become one's warrant to believe the conclusion.

[42] Indeed, even the following extreme response, I take to count in its favour: once I know (1), never mind how, I'll be able to *exploit* (1) as evidence for (3).

6. Conclusion

6.1 I take myself to have shown that motivated transmission failure conditions can be constructed which are applicable to — capture adequately — all, or most, plausible accounts of the sources of warrant-or-evidence for future reasoning. I haven't shown that there are in fact genuine cases of transmission failure. I have, though, demonstrated that the fallibilist+ and infallibilist cannot evade questions of transmission failure as easily as they might have hoped. Williamson's, Hawthorne's, and Silins's hard line against genuine instances of transmission failure is not warranted.[43]

---

43 It is a further task — one not attempted in this chapter — to show why, for example, an infallibilist might plausibly *take* (MOORE)-reasoning to suffer from some kind of epistemic circularity. Finally, see Tucker (2010: esp. 517ff.) for another hard line against transmission failure, although it is different in form from those targeted in this chapter, in not (as I understand it) being reliant on any particular conception of evidence.

5. A Puzzle for Dogmatism

Returning to dogmatism and the pattern of objection, I present an apparently more serious puzzle for dogmatism. It seems that one must have had warrant to believe the conclusion of (EK)-reasoning antecedently to the perceptual evidence.

0.1   I want to consider a puzzle in the realm of confirmation theory. The puzzle arises from consideration of reasoning with an argument, given certain epistemological commitments. Here is the argument (preceded by the stipulated justification for the first premise):

(JUSTIFICATION FOR 1) The table looks red.

(EK)

(1) The table is red.

(2) If the table is red, then it is not white with red lights shining on it.

(3) The table is not white with red lights shining on it.

As we've seen, (EK) — the easy knowledge argument (aka (TABLE)) — has received much epistemological scrutiny of late.[1]

0.2   The plan: First, I set out the epistemological commitments in play. Second, I set out an example, leading to the puzzle, which is putatively

---

[1]   See, notably, Cohen (2002, 2005). Likewise for our (MOORE) argument (in respect of which the puzzle to come can, *mutatis mutandis*, also be run).

troubling for *dogmatism*. Finally, I consider the implications of the puzzle for dogmatism.

1. Epistemological Commitments

1.1 Suppose that the *mere having* of the experience described in (JUSTIFICATION FOR 1) can give one defeasible perceptual *justification*[2] to believe (1) — that is, it is the subject's having the experience, rather than the subject's beliefs about the experience, that makes it epistemically appropriate for the subject to believe (1). And we might go further in claiming that this justification can (suffice to) give one *knowledge* of (1). This supposition and claim are distinctive features of dogmatist accounts of justification and knowledge respectively (see Pryor 2000, 2004). To refer specifically to dogmatism about justification, I'll use 'j-dogmatism', to refer to dogmatism about knowledge, I'll use 'k-dogmatism', and to refer to dogmatism generically, I'll use 'dogmatism'. I take it the truth of k-dogmatism entails the truth of j-dogmatism; but the converse entailment does not hold.

Dogmatists are (necessarily?) *fallibilists* about knowledge: "[W]e can have knowledge on the basis of defeasible justification, justification that does not *guarantee* that our beliefs are correct" (Pryor 2000: 518).[3] It's the defining feature of dogmatism that the justification one gets for (1) is *immediate*: you don't need antecedent justification for any other propositions in order for the having of the experience described in (JUSTIFICATION FOR 1) to give one justification for (1). Some find dogmatism an appealing way to think of perceptual justification and knowledge. So let's suppose, *pro tem*, we're dogmatists and fallibilists — that is, we are fallibilists in this dogmatist sense.[4]

---

[2] 'Justification' is used in this chapter as a broad term of epistemic appraisal and is interchangeable with 'warrant'.

[3] If one wants to frame fallibilism in terms of conditional probabilities (cf. Pryor MS), one will claim that a subject, S, can know a proposition, p, when the probability of p conditional on S's evidence, e, is less than 1. Note that conditional probabilities involve two propositions: one about the world, p, and one about the subject's evidence, e. However the subject does not have to believe the proposition about evidence in order to possess the evidence.

[4] This supposition keeps things manageable. Our puzzle assumes fallibilism. Note, however, that one can (see Hawthorne 2004: 75–77) give a rendering of a similar puzzle on the assumption of *infallibilism* (fallibilism's negation).

1.2 At a highly general level, it seems that dogmatists must give some account of the defectiveness of (certain instances of) reasoning by means of (EK). Why so? Here's the worry: on a dogmatist view, the mere having of a perceptual experience (giving justification for and, say, knowledge of, (1)), combined with some elementary logical reasoning (via (2)), can seemingly lead us — all too easily — to knowledge of the falsity of certain sceptical hypotheses ((3)). Thus the *problem of easy knowledge* (discussed at length in Chapters Two and Three). Our ensuing puzzle uses tools from confirmation theory to challenge dogmatism more directly.

2. Example, Leading to the Puzzle for Dogmatism

2.1 *Example*: Let us, for simplicity, consider only red tables and white tables,[5] and only red light and white (natural) light. Suppose that the prior probabilities are divided equally between red table (RT) (0.5) and white table (WT) (0.5) and in the ratio 1:2 between red light (RL) (0.33) and white light (WL) (0.67). So the prior probabilities of the four hypotheses (assuming the table colour and the light colour are independent) are: (RT&RL) 0.167; (RT&WL) 0.33; (WT&RL) 0.167; (WT&WL) 0.33.[6] Now I have a visual experience as of a red table. We know that the posterior probability of each of the four hypotheses is proportional to the product of the prior probability and the *likelihood* (that is, the probability of the evidence given the hypothesis). Keeping things simple, suppose that the probability of a table looking red is the same given (RT&RL), or given (RT&WL), or given (WT&RL). Suppose (idealising) that the probability of a table looking red given (WT&WL) is zero. Then the posterior probabilities are: (RT&RL) 0.25; (RT&WL) 0.5; (WT&RL) 0.25; (WT&WL) 0.

Thus, given the evidence described in (JUSTIFICATION FOR 1), the probability of premise (1) [that is, red table with either red light or white light] is raised from 0.5 to 0.75; the probability of premise (2) is 1 because it is *a priori* true; and the probability of the conclusion (3)

---

5 One could, to make things more realistic, generate a similar example by considering, say, ten equiprobable colours the table might be.

6 The prior probability assigned to the 'sceptical hypothesis' (WT&RL) is low because the prior probabilities favour the white (natural) light hypothesis over the red (tricky) light hypothesis. It might seem like a *reasonable* prior, but it would not be acceptable to the (local) sceptic (cf. Wright 2007, 2008).

[~(WT&RL)] is decreased from 0.833 to 0.75. That is, the probability of the 'sceptical hypothesis', (WT&RL), is increased from 0.167 to 0.25 (essentially because one of the hypotheses, (WT&WL), has been eliminated by the evidence and its share of the prior probability has been redistributed amongst the remaining three hypotheses). The ratio of the posterior probabilities of premise (1) — that is, RT — and the 'sceptical hypothesis' (WT&RL) is 3:1. But this is so only because the ratio of their prior probabilities was 3:1. The evidence described in (JUSTIFICATION FOR 1) is not diagnostic between these two hypotheses.

2.2   The foregoing worked example, though simplified and idealised, serves to support premise (iii) in the following argument against j-dogmatism, *viz.* getting (JUSTIFICATION FOR 1) diminishes the credence one ought to have in (3).[7] Similarly, the worked example serves to support premise (iii*) in the subsequent argument against k-dogmatism. Here, first, is the argument against j-dogmatism:

---

7   In itself, that a piece of evidence disconfirms a hypothesis (known to be) entailed by a hypothesis that the evidence confirms is not problematic. Consider the following thesis (cf. Hempel 1945, whose theory of confirmation lacks the following property):

(CC) If E confirms H and H entails H', then E confirms H'.

Due to counterexample(s), we have good reason to reject (CC). (Of course, principle (CC) is fine if by 'E confirms H' we mean only that the probability of H given E is greater than some threshold (e.g. 0.9). If the probability of H given E > 0.9 and H entails H', then the probability of H' given E > 0.9. However the principle (CC) is not fine if by 'E confirms H' we mean that E *raises* the probability of H (i.e. the probability of H given E is greater than the prior probability of H). It is thus this latter understanding of confirmation with which we are operating here.) Consider: E = card is black, H = card is the ace of spades, and H' = card is an ace. Clearly, H entails H' while E confirms H but not H'. Note the following weaker thesis, however:

(CC*) If E confirms H and H entails H', then E doesn't disconfirm H'.

While the counterexample we considered to (CC) *is not* a counterexample to (CC*), Pryor's (2004: 350–51) case of 'Clio's pet' plausibly *is*.

5. A Puzzle for Dogmatism

(i) If one has justification to believe (1) after getting (JUSTIFICATION FOR 1), one has justification to believe (3) after getting (JUSTIFICATION FOR 1).

(ii) If having a certain experience diminishes the credence one ought to have in a proposition, then, if one has justification to believe the proposition after having the experience, one must have had justification to believe the proposition antecedently to the experience.

(iii) Getting (JUSTIFICATION FOR 1) diminishes the credence one ought to have in (3).

(iv) Therefore, if one has justification to believe (1) after getting (JUSTIFICATION FOR 1), one must have had justification to believe (3) antecedently to getting (JUSTIFICATION FOR 1).

(v) Therefore j-dogmatism is false: (JUSTIFICATION FOR 1)'s ability to provide justification to believe (1) is *not* independent of whether one has antecedent justification to believe (3).[8]

---

8   I take something like this argument to be extractable from White (2006), whose focus is specifically on j-dogmatism. Cf. also Schiffer (2004) and Wright (2007). Note premises (i) and (i*) each rest on a *closure* principle; I explore this further in section 3. Note also premises (iii) and (iii*) can form the basis for an explication of the phenomenon of *transmission failure* (cf. Okasha (2004), Chandler (2010), and Moretti (2012)). Note, finally, that if one added a further premise to these arguments that we don't in fact have justification to believe — aren't in fact in a position to know — (3) prior to experiencing (JUSTIFICATION FOR 1), one would have the makings of a full-fledged argument for scepticism.

The argument against k-dogmatism is similar:

(i*) If one knows (1) after getting (JUSTIFICATION FOR 1), one is in a position to know (3) after getting (JUSTIFICATION FOR 1).

(ii*) If having a certain experience diminishes the credence one ought to have in a proposition, then if one is in a position to know the proposition after having the experience, one must have been in a position to know the proposition antecedently to the experience.

(iii*) Getting (JUSTIFICATION FOR 1) diminishes the credence one ought to have in (3).

(iv*) Therefore, if one knows (1) after getting (JUSTIFICATION FOR 1), one must have been in a position to know (3) antecedently to getting (JUSTIFICATION FOR 1).

(v*) Therefore k-dogmatism is false: (JUSTIFICATION FOR 1)'s ability to confer knowledge of (1) is *not* independent of whether one is antecedently in a position to know (3).[9]

Note that this second argument contains the locution 'in a position to know' at several junctures. I take it that one is in such a position just in case one has (evidential) justification for the true proposition in question, and some anti-luck condition is fulfilled thwarting *Gettierisation*. Admittedly this account is vague and context-dependent at a number of points (cf. Williamson 2000: 95), but this working definition will do for our purposes.

I take it that, with these two arguments, we've identified the major puzzle in confirmation theory for dogmatism. They purport to establish, *contra* dogmatism, that the role of a perceptual experience (of the table looking red) in providing justification to believe (1), and ultimately knowledge of (1), depends on an antecedently available justification to believe (3), or on being antecedently in a position to know (3). Each argument has three premises. Unless there is some flaw in the reasoning

---

9   I take something like this argument to be extractable from Hawthorne (2004: 73–75), whose (effective) focus is specifically on k-dogmatism. Cf. also Cohen (2005: 425).

that takes us from the three premises to the interim conclusion, and thence to the conclusion, the dogmatist must identify a false premise. Each of the premises, however, is plausible.

3. Implications of the Puzzle

3.1 The arguments comprising our *puzzle* for dogmatism (see 2.2) are valid, so let's isolate a premise on which some doubt might be cast. An obvious move at this stage, given the *apparent* security of the second and third premises,[10] is to flag premises (i) and (i*):

> (i) If one has justification to believe (EK1) after getting (JUSTIFICATION FOR 1), one has justification to believe (EK3) after getting (JUSTIFICATION FOR 1).

> (i*) If one knows (EK1) after getting (JUSTIFICATION FOR 1), one is in a position to know (EK3) after getting (JUSTIFICATION FOR 1).

Each premise, respectively, presupposes (something like) the following (single-premise) closure principles:

> (J-Closure) If one has justification to believe P and can tell that P entails Q then — *ceteris paribus* — one has justification to believe Q.

> (K-Closure) If one knows P and competently deduces Q from P, thereby coming to believe Q, while retaining one's knowledge that P, one comes to know that Q.

A defender of j-dogmatism or k-dogmatism who wants to question the truth of (i) or (i*) should offer reasons to reject (J-Closure) or (K-Closure),

---

10 In the coming Interim Review, I suggest a line of argument to the effect that their security is *only* apparent. I thus do not mean to commit to the ensuing move being *the most promising* way for dogmatism to get out of the puzzle; just *an obvious* way.

respectively.[11] However, these are highly plausible closure principles. Thus dogmatism is — or seems very likely to be — false.[12]

---

11 Note that *(K-Closure)* is difficult to distinguish from a principle about transmission (here, transmission of epistemic status). One might then ask: would there not be a similar principle about justification, that would speak of coming to have a justified belief? The principle that White calls '**Justification Closure**' (2006: 528) would seem to be like this (using, as it does, the 'justified in believing' nomenclature — a nomenclature I noted in the Introduction to be associated with doxastic justification).Why, then, is it important here to have *(J-Closure)* be a principle about (propositional) justification to believe rather than about (doxastic) justified belief (or being justified in believing)? First, even though White uses nomenclature associated with doxastic justification, it is not unequivocally so associated, and White's surrounding remarks suggest instead a propositional focus. Second, as can be seen from the argument, a propositional justification closure principle is all White needs — and this is a good thing, given the familiar counterexamples to doxastic justification closure principles. Finally, see Lasonen-Aarnio (2008) for an interesting exploration of so-called *deductive risk* — a phenomenon which provides a novel basis for questioning *(K-Closure)*.

12 As hinted (n. 10), I consider, and canvass, a *range* of possible dogmatist responses to these arguments in the coming Interim Review.

Interim Review

As we now transition from Part One to Part Two of the book, let's take stock of what has been achieved in Part One and what remains to be achieved in Part Two. First, what has been achieved? Essentially, immediate justification (such as perceptual justification as understood by the dogmatist) allows for basic knowledge, and basic knowledge seems to give rise to at least two problems. (A) It would allow that provides an adequate response to the sceptic. (B) It would allow a 'too easy' inferential route from basic knowledge to other knowledge. This was my *pattern of objection* to dogmatism, immediate justification, and basic knowledge. In Chapter One, I argued that Wright's position (which does *not* accept that there is immediate perceptual justification to believe the Moorean premise 'I have hands') still faces the (MOORE)-transmit problem. In Chapter Three, I argued that, even if (MOORE)-reasoning and (EK)-reasoning do transmit warrant and do not involve any epistemic circularity, they still exhibit an epistemological limitation. At that point we could have concluded that the prospects of allowing for immediate justification and basic knowledge would be rather good.

In Chapter Four I argued that a concept central to the work of philosophers debating over immediate justification and basic knowledge — *viz.* transmission failure — is secure from a particular challenge. Specifically, I argued that transmission failure is *possible* on *all or most* plausible accounts of the sources of warrant-or-evidence for future reasoning. Of course, the notion of transmission failure discussed in that chapter is connected with epistemic circularity; and a core upshot of dogmatism is that there is *no* epistemic circularity in

(MOORE)-reasoning. The challenge faced by the dogmatist is to respond to problems (A) and (B) *without* appeal to epistemic circularity. Thus, the importance of Chapter Four is more theoretical than dialectical.

The dialectical importance of the final chapter in Part One is, by contrast, extreme. There, I argued that epistemological dogmatism is vulnerable to a strong objection. Here, I consider whether there are any good responses to that objection.

1. Reacting to Chapter Five's Objection to Dogmatism

I closed Chapter Five by suggesting that a defender of dogmatism about justification or dogmatism about knowledge may well look to offer reasons to reject (*J-Closure*) or (*K-Closure*), respectively. In the coming chapters — Chapter Six and, in particular, Chapter Seven — I oppose, specifically, John Hawthorne's recent defense of (*K-Closure*). Those chapters join Hawthorne in, *arguendo*, assuming that something in the region of conclusive reasons or sensitivity is a condition on knowledge, before going on to render those conditions in as plausible a form as possible.[1]

In section 5 of the Introduction I mentioned a way — involving taking conclusive reasons or sensitivity to *characterise* justification — of extending any rejection of closure from *(K-Closure)* to *(J-Closure)*.[2] I noted, though, that even with conclusive reasons or sensitivity conceived as a necessary condition for justification, that would not guarantee an exception to *(J-Closure)*. This is because: although if the conclusion did not meet the conclusive reasons or sensitivity

---

1   It might seem that a defense of dogmatism about knowledge (a position which, concededly, hasn't clearly been endorsed by any philosopher thus far, but which has been articulated and which is independently interesting) ideally ought not to rest on such an assumption. This is not because these conditions are peculiarly anti-dogmatist in spirit; it is rather just that a defense of dogmatism should rely on as few assumptions as possible, in order to avoid creating hostages to fortune. But note: if such a defense works, there couldn't be knowledge by inference of the conclusion of (EK) (or (MOORE)).

2   If this extension works, there couldn't be justification by inference of the conclusion of (EK) (or (MOORE)). So (EK)-reasoning would be an example of transmission failure. So, apparently, there could be transmission failure that was not related to epistemic circularity.

condition it would not be justified, the premise might also not be justified, despite meeting the conclusive reasons or sensitivity condition. However, I noted that in any actual case there might be no reason to suppose that the premise, which meets the conclusive reasons or sensitivity condition, nevertheless fails to meet some other necessary condition for justification. Consider the dialectical context where someone is trying to pin a problem on dogmatism by using *(J-Closure)* to proceed from justification to believe (1) to justification to believe (3). The person posing this problem is content to assume that the conditions for justification to believe (1) are met, and we can add that (1) meets the conclusive reasons or sensitivity condition. So it is hard to see that the problem-poser has any good reason to reject the continuing assumption that there is justification to believe (1) or justified belief in (1), even with conclusive reasons or sensitivity now added as a necessary condition on justification. But (3), though putatively justified, fails the conclusive reasons or sensitivity test. So there *is* plausibly an exception to *(J-Closure)*.

In sum, while I believe such an extension is worthy of serious consideration, it must be conceded that I have offered no *decisive* argument against *(J-Closure)*.[3] So, even if I can make out a successful (fully general) case for rejecting *(K-Closure)* — and so for rejecting the argument against dogmatism about knowledge — I cannot presently claim that that success *carries over* to vindicate rejection of *(J-Closure)* — and so rejection of the argument against dogmatism about justification.

However, I am not resigned to accepting that dogmatism about justification is false, and one might reject the arguments against dogmatism by other means than a rejection of closure principles. Here, I briefly suggest an alternative way of responding to the arguments presented in Chapter Five against dogmatism. This alternative — not pursued in Chapter Five — involves a form of *departure from the standard Bayesian picture*. To some degree, which of these two routes a defender of dogmatism pursues — and I do not claim them to be exhaustive — will depend on the costs associated with, respectively,

---

3   Recall, *(J-Closure)* is defined in terms of justification to believe. While there any surely reasons to reject a closure principle defined instead in terms of justified belief, such a principle is not presently germane.

rejection of closure principles and a departure from standard Bayesian assumptions.

Davies's (2009) account, on which I build in Chapter Three, "involve[s] some departure from the standard Bayesian requirement that a probability distribution must assign some probability, high or low, to each proposition, including [MOORE(3) An external world exists]" (356).[4] We can take it that this also includes: The table is not white with red lights shining on it.

These propositions — the conclusions of (MOORE)-reasoning and (EK)-reasoning respectively — may be outside the subject's conceptual repertoire when the subject first comes to believe the premise, 'I have hands' or 'The table is red', on the basis of a perceptual experience as of having hands or as of a red table. Once the conclusion proposition is grasped, and the entailment is recognised, the subject is committed to assigning a posterior credence to the conclusion that is no lower than the posterior credence assigned to the premise. However, we might depart from the requirement that a coherent assignment of *prior* credences should encompass propositions of which the subject has, at that stage, no understanding. While much work would need to be done, it might be that this kind of departure from the standard Bayesian picture could offer another way to respond to Chapter Five's arguments against dogmatism.

We have briefly reviewed two possible methods of resisting Chapter Five's arguments against dogmatism. I now want to review a third possible method. Nico Silins (2007) can be taken to claim that White's arguments — which I sought to capture in Chapter Five — *only* establish **(I)** that it is impossible for anyone ever to acquire evidence

---

4   A departure of this kind, for Davies (2009: 356) results from "[s]upposing […] that there were a theory of evidential support with the following two features. First, Moore's experience as of hands *would provide no support* for MOORE(1) [I have hands] given the *negation* of MOORE(3) as background assumption but, second, Moore's experience *could provide support* for MOORE(1) even *without* the positive adoption of MOORE(3) as a background assumption." Indeed, more generally Davies's distinction between two epistemic projects (and associated resultant distinctions) may be difficult to capture in the standard Bayesian framework. Cf. Pryor (2012: 282–83) for a related "propos[al] to set […] probabilistic considerations aside for […] discussion [of transmission-failure]" on account of "many complications at play". More generally on this issue — that is, resolution of potential conflict between formal considerations and a family of views of which dogmatism is a member — see Pryor (2013).

that justifies ordinary empirical propositions unless they already had, prior to acquiring that evidence, propositional justification for rejecting sceptical hypotheses, and so *do not* establish **(R)** that our justification for ordinary empirical propositions *essentially rests on* or *is supported by* our justification for rejecting sceptical hypotheses.[5]

This is a promising strategy. Does Silins make good on his claim? (To the extent that he does, of course, the dogmatist will have another possible escape route from Chapter Five's objection.) Consider the following example: (*Prime*) If it is a necessary truth that every thinker always has (propositional) justification for certain *a priori* knowable propositions, then it is impossible ever to acquire evidence that justifies me in believing that I have hands unless I already had, prior to acquiring that evidence, propositional justification for believing the *a priori* proposition that there is no largest prime number; however it would not be that my justification for believing that I have hands essentially rests on or is supported by my justification for believing that there is no largest prime number. A supporter of Silins might suggest there is an analogy between *Prime* and the case(s) involving sceptical hypotheses.[6] This analogy would suggest that, even if, for example, it is impossible to be justified in believing that I have hands on the basis of a perceptual experience as of hands unless I have antecedent warrant to believe the anti-sceptical proposition that there is an external world, still the warrant to believe that I have hands might not *depend on* the antecedent warrant to reject the sceptical hypothesis.

Here is a dogmatist-friendly view of what the *Prime* example establishes:

---

5   Let us not probe further into some of the notions introduced in **(R)** — e.g. essentially rests on, is supported by — other than to note that they are not *Bayesian notions* as such (likewise for the notions of immediate versus mediate evidential support). White (2006: 555, n. 14) gestures towards this Silins point, appealing to the "*in virtue of*" relation. Put somewhat vernacularly, the point might be that there is some slippage here between different notions of *independence* in the arguments as formulated in Chapter Five.

6   Note, though, while justification for believing that there is no largest prime number, *ex hypothesi* in *Prime*, is necessary *a priori*, it's plausible that default justification for rejecting sceptical hypotheses, if it exists, is contingent *a priori* (cf. Hawthorne 2002 and Cohen 2002: 320–22).

(iv**) If one has justification to believe 'I have hands', after having perceptual experience as of having hands then one must have had justification to believe there is no largest prime number antecedently to having perceptual experience as of having hands.

This is of the same form as (iv) in the argument against j-dogmatism in Chapter Five. The point of the *Prime* example is that it obviously does not follow that j-dogmatism is false. It does, let us accept, follow from (iv**) that:

(v**) Perceptual experience as of having hands' ability to provide justification to believe 'I have hands' is *not modally* independent of whether one has antecedent justification to believe that there is no largest prime. (One cannot have one justification without having the other.)

However, there is clearly a gap between that (allowing that it does follow) and 'j-dogmatism is false', which does not follow. The point is that from the modal dependence in (v**) it clearly does not follow that justification to believe 'I have hands' depends *constitutively* on justification to believe that there is no largest prime — even though one cannot have one justification without having the other. Having a justification to believe that there is no largest prime does not partly constitute having a justification to believe 'I have hands'; it is not part of *what it is for* one to have a justification to believe 'I have hands'. And I take it that epistemic dependence is a kind of constitutive, and not merely modal, dependence.

I think there is much merit in Silins's strategy. I also think that we might not need even to grant that the argument of Chapter Five establishes the relation of modal dependence between epistemic warrants. We could allow that the argument does establish:

(iv—) If one has justification to believe 'I have hands', after having perceptual experience as of having hands then it must be that a coherent assignment of credences would have assigned a high credence to an anti-sceptical hypothesis antecedently to one's having perceptual experience as of having hands.

And then we could ask, with Pryor (2012: 282): "What's the relation between probabilistically confirming and supplying warrant?".

Still, it is not entirely clear to me, at this point, how best to respond to Chapter Five's objection to dogmatism. While I have reviewed several options for the dogmatist — options which I take to be very much *live* and, indeed, promising — much remains to be done before any utterly convincing response to the objection could be presented.

I certainly do not at all assume that the objection to dogmatism is unanswerable. Indeed, my provisional view is that dogmatism remains a tenable position. Nevertheless, it is reasonable to consider the worst-case possibility that, ultimately, dogmatism cannot be defended against the objection. It would be natural, at that point, to consider taking Roger White's (2006) line, whose focus, recall, is specifically on dogmatism about justification.

White (2006: 552–53), not interested in questioning (*J-Closure*), considers retreating from dogmatism about justification to a distinct thesis which he calls JUSTIFICATION BY DEFAULT (cf. Pryor 2000: 519).[7] At points in the book up until now, we've had cause to highlight elements of White's position as they were relevant. At this point, we do well to state it in full:

> Suppose that we abandon dogmatism, and insist that in order to gain perceptual justification for believing that P, we must have independent justification for believing that we are not victims of a visual illusion that P. We could nevertheless insist that we have a kind of default justification for assuming the general reliability of our perceptual faculties. We are entitled to believe that our faculties tend to deliver the truth unless we have some positive reason to doubt this.[8] Our faculties are generally reliable only if skeptical alternatives rarely obtain. So if I'm justified in taking my faculties to be reliable, then I need give very little credence to skeptical hypotheses (unless of course I have reason to suspect that one obtains). On the view that I'm sketching I do not need to explicitly believe in the reliability of my faculties or the falsity of sceptical alternatives in order to gain justification from perceptual experience, but justification for this reliability is available to me nevertheless [...][9] [I]t is

---

7   As White notes, JUSTIFICATION BY DEFAULT bears obviously similarities to Wright's appeal to the notion of unearned warrant; Pryor rejects these stances.

8   Cf. Burge's (1993, 2003) view, on which we have such an entitlement to rely instead on our faculties.

9   Thus, White has in mind propositional, and not doxastic, justification.

denied that the justification for ruling out skeptical alternatives requires some prior empirical ground. This justification is available a priori by default. I am justified in my perceptually based beliefs, according to this view, in just the circumstances that the dogmatist claims that I am. Such a view seems to have all of the advantages of dogmatism but avoids all of my objections. No doubt the view requires closer examination and development. But if we are attracted to something in the ball park of dogmatism, it seems to be the right place to look.

What follows? Suppose we retreat from dogmatism, allow that justification to believe quotidian propositions epistemically depends on justification to believe an anti-sceptical hypothesis or reliability hypothesis, and accept — with White — that we have such JUSTIFICATION BY DEFAULT. A corollary of such a retreat would appear to be that we could then say that the solution to problems (A) and (B) — outlined at the outset of this Interim Review — is that the relevant reasoning involves epistemic circularity in each case.[10] However, the situation is not so straightforward. I showed in Chapter One (in effect) that there can still be transmission of some warrant even where there is a kind of epistemic circularity. More on this later, in section 2.

Now if we have justification by default for a reliability hypothesis, we might not need to *believe* it, still less to *know* it, in order to know quotidian propositions: there could be antecedent justification to believe, but no antecedent belief and so no antecedent knowledge. Still, any such knowledge of quotidian propositions wouldn't be (the logically stronger) Pryorian basic knowledge, because it depends epistemically (constitutively) on one's having justification to believe the reliability proposition. Could it, though, be (the logically weaker) Cohenian basic knowledge? Interestingly, this is precisely the case about which it was said in the Introduction (p. 10) that it is at best unclear that it is a case of Cohenian basic knowledge.

Though White's focus is on justification, the argument of Chapter Five did apply to knowledge, and not just justification. But the most that the argument in Chapter Five would establish is that if one knows, with source K, some quotidian proposition, then one was antecedently *in a*

---

10 Insofar as Cohen doesn't appeal to epistemic circularity to solve problems (1) and (2), we can be sure — confirming Chapter Three's account of his position — that his position is not simply described in terms of such a retreat.

position to know that K is reliable. That is not the same as saying that one would antecedently *know* that K is reliable. So far, so good for Cohen's basic knowledge. However, if the argument in Chapter Five establishes that the justification to believe the quotidian proposition depends epistemically (constitutively) on the antecedent justification to believe that K is reliable, then I have said that it is at best unclear whether this is Cohenian basic knowledge. On the other hand, if the argument does not establish the constitutive epistemic dependence, then we should say that knowledge of the quotidian proposition is Pryorian (and thus Cohenian) basic knowledge — and that the challenge to dogmatism was unsuccessful.

2. Looking Back to Part One and Ahead to Part Two

Now what follows with respect to the work done in Part One and the work to be done in Part Two? First, what follows with regard to Part One? In Chapter One we saw that Wright, contra the standard view, faced the difficult (MOORE)-transmit problem — a problem standardly only taken to be faced by dogmatists. This problem — the particular problem of giving a plausible account of why something seems wrong with (MOORE)-reasoning given it can transmit warrant — cannot be answered by Wright by pointing out that there's non-transmission of (disjunctive) warrant by the lights of his (non-)transmission theses. Wright cannot so answer because there's transmission of evidential warrant by the lights of two other plausible (non-)transmission theses.[11] Crucially, in each case — that is, in both the case involving Wright's theses and the case involving the two other plausible theses — the warrant under consideration is provided by the *same experience*, a visual

---

11 It might be objected that Moore's argument fails completely to reveal why our acceptance of its conclusion has the status of having any warrant whatsoever. One way of understanding this objection is that the evidential warrant that is transmitted from premise (1) of (MOORE) is — according to Wright's view — dependent on the unearned warrant to accept premise (3) of (MOORE). Wright (2004) indicates a philosophical theoretical account of the nature of that unearned warrant but, of course, this piece of philosophical theory will not be within the grasp of ordinary non-philosophical thinkers. It will therefore be correct that *Moore's argument* does not itself reveal why (3) has any warrant whatever — just as it does not reveal why (1) has any warrant whatever. On this understanding of this objection, (3) is in no worse shape than (1).

experience as of having hands. (For why invocation of the two theses that license transmission of evidential warrant is not question-begging against Wright, see my introduction, and subsequent discussion, of theses (A)-(D) in Chapter One, section 2.4ff.) One natural idea would be for Wright to borrow the kind of story that I tell in Chapter Three (on behalf of the dogmatist) about the problem of easy knowledge. But Chapter One has shown that Wright cannot happily borrow that kind of story, especially given his (1985) position on the non-factuality of the proposition that there is an external world.

Insofar as dogmatism turns out not to be a live option, Wright would no longer be at a dialectical disadvantage *vis-à-vis* dogmatism. Nevertheless, insofar as Wright *faces* the (MOORE)-transmit problem, Chapter One can be taken to pose the following question to Wright: how do you *answer* the (MOORE)-transmit problem? Note also that in Chapter One (at 1.1) I wrote: "Assume, then — with the dogmatist and Wright — that something (at least) *seems* wrong with (MOORE)-reasoning." Meanwhile, in Chapter Three I claimed that reasoning fundamentally the same as (MOORE)-reasoning — namely, (EK*)-reasoning — is *less* unsatisfactory than (EK)-reasoning. Is there any conflict between these claims from Chapter One and Chapter Three? No. All that the main argument of Chapter Three requires is that (EK)-reasoning and (EK*)-reasoning are *different*, in that (EK*)-reasoning seems *less* unsatisfactory than (EK)-reasoning. Importantly, it does not require that either (EK*)-reasoning or (MOORE)-reasoning is *wholly* satisfactory. Indeed it diagnoses an epistemic limitation in each form of reasoning, namely that neither argument can be used in the epistemic project of settling the question — albeit that limitation doesn't preclude knowledge.

Moreover, we can note that, if Wright ends up with a first time perceptual warrant for the proposition that there is an external world, then his position is, to that extent, similar to the dogmatist's position, and Wright needs to explain why (MOORE)-reasoning seems not to be a satisfying response to the sceptic. That is quite consistent with the idea that (EK)-reasoning seems to be somehow epistemically worse than (EK*)-reasoning. I take Chapter Three to have established that none of the principles that have been proposed can account for this difference.

Chapters Two and Three then looked at the problem of easy knowledge. These chapters explore a legitimate question: is there a solution to the problem of easy knowledge that is available to the dogmatist? My answer is: yes, there is. So if there is something wrong with dogmatism, it is not that it cannot respond to the problem of easy knowledge. Of course, we must now ask how things stand if the argument of Chapter Five shows dogmatism to be untenable. Then, the fact that justification for (EK1) depends on justification for (EK3) means that we have a kind of epistemic (justificatory) circularity. So that is at least part of the solution to the problem of easy knowledge (unlike the situation in Chapter Three). There might still be an additional problem if an argument like that made in Chapter One shows that there is an (EK)-transmit problem (despite the circularity). However, that raises issues quite different from those in Chapter Three.

Finally, what follows with regard to the ensuing Part Two — our exploration of certain conditions that some philosophers have claimed are necessary for knowledge, *viz.* conclusive reasons, sensitivity and safety? It bears emphasising that we need not assume that we have basic knowledge to make exploration of conclusive reasons, sensitivity,[12] and safety worthwhile. Moreover, now that we have seen that a defender of dogmatism about knowledge may well want to offer reasons to reject (*K-Closure*), the outcome of our enquiry into (*K-Closure*) in Chapters Six and Seven (and an additional closely related knowledge-closure principle in Chapter Six)[13] becomes of increased interest.[14]

---

12 It is noteworthy that Kripke (2011: 189–90) says: "Even if [Nozick's sensitivity] account is restricted to perceptual ('noninferential,' or 'basic') knowledge — and I think [it is] much more plausible if so restricted — the red barn problem can still arise." We encounter the 'red barn' problem, and related issues, in Chapter Seven.
13 This is the principle on which Dretske was originally focused which, unlike (*Closure*), does not involve the performance of a competent deduction.
14 We've seen several times that one might consider an effort to 'carry over' arguments against (*K-Closure*) to (*J-Closure*) by, for example, taking the conclusive reasons or sensitivity condition to *characterise* justification.

PART TWO
CONDITIONS ON KNOWLEDGE: CONCLUSIVE REASONS, SENSITIVITY, AND SAFETY

Overview of Part Two

Our Overview of Part Two — in which, by turn, the status of conclusive reasons, sensitivity, and safety as necessary conditions on knowledge is considered — can be refreshingly brief. In large part this is because the bulk of the heavy lifting in setting out the overall narrative of the book has been completed. (The final chapter — looking at an application of safety to the domain of legal proof — is, of necessity, something of an outlier.)

It simply remains to (re)affirm the following. (1) Our Interim Review made clear that a rejection of closure is one — but not the only — means of responding on behalf of the dogmatist to the serious objection to dogmatism considered in Chapter Five. Insofar as conclusive reasons or sensitivity is necessary for knowledge, *(K-Closure)* fails. (2) Our Introduction outlined, in a very broad-brush manner, Martin Smith's (2009) proposal to explain (a Part One issue) transmission failure (of knowledge) in terms of the safety condition (a Part Two issue). This proposal is considered in detail in the conclusion. Let us note for now, though, that safety's status as a necessary condition on knowledge is essential if Smith is to establish his proposal.

Do I then, in the following chapters establish the status of any of the aforementioned conditions as genuinely necessary for knowledge? Not quite. Taking first the closely related conclusive reasons and sensitivity conditions, my aim is simply to make them as plausible as they can be as necessary conditions on knowledge. I explicitly disavow the challenge of rendering them bulletproof to counterexample(s). To the extent that I have rendered them more plausible, I will also have rendered more plausible the *(K-Closure)*-rejecting (and, possibly, *(J-Closure)*-rejecting) response of the dogmatist to Chapter Five's arguments.

The following objection to this as a dogmatist response may be raised at this point: the root idea behind standard dogmatisms is that *seemings* necessarily constitute *prima facie* justification for their contents. This is dogmatism's core. The implication would appear to be that seemings provide this justification even if they aren't backed by conclusive reasons and even if the resulting belief wouldn't be sensitive. Therefore, dogmatism about justification and knowledge is incompatible with requiring conclusive reasons or sensitivity. (This objection, and my ensuing reply, carries over, *mutatis mutandis*, to the safety condition, though safety *is*, by contrast, preserved across competent deduction.)

My reply is that, while the premise(s) is true, this conclusion doesn't follow therefrom. To be sure, conclusive reasons or sensitivity as necessary conditions on knowledge is no part of the core of dogmatism; but there is nothing incompatible about augmenting dogmatism therewith. Two routes for securing this compatibility (between which I can remain agnostic) present themselves. First, one might (arguably, taking these conditions at face value) insulate conclusive reasons or sensitivity from any role in justification — that is, from any load-bearing weight in *justification*. Then, straightforwardly, the core of standard dogmatisms can be preserved, compatibly with conclusive reasons or sensitivity as necessary conditions on *knowledge*. (On this first route, this dogmatist response will only bear on *(K-Closure)*.) Second, one might, plausibly, give conclusive reasons or sensitivity a role in justification — that is, give it load-bearing weight in justification. Still the core of standard dogmatisms can be preserved: *seemings* still necessarily constitute **prima** *facie* (or *pro tanto*) justification for their contents, but such justification would fail to be **ultima** *facie* (or all-things-considered) should conclusive reasons or sensitivity not be met. (On this second route, this dogmatist response will bear additionally on *(J-Closure)*.)

A final note on Chapters Six and Seven, and the relationship between conclusive reasons and sensitivity. It must be acknowledged up front that these two putative conditions on knowledge are very similar. It is correspondingly no surprise that my initial fixes for the two conditions are also very similar. Several remarks are therefore in order. First, as I note in Chapter Seven, while the two requirements are similar, Dretske

(2005: 24, n. 4) himself is at pains to point out situations in which the requirements come apart. I think there is further interesting work to be done exploring this matter. Second, while the initial fix I propose for the two conditions is similar, in Chapter Seven's treatment of sensitivity I go far beyond that initial fix to explore more wide-ranging modifications of sensitivity. Those more wide-ranging modifications have obvious potential to be carried over to conclusive reasons also. Finally, and most generally, the chapter ordering reflects the chronological sequence in which they were written (reflecting, in turn, a maturation of my thoughts on these conditions). Ideally, within the overall structure of the book, these two chapters should be read as a pair. While general morals are offered in Chapter Six for the future of conclusive reasons as a condition on knowledge, those morals are offered within the comparatively narrow context of the debate between Dretske and Hawthorne. Chapter Seven, meanwhile, while engaging with Hawthorne, operates at a more detached level, and explores sensitivity *in abstracto*.

Regarding safety, again, I aim to have made it as plausible as it can be as a necessary condition on knowledge, and take myself to have staved off a group of putative counterexamples thereto. Nonetheless, I also concede I cannot be taken to have definitively established (my) safety (condition) as a necessary condition on knowledge. Once again, though, to the extent that I have rendered it more plausible, I will also have rendered more plausible Smith's explanation of transmission failure (of knowledge) in terms of the safety condition.

Finally, the *weakness* of my dialectical aims with respect to these putative conditions on knowledge should be emphasised. I'm attempting to defend these conditions as necessary for knowledge. In fact, it is slightly weaker than that still: I'm attempting to make these conditions as plausible as they can be — render them in as plausible a form as possible — as necessary conditions on knowledge. That aim is independently interesting, and also (for reasons already given) has a payoff for upshots of allowing for basic knowledge. My aim is avowedly *not* to provide an *analysis* of knowledge with one or more of these conditions forming a component part. In this context, consider a recent fascinating case presented by John Williams and Neil Sinhababu (2015 *et al*) — the Backward Clock:

You habitually nap between 4 pm and 5 pm. Your method of ascertaining the time you wake is to look at your clock, one you know has always worked perfectly reliably. Unbeknownst to you, your clock is a special model designed by a cult that regards the hour starting from 4 pm today as cursed, and wants clocks not to run forwards during that hour. So your clock is designed to run perfectly reliably backwards during that hour. At 4 pm the hands of the clock jumped to 5 pm, and it has been running reliably backwards since then. This clock is analogue so its hands sweep its face continuously, but it has no second hand so you cannot tell that it is running backwards from a quick glance. Awaking, you look at the clock at exactly 4:30 pm and observe that its hands point to 4:30 pm. Accordingly, you form the belief that it is 4:30 pm.

This innovative case is set up to be one in which the belief formed is sensitive (and presumably one for which one has conclusive reasons) and safe, but yet which is intuitively non-knowledge — the belief is too luckily true. Now, to be sure, the core cases I use as motivation to prompt fixes to conclusive reasons and sensitivity in Chapters Six and Seven are cases in which these conditions are met but which are clearly non-knowledge. Moreover, as I note in Chapter Eight (after stressing my weak dialectical aims), being readily able to invent cases of non-knowledge meeting my proposed safety condition is *prima facie* troubling; and I go on to consider possible such cases *in the ballpark* of the core case motivating my proposed fix to safety in that chapter. However, the fact remains: fascinating as the Backward Clock is, it does not dent my limited dialectical ambitions with respect to these conditions.

6. Conclusive Reasons

I explain Dretske's challenge to knowledge-closure, based on his conclusive reasons condition on knowledge. I argue that his (1971) account of conclusive reasons can be supplemented so that his challenge to closure remains unmet.

0.1 Take the following principle (or schema)[1] as the focus of the ensuing discussion ('P' and 'Q' are placeholders for propositions):[2]

> (*Closure*) If one knows P and competently deduces Q from P, thereby coming to believe Q, while retaining one's knowledge that P, one comes to know that Q. (Hawthorne 2005: 29)[3]

0.2 Some remarks about (*Closure*). First, it is defensible. Many closure principles are not worth defending. Consider, for example, the following:

> (*Closure'*) If one knows P and, necessarily, P entails Q, then one knows Q.

---

1 As a schema it is assessable as valid/invalid (and not true/false).
2 And are so used throughout this chapter.
3 Precisely stating (*Closure*)'s relationship with transmission principles is a difficult thing to do. One way into this is to say that (*Closure*) is to be distinguished from transmission principles which, in addition to (*Closure*), require that one's deduction furnishes one with — in a sense left intuitive here — a *first-time* warrant for Q. But, of course, (*Closure*) doesn't explicitly mention warrant, so even this effort at a broad-brush statement may be too rough and ready to be particularly serviceable. Another way into this (anticipating the Conclusion's discussion of Smith (2009)) is to distinguish between knowledge-closure (preservation) and knowledge-transmission: to reach our knowledge-transmission principle, perhaps we could simply say at the end of the principle: 'one comes to know *for the first time* that Q'. (*Quaere*: does 'comes to know' already include that it is for the first time?)

This schema is not defensible. If P's entailing Q is not known to the relevant subject, it is readily conceivable that the subject could know P without knowing Q.[4]

Second, to challenge (*Closure*) is not to challenge a fundamental rule of inference, *modus ponens*. Here is what Fred Dretske (2005a: 13) has written on the matter:

> Closure is stronger [than *modus ponens*]. *Modus ponens* says that if P is true, and if P implies Q, then Q must be true. Closure tells us that when S knows that P is true, and also knows that P implies Q, then not only must Q *be* true (*modus ponens* gets you this much), S must *know* it is true.

Third, (*Closure*) respects Timothy Williamson's view — endorsed by Hawthorne (2004: 33)[5] — on the source of epistemic closure intuitions, namely that "deduction is a way of extending one's knowledge" (Williamson, 2000: 117). Fourth, (*Closure*) is restricted to single premise inferences. (For remarks about closure principles involving multiple premises — in which issues concerning aggregation of risk become salient — see Hawthorne 2004: 46–50.)

Finally, what sense of *entailment* is *in play* in (*Closure*)? ((*Closure*) involves competent deduction of Q from P. I take it one can do this only if P entails Q — in some sense or other.) Closure principles are generally formulated in a way that requires the entailment to be *strictly logical*, but James Pryor (2012) notes:

> [I]n practice epistemologists are pretty relaxed about what they count as "logical" [...] [S]ay that a premise [P] implies for you a premise [Q] whenever you're in a position to be reasonably certain that [P → Q], regardless of whether there's really any strictly logical entailment.

I will follow Pryor's lead in taking 'implies for you' to be a sufficient 'entailment' relation for closure principles.

---

[4] (*Closure*) is defended by Stalnaker (1984), but Stalnaker's conception of belief is unorthodox.

[5] Hawthorne (2004) (tentatively) defends a position he calls *sensitive moderate invariantism* (and is often referred to as *subject-sensitive invariantism*) about knowledge on the back of consideration of a series of *lottery puzzles*. These puzzles "derive their force from the idea that [...] some sort of closure principle holds for knowledge" (Hawthorne 2004: 31).

1. The Challenge to (Closure)

1.1 My strategy in outline: first, I want to set out Dretske's classic challenge to (*Closure*) — a challenge which began in 1970–1971. Then I want to consider a specific counter-challenge to Dretske's challenge to (*Closure*) mounted by John Hawthorne (2005), and to defend Dretske's challenge from Hawthorne's counter-challenge. Doing this is not to invalidate (*Closure*). In this regard my conclusions are modest: Dretske's challenge to (*Closure*) is — or, better: can be made — sophisticated and, so far, unmet.

1.2 Dretske (1970: 1007) draws our attention to "*sentential operators*"; that is, terms or phrases which operate on a sentence or statement to give another sentence or statement. A focus on 'S regrets' and 'S knows' (where 'S' is a placeholder for a subject) will be useful. First, consider the following argument:

(R)   S regrets P

S knows P implies Q

Therefore, S regrets Q

Is (R) valid? No. Consider a subject, Sam, who regrets that he drank ten beers last night, and who also knows that drinking ten beers entails drinking some alcohol. It does not thereby follow that Sam regrets drinking some alcohol last night.

Consider, more germanely to our present discussion, the following argument:

(K)   S knows P

S knows P implies Q

Therefore, S knows Q

Is (K) valid? (K) is Dretske's original (1970–1971) target, and he there concludes (K) is not valid.[6] (K), while similar to (*Closure*), is distinct

---

6   Nozick (1981: 240–42) also denies (K)'s (and *(Closure)*'s) validity. In the next chapter we come to engage directly with Nozick.

from (*Closure*) in a number of respects. Most notably (*Closure*), but not (K), requires the performance of a competent deduction. (Equally, (K), but not (*Closure*), explicitly requires that S knows that P implies Q.) In his (2005) debate with Hawthorne, Dretske shifts his focus squarely to attacking (*Closure*).

1.3 To understand Dretske's attack on (*Closure*) (and (K)) we need to introduce three interrelated pieces of (Dretskean) terminology: *conclusive reasons, relevant alternatives,* and *heavyweight implications.*

Let's introduce these concepts in one go by means of consideration of two closely related arguments (assume a subject marshalling these arguments claims knowledge of premises and conclusion):

(HANDS1)   I have hands

(HANDS2)   If I have hands then I have a hand

Therefore:

(HANDS3)   I have a hand

(BIV1)   I have hands

(BIV2)   If I have hands then I'm not a handless BIV[7]

Therefore:

(BIV3)   I'm not a handless BIV

Suppose, in line with Dretske, that one's evidence for the first premise of both (HANDS) and (BIV) is an experience as of having hands: an experience neutral between veridical and non-veridical cases.[8]

---

7   BIV = as before, Brain-in-a-Vat being fed pseudo-perceptual experiences by an evil scientist.
8   Klein (1995) gives an analysis of closure principles sensitive to different conceptions of evidential warrant. Note also — as a dialectical matter — Hawthorne (2005) does not contest this Dretskean conception of evidential warrant (notwithstanding it would not be his independently favoured way of viewing the matter).

1.4 Here is Dretske's (2005a: 19) definition of a conclusive reason (where 'P', again, is a placeholder for a proposition):

R is a conclusive reason for P = $_{df}$ R would not be true unless P were true

Dretske's original (extensionally equivalent — cf. n. 9) formulation of a conclusive reason (1971: 1) better brings out the *modal* character of conclusive reasons:

R is a conclusive reason for P if and only if, given R, $\sim\Diamond\sim$P (or, alternatively, $\sim\Diamond$ (R.$\sim$P))[9]

Dretske makes clear later that the appropriate modality is *empirical* "possibility as it exists in relation to one's evidence or grounds for believing P" (1971: 14). However, as the debate between Dretske and Hawthorne, which we will be entering here, centres on the former (2005a)-definition, it is that former definition on which we will focus. This (2005a)-definition (a close relative of the sensitivity condition to be encountered in the ensuing chapter) essentially asks whether, in (all) nearby possible worlds where P is false, is R also false? Iff this is so, R is a conclusive reason for P.

How does this piece of terminology map onto analysis of (HANDS) and (BIV)? Well the subject's perceptual experience as of having hands *is* a conclusive reason for (HANDS1). The relevant alternative[10]

---

9   The '$\sim$' sign, here and elsewhere in this chapter, refers to negation. Although these formulations are both Dretske's, one might, at first blush, think that they seem importantly different. One might think: the first formulation is naturally interpreted as saying that, in (all) **nearby** possible worlds where R is true, P is also true; but the second formulation (particularly the part in brackets) is more naturally interpreted as saying that, in **all** possible worlds where R is true, P is also true. Now it was not Dretske's intention that these two formulations should be interpreted differently. Thus, one might ask: which formulation or interpretation would he have wanted? And — more on this later in this chapter — Dretske's idea was that in (all) **nearby** possible worlds in which the proposition P is not true, the evidence proposition, R, is also not true.

10 What counts as a relevant alternative (strictly: a *set* of relevant alternatives), in this or that context, is an intuitive datum. There is no set of severally necessary and jointly sufficient criteria for relevance. We can say, though, if an alternative is a *genuine objective possibility* (a vague notion), it counts as relevant. (Heller (1999) defends Dretske's notion *and use* of 'relevant alternatives' from attacks from Stine (1976), Cohen (1988), DeRose (1995) and Lewis (1996).) Finally, it is because only relevant (and not *far-fetched*) alternatives, for Dretske, need be 'ruled out' in order for a subject to have knowledge, that Dretske can be classed an *infallibilist* about knowledge.

to having hands in the context of (HANDS1), is the subject having a stump in place of one hand, or a hand amputated, etc., and it is clear that the subject would not[11] have an experience as of having hands were he to have a stump in place of one hand or be a hand-amputee. The subject's evidence is, then, a conclusive reason for (HANDS1). The idea, then, is that a **conclusive** reason just is one that rules out **all relevant** alternatives. And a piece of evidence (described by a proposition, R) rules out all relevant alternatives to a proposition, P, iff in (all) nearby possible worlds where P is false, R would also be false.

And, moving on to (HANDS3) — (HANDS2) is knowable *a priori* — the relevant alternative to having a hand in the context of (HANDS3) is the subject being handless, perhaps through having both his hands cut off. It is clear that our subject's experience as of having hands would not persist were he to become handless. The subject's evidence is, then, also a conclusive reason for (HANDS3). We thus have, with (HANDS), an instance of closure of knowledge under known entailment.

1.5   But that there are instances of closure here and there is not good enough for closure supporters: closure must hold across the board if (*Closure*) is to be valid. This is where we must consider (BIV) and Dretske's concept of heavyweight implications. As with (HANDS1), the subject's perceptual experience as of having hands provides him with a conclusive reason for (BIV1). Likewise, the second premise of (BIV) is knowable *a priori*. The difference in the two arguments is brought out in the conclusion: in (BIV) — unlike with (HANDS) — the subject's experiential evidence *is not* a conclusive reason for (BIV 3). The relevant alternative is different. Were our subject not *not* a handless BIV he would straightforwardly be a handless BIV. And, by hypothesis, our subject *would still have* an experience as of having hands were he a handless BIV. So, by Dretske's lights, (BIV) is an instance of a counterexample to (*Closure*). (*Closure*) is thereby, for Dretske, invalidated.[12]

1.6   The final piece of the jigsaw is the concept of a heavyweight implication. Dretske wants to say something about when we will

---

11   In the relevant sense of empirical possibility. (Read this modal claim in, where appropriate, in subsequent counterfactuals.)
12   Note, for the (standard) contextualist, (*Closure*) is valid in *all fixed contexts*.

have instances of (*Closure*), and when we will have counterexamples. Dretske's answer is that we will have counterexamples to (*Closure*) if there is a heavyweight implication as our conclusion. Clearly (BIV3) must count as a 'heavyweight implication'. But can Dretske give an account of this concept without merely pointing to paradigms thereof when it suits his purposes?

Dretske is content simply to point to paradigms of heavyweight implications — for example, that there is a material world; that humans are not mindless zombies; that there was a yesterday — and to assert that "[t]here are some known implications of what we know [...] that we do not have to know to be true in order to know to be true what implies them" (2005a: 23). It would be somewhat unsatisfactory to leave things there, so let's invoke Hawthorne's (2005: 33) take on what he calls a "heavyweight proposition":[13]

> Let P be a "heavyweight proposition" just in case we all have some strong inclination to think that P is not the sort of thing that one can know by the exercise of reason alone and also that P is not the sort of thing that one can know by the use of one's perceptual faculties (even aided by reason).

In sum, Dretske views the denial of (*Closure*) as the only way to preserve ordinary knowledge — we do not have to know the heavyweight implications of (quotidian proposition) P to know P.

2. Hawthorne's 'Heavyweight Conjunct' Counter-Challenge

2.1 First, an overview of Hawthorne's (2005) strategy. His counter-challenge to Dreske's challenge has two strands. First, he aims to show how we *can* have conclusive reasons for heavyweight propositions — but in such cases, as we have seen from our analysis of Dretske in section

---

13 A heavyweight *implication* just is, I take it, a heavyweight *proposition* which is entailed by a quotidian proposition. To link this back to Chapter Two, it is not clear whether the notion of 'heavyweight implication' will distinguish between the conclusions of (EK)- and (EK*)-reasoning. One view would be that in both cases, the conclusion is not the sort of thing that one can know by perception and reasoning alone; but the difference is that in one case, and not in the other case, there is the possibility of gathering evidence that would favour the conclusion over its negation.

1, Dretske's machinery gives us no account of how knowledge of such propositions is blocked. (Although on the face of it Dretske is simply offering conclusive reasons as a necessary condition on knowledge, the first strand challenge makes sense when we see that Dretske accepts the challenge of explaining why we don't know heavyweight propositions.) Secondly, he aims to show how we can "all too often lack conclusive reasons for *a priori* consequences of known propositions, even though those consequences are not [heavyweight implications]" (Hawthorne 2005: 35). That is, he aims to show that there are propositions for which we lack conclusive reasons (according to Dretske's account of conclusive reasons) — in consequence, propositions that Dretske is bound to say we do not know — but which are not heavyweight propositions. (More on the dialectical efficacy of the second strand later in this chapter.)[14]

2.2   Our principal focus will be on the first strand: putative cases in which conclusive reasons *are present* for heavyweight implications. Hawthorne has three imaginative cases putatively exemplifying this property. I want to focus (initially) on *Case 1*: what I will call the case of the *'heavyweight conjunct'*. Here is case 1 (Hawthorne, 2005: 35–36):

> [W]hile I might lack conclusive reasons for the proposition ~I am a brain in a vat, I will (supposing I have a headache) have conclusive reasons for I have a headache and ~I am a brain in a vat. My reason for that conjunction include my headache. Were the conjunction false I would not, then, have had my reasons.

So let's consider this step by step. First a *contrast proposition* is set out: a heavyweight proposition — ~I am a brain in a vat — is asserted to *lack* the backing of conclusive reasons. The proposition in question — ~I am a brain in a vat — is a proposition for which we do not have conclusive reasons: the relevant alternative is that I am a brain in a vat, and it difficult to produce evidence that excludes that alternative.

Next a closely related proposition — I have a headache and ~I am a brain in a vat — is considered for which one *does* have conclusive reasons, in part, here, one's headache. Why is the headache a conclusive reason for this proposition? Well, to use possible worlds discourse, the

---

14   Dretske's (2005b: 43–44) irenic reply to Hawthorne is, essentially, 'confession and avoidance'.

closest worlds where the conjunction is false are worlds in which one does not have a headache.[15] Crucially, such worlds are not as *outré* as BIV-worlds: they are standard non-BIV-worlds.[16] So my reasons for the conjunction are conclusive, but Hawthorne (2005: 36) contends that:

> [T]he [conjunction] is every bit as apt to raise inner alarm bells as the proposition that ~I am a [BIV] and will thus come out as [...] heavyweight.

2.3 What are we to make of case 1? An appealing response to Hawthorne is to deny one has conclusive reasons for the conjunction. This response will involve patching up Dretske's definition (see 1.4) of a conclusive reason. (In this sense, Hawthorne is not criticisable for offering case 1 as a counterexample to *Dretske's* challenge.)

2.4 To answer Hawthorne on behalf of Dretske, we need, I'll contend, to supplement Dretske's definition of a conclusive reason with a further (necessary) thesis for being a conclusive reason:

> *(SUPP)* If P is a conjunctive proposition, R would not be true unless each of the conjuncts of P, *taken separately*, were true.

That is, R must be a conclusive reason for each of the conjuncts, *taken separately*, of a conjunctive proposition. What is the force of the italicised 'taken separately'? In essence, the point is that *(SUPP)* comes into play when we are faced with a conjunctive proposition, and requires the relevant modal relation to hold between R and *each of P's conjuncts* (and not just instead, as in the original formulation of conclusive reasons, between R and *P itself*).[17] More specifically, suppose that proposition, P, is a conjunction: (P_1 & P_2). Alternatives to P are possibilities in which P is false. Conclusive reasons do not need to exclude *all* possible alternatives

---

15 So there is a crucial difference between this case and the (BIV) case. (BIV3) is 'I am not a handless BIV', which is equivalent to a disjunction: 'Either I have hands **or** ~I am a brain in a vat'. Hawthorne's example is a conjunction: 'I have a headache **and** ~I am a brain in a vat'.

16 As we are not debating with the sceptic, we can join Dretske and Hawthorne in making the assumption that we are not presently in a BIV-world.

17 This is why *(SUPP)* is a genuine supplementation of the original conclusive reasons account. On the original account, and where P is a conjunctive proposition, the relevant modal relation must hold between R and P, and when P is true, each of P's conjuncts is true; however it doesn't follow that the relevant modal relation must hold between R and each of P's conjuncts (and this is because it isn't the case that whenever P is false, each of P's conjuncts is false).

to P. However, by *(SUPP)*, when P is conjunctive, conclusive reasons need to do more than exclude the most nearby alternatives to P. The nearby alternatives *might* be possibilities in which P_1 is false. But, by *(SUPP)*, conclusive reasons need to exclude nearby possibilities in which P_1 is false *and also the nearest possibilities in which P_2 is false*. That is, by *(SUPP)*, both $\sim P_1$ and also $\sim P_2$ are relevant alternatives to P. What needs to be shown is (1) that in the nearest $\sim P_1$ worlds, R is false and also (2) that in the nearest $\sim P_2$ worlds, R is false.

With all this said: first I need to explain how this supplementation will solve case 1 for Dretske; then I need to defend the supplementation from a charge of being *ad-hoc*.

2.5 The first, explanatory part is straightforward. While having a headache is a conclusive reason for having a headache (first conjunct), I might well still have a headache were I a BIV (second conjunct), and this counterfactual precludes one's having a headache from being a conclusive reason for one's not being a BIV.[18]

2.6 More trickily, how do I *justify* appeal to *(SUPP)*? (I take it Hawthorne is committed – even if only: *arguendo* — to the denial of this supplementation as a necessary condition for a conclusive reason. So much is clear from Hawthorne's treatment of case 1: with *(SUPP)* in place the headache is no longer, as Hawthorne requires, a conclusive reason for the conjunction.) I want to generate a *reductio* for this *undeveloped* Dretskean view of conclusive reasons, leading to justification of a Dretskean appeal to *(SUPP)*.[19] Consider the following case: suppose I have a headache. It seems, absent supplementation by *(SUPP)*, that that experience can be a conclusive reason for the following proposition, *(P)*: I have a headache and I have all my limbs. Without supplementation by *(SUPP)* this experience will count as a conclusive reason for this conjunction. After all, worlds in which I fail to have a headache are palpably closer than worlds in which I lose a limb. (Multiple like

---

18   As the headache is *internal* to the BIV, I take it Putnam's (1981: ch.1) objections to the capacity of a BIV to refer to external things are not germane.

19   In the next chapter I develop a like case against Nozick's sensitivity condition. There I consider in detail a possible response to the case extractable from Peacocke (1986). Though Peacocke's response is relevant here, I reserve treatment of the response until Chapter Seven.

examples can be constructed. The form of such examples is developed in more detail in the next chapter. It is the case's generalisability which makes it so pressing.)

Intuitively, however, the idea that this experience counts as a conclusive reason for this conjunction is nonsense (insofar as conclusive reasons in some sense *justify* belief in propositions for subjects).[20] (*SUPP*) tells us why. (*SUPP*) rules out this result, as I might very well still have a headache were (*P*)'s second conjunct false. (Note that the second conjunct of (*P*) does not count as *heavyweight* by our definition of 1.6. This distinguishes my *reductio* from case-1-type examples: it is much more dialectically effective, in motivating a modification to Dretske's account, to appeal to quotidian propositions, on account of their generalisability. The fact that the second conjunct of (*P*) is not heavyweight is developed in 3.1 – 3.3.)

My supplementary account of a conclusive reason hence provides a non-*ad-hoc* solution to case 1. I have not, as Hawthorne (2005: 34) scoffs: "scurr[ied] back to the epistemological laboratory to contrive an account which delivers the welcome result while avoiding the embarrassing one". Rather my supplementation is necessary to avoid the absurdity into which an undeveloped Dretskean account leads us.

2.7 Hawthorne has two more imaginative cases involving propositions supposedly exemplifying the property of being heavyweight propositions for which we have conclusive reasons. I believe a (supplemented) Dretskean notion of conclusive reasons has the resources to accommodate them. Let's quickly deal with them here.

Case 2: Suppose at the zoo I have experiences as of a bird flying around in a cage; and suppose that experience is my reason for thinking I am not looking at a cleverly disguised inanimate object in the cage. Suppose finally that it is much easier to make an inanimate object look like an animate object by making it turtle-like than by making it bird-like. Now Hawthorne posits that, while the proposition that I am not looking at an inanimate object cleverly disguised to look like an animate object

---

20 This parenthetical claim is not explicit in Dretske's account of conclusive reasons. However, insofar as Dretske affirms "knowledge is belief based on [...] conclusive reasons" (2005a: 19), we might take the parenthetical claim to be *in keeping* with a *Dretskean* account of knowledge.

is manifestly heavyweight, I have conclusive reasons for it: the 'closest worlds' where there is an inanimate object in the cage are worlds in which I fail to have a bird-like experience. In sum, there are two points that Hawthorne needs to make (here, and in the coming case 3). One is that, intuitively, reason plus perception cannot tell me that P is true; that is, that I am not looking at an inanimate object cleverly disguised to look like an animate object. Thus, by Hawthorne's account of heavyweight propositions, the proposition (P) that I am not looking at an inanimate object cleverly disguised to look like an animate object, is heavyweight. The other point Hawthorne needs to make is that, when I have an experience as of a bird, this (R) counts as a conclusive reason for the proposition P. As noted, this second claim seems correct on Dretske's account of conclusive reasons. In the nearest worlds in which P is false, I am looking at an inanimate object cleverly disguised to look like a turtle. So I do not have an experience as of a bird.[21]

Answer: Taken at face value, Hawthorne's case 2 fails to set out a genuinely manifestly heavyweight proposition (and so is not ripe to be a counterexample to Dretske). Why not? If, as a matter of fact, the possibility of bird-like inanimate objects is as remote as Hawthorne stipulates, then I can (and do) know the proposition in question on the basis of my perceptual experience. (Whether I know that I know the proposition in question will depend on my knowledge of the germane objective facts about the circumstance of evaluation.) The possibility of bird-like inanimate objects in the cage is, by stipulation, too remote to be relevant, and it is of no matter that my evidence cannot discount such a counter-possibility. It is only if we — counter to how the case is set up — countenance bird-like inanimate objects in the cage as relevant alternatives that we fail to know the proposition in question. But on *this supposition* the proposition in question *is* manifestly heavyweight, and

---

21 Before coming to my answer, there is a possible extrapolation from case 1. Arguably, P can be taken as equivalent to (P_1 & P_2), where P_1: I am not looking at an inanimate object cleverly disguised to look like an animate turtle, and P_2: I am not looking at an inanimate object cleverly disguised to look like an animate bird. Now, by parity with my treatment of case 1, we allow that, if P_1 were false then I should not have evidence R. But we also point out that if P_2 were false then I should still have evidence R. Thus, as before, R does not exclude relevant alternatives to P_2 although it does exclude relevant alternatives to P_1. My reason for not pursuing this answer lies in my doubts over whether P is indeed equivalent to (P_1 & P_2).

now Dretske's conclusive reasons machinery gives the welcome result that we fail to know the proposition in question on the basis of our perceptual evidence. The basic point is that this supposition, contrary to Hawthorne's dialectical aims, brings Hawthorne's case 2 in line with *standard Drestkean cases*.

Case 3: I see a cookie. Suppose I have an experience as of a cookie five feet in front of me and, on this basis, form the belief that there is a mind-independent object roughly five feet in front of me. Again, Hawthorne opines, we have a ("highfalutin") manifestly heavyweight proposition. On this first point, it must be conceded that there is some strong inclination to think that reason plus perception does not suffice for knowledge that there is a mind-independent object roughly five feet in front of me. Reason plus perception does not exclude the possibility that the causes of my perceptual experience are mind-dependent. And, moreover — the second point — Hawthorne shows it is a proposition for which we have conclusive reasons: the 'closest worlds' in which there isn't a mind-independent object roughly five feet in front of me are worlds with laws like the actual world in which there is no physical object at all in front of me (and not worlds where "some bizarre metaphysics holds"). Therefore, on this analysis, in such close possible worlds I will fail to have an experience as of a cookie five feet in front of me. Put differently, in the nearest possible worlds in which there is *not* a mind-independent object roughly five feet in front of me, I do not have the same kind of perceptual experience as of a cookie roughly five feet in front of me.

Answer: My strategy, in a nutshell, is to side with Hawthorne on the second 'conclusive reasons' point, but to depart on the first 'heavyweight proposition' point. More specifically: as with case 2 I just do not see that we have a genuinely manifestly heavyweight proposition here.[22] And

---

22 To anticipate my reasoning, and speaking metaphorically: the 'highfalutin' stain Hawthorne detects in the proposition in question, brought about by reference to a "mind-independent object", is removed by the *down-to-earth* reference to "roughly five feet in front of me". Everything turns on my rejecting Hawthorne's claim that the proposition P meets the definition of a heavyweight proposition. It is important here that, in order not to beg the question against Hawthorne and in favour of Dretske, we must not take the fact that we have a conclusive reason for P to show that P is not heavyweight (that is, is not heavyweight by Hawthorne's criterion).

on the intuitively plausible view of what counts as the closest possible world in this context of inquiry, we do indeed — as the Dretskean machinery predicts — have a conclusive reason for the proposition in question. The closest world in which there fails to be a mind-independent object roughly five feet in front of me is surely the world in which there *is* a mind-independent object *failing* to count as roughly five feet in front of me (and not either the world Hawthorne posits or worlds in which some bizarre metaphysics holds). Let's suppose the cookie has been moved from its position; it is still in front of me, but not *roughly five feet* in front of me. Now I will not have an experience as of a cookie five feet in front of me when there is a mind-independent object failing to count as roughly five feet in front of me. And so I have a conclusive reason for this non-heavyweight proposition.[23] The *genuinely* manifestly heavyweight proposition in this neighbourhood — indeed an entailment of Hawthorne's proposition — is: there is a mind-independent object. *Now* the relevant alternative *is* a world in which there is no mind-independent object. (We are in the 'bizarre metaphysics' world, or some equally distant world.) And now I straightforwardly fail to have a conclusive reason for the heavyweight proposition in question.[24]

Assuming I am right on all this, the dialectical situation is as follows: Dretske's conclusive reasons machinery, supplemented by (SUPP),[25] can explain failures of closure satisfactorily by establishing the lack of conclusive reasons for heavyweight propositions.

3. Hawthorne's Second Strand

3.1 In section 2.1, I mentioned the second strand to Hawthorne's counter-challenge to Dretske. Hawthorne maintains we "all too often lack conclusive reasons for *a priori* consequences of known propositions,

---

23 There are delicate issues here about the fine-grainedness of perceptual experiences and judgments (see Schaffer 2003). But to reject my analysis here is to allow that one fails to have conclusive reasons for quotidian perceptual judgments, such as: there is a cookie roughly five feet in front of me.

24 It has been put to me that, in light of cases 2 and 3, Hawthorne perhaps ought to be operating with an account of heavyweight propositions (cf. 1.6 *supra*) *relativised* to *perceptual reasons* or to *empirical investigations*. In advance of any such account being developed further, however, I prescind from further comment thereon.

25 (SUPP) enters the picture only for Hawthorne's case 1 (but cf. n. 21 *supra*).

even though those consequences are not [heavyweight implications]" (2005: 35). He proceeds to construct two fun cases putatively establishing this point (36—7).²⁶ Even if Hawthorne is granted this, insofar as he presents these cases as counterexamples to (better: problematic or challenging cases for) Dretske he commits an *ignoratio elenchi*.²⁷ Of the following three theses, Dretske is — as pointed out at 1.6 — (and should be) committed to neither (I) nor (II), but only to (III):

(I) One lacks conclusive reasons for a proposition, *p*, *iff* the proposition is heavyweight.

(II) One lacks conclusive reasons for a proposition, *p*, *only if* the proposition is heavyweight.

(III) One lacks conclusive reasons for a proposition, *p*, *if* the proposition is heavyweight.²⁸

3.2 Now Hawthorne has already — in the first strand — offered putative counterexamples to (III), and I have attempted to parry those counterexamples. In the second strand he goes on to argue that heavyweight propositions are neither necessary nor sufficient for failure of closure on Dretske's account. Unfortunately for Hawthorne, however, these second strand cases count only against theses (I) and (II) — theses to which Dretske is not committed. In fact, these second strand cases provide the basis for further counterexamples to (*Closure*): grist to Dretske's mill, one might think. Indeed, my *reductio*

---

26 For why Kripke's (2011) 'red barn' case is not a candidate to be a 'second-strand' case, see Dretske (2005a: n. 4).
27 As I grant Hawthorne his point here — *viz*. Dretske allows for non-heavyweight implications not backed by conclusive reasons — I do not set out his intricate cases.
28 In fact, (*Closure*) would be denied with the weaker still:

(IV) *Some* heavyweight propositions lack conclusive reasons.

Without more by way of explanation, however, any such denial might seem unprincipled. Equally unmotivated would be the following (*Closure*)-denying principle which Hawthorne (2005: 37) considers:

If one knows P and deduces Q from P then one knows Q, unless Q is a manifestly heavyweight proposition.

Without being told *what feature* of manifestly heavyweight propositions allows them to fulfil this role, any such principle must seem *ad hoc*.

of the undeveloped Dretskean account in 2.6 is a further example of the phenomenon exemplified by these second strand cases (provided, of course, Dretske's definition of conclusive reasons is supplemented with (*SUPP*)).

3.3 It would be better still for the Dretskean 'anti-(*Closure*)' project if Dretske could give an account of when non-heavyweight implications will lack conclusive reasons, but the project is hardly vitiated by the absence of any such account.[29]

4. Conclusion

4.1 My project is complete: (*Closure*) has certainly not been invalidated, but a sophisticated (suitably supplemented) Dretskean challenge thereto remains unmet. Deduction — *pace* Hawthorne (and Williamson) — may not always be a way of extending one's knowledge.

---

29 It must be conceded that Hawthorne seems to read Dretske as offering a kind of explanation of when, and only when, these failures of *(Closure)* arise, *viz.* they arise when, and only when, the implied proposition is heavyweight. An implied proposition's being heavyweight is not, however, what failure of closure *consists in*. Rather, on Dretske's account, what failure of closure consists in is that the implied proposition does not meet the conclusive reasons criterion for being known. It is hard to see the idea of a heavyweight proposition being *at the heart of* an explanation of failures of closure if there are plenty of examples of failures of closure that do not involve heavyweight propositions. Again, though, it must be conceded that Hawthorne will take himself to have argued already that there is something wrong with Dretske's account because examples that seem to be relevantly similar (e.g. both seem to involve heavyweight propositions) can receive different verdicts from the conclusive reasons test.

7. Sensitivity

Continuing to engage with the issue of knowledge-closure, I turn to Nozick's (1981) sensitivity condition on knowledge. I propose some modifications of the sensitivity condition, argue that a sensitivity account should reject the Equivalence Principle ('If you know a priori that p and q are equivalent and you know p, then you are in a position to know q'), and assess the costs of this rejection.

0.1 John Hawthorne (2004: 39–41) has two forceful arguments in favour of:

> *Single-Premise Closure* (SPC). Necessarily, if S knows p, competently deduces q from p, and thereby comes to believe q, while retaining knowledge of p throughout, then S knows q.

Each of Hawthorne's arguments rests on an intuitively appealing principle which Hawthorne calls the *Equivalence Principle*. I show, however, that the opponents of SPC with whom he's engaging — namely Fred Dretske and Robert Nozick — have independent reason to reject this principle, and resultantly I conclude that Hawthorne's arguments in favour of SPC are not knock-down.

0.2 The plan: First, I introduce Hawthorne's Equivalence Principle, and a Sensitivity condition (see 1.2 *infra*) — a condition which features in, and is, *arguendo*, presupposed by, Hawthorne's pro-closure arguments. (Presupposed, in the sense that Hawthorne assumes Sensitivity, *pro tem*, and seeks to chart serious costs — in addition to abandoning SPC — involved with such an acceptance.) Second, I set out one of

Hawthorne's pro-closure arguments in which the Equivalence Principle features. Third, I set out and motivate, by means of *reductio*, a modification to the Sensitivity condition. Fourth, I use this motivated modification to the Sensitivity condition to reject the Equivalence Principle, and thus to cast doubt on the decisiveness of both of Hawthorne's arguments for SPC. In so doing, a further principled modification to the Sensitivity condition emerges. None of the foregoing is to clinch the *truth* of a view in the ballpark of Sensitivity, but is rather to show a principled way to resist Hawthorne's arguments, by means of well-motivated modifications to Sensitivity (cf. 3.3 *infra*).

1. Hawthorne's Equivalence Principle and Sensitivity

1.1   Hawthorne notes the following intuitively appealing principle:

Equivalence. If you know a priori that p and q are equivalent and you know p, then you are in a position to know q.

(Here, p and q are equivalent iff they have the same truth-value.)

1.2   Hawthorne, while explicitly addressing both Nozick and Dretske, glosses his arguments using just Nozick's Sensitivity condition on knowledge:

Sensitivity. S knows p only if S Sensitively believes p, where S Sensitively believes p just in case, were p false, S would not believe p.[1]

---

1   I suppress mention of *methods* (see Nozick 1981: 179–85, 188–96); I'm confident nothing major is lost, in this chapter, by so doing. While mention of methods is suppressed, and so not foregrounded, see n. 21 *infra*, where I briefly address an effort of some philosophers to appeal to methods — in particular, principles governing the *individuation* of methods — to solve some problem cases for the Sensitivity theorist. In a nutshell, though I suggest where my sympathies lie in debates over the individuation of methods, I am not presently in a position to offer an argument defending my sympathies, and the nub of my current position is that I do not need to commit on this issue for present purposes. Although Nozick confronts issues over methods much more directly than I, I essentially, on these issues, follow Nozick (1981: 184): "I do not want to underestimate […] difficulties [about how to individuate methods] but neither do I want to pursue them here." (Moreover, Nozick (185) observes that "[a]lthough sometimes it will be necessary to be explicit about the methods via which someone believes something, often it will cause no confusion to leave out all mention of method.") For why this is a

Dretske (1971) does not endorse Sensitivity. Instead he requires that, in order to know *p*, one must have a *conclusive reason* to believe *p*. While the two requirements are similar, Dretske (2005: 24, n. 4) himself is at pains to point out situations in which the requirements come apart. Hawthorne's (2004) criticisms of Sensitivity, however, carry over to Dretske's conclusive reasons account (see Hawthorne 2004, 2005), and their differences play no role in my arguments. I'll follow Hawthorne (2004) by concentrating on Nozick's Sensitivity account (though what I come to say about Nozick goes, *mutatis mutandis*, for Dretske also).[2]

2. Hawthorne's 'Equivalence and Distribution' Pro-Closure Argument

2.1 Hawthorne (2004: 41) notes:

The following principle [...] seems extremely intuitive:

> *Distribution.* If one knows that *p* and *q*, then one is in a position to know *p* and to know *q*.[3]

Suppose I know

(9) That is a zebra.

By Equivalence, I can know

---

permissible strategy on my part, again see n. 21 *infra*. Finally, for a recent overview of, and substantive position on, methods, see Becker (2012). Becker's aim is to "sketch a particular conception of methods that [he] think[s] Nozick would have accepted, explaining how finely methods are to be individuated and how methods can be conceived internalistically within a broadly externalist epistemology" (82). (Cf. Nozick's (184–85) "clarifying remarks" on — though not precise formulations of — individuation conditions for methods.)

2   It should be noted that SPC was not Nozick's (or Dretske's) conception of closure. This can be safely bracketed in what follows.

3   I use Hawthorne's (2004: 41, n. 100) weaker formulation of Distribution which, he notes, "serve[s] [his] current purposes just as well [as the formulation in the main text]". Is even this weaker principle true? Suppose one knows that one has hands and that one never performs conjunction elimination; one is not, then, in a position to know that one never performs conjunction elimination, *by performing conjunction elimination*. However, one may know the conjunction by conjunction introduction, or else one's knowing the conjunction might constitute one's knowing its conjuncts (cf. Williamson 2000: 283). In either case, knowledge of this conjunction does not undermine Distribution.

(12) That is a zebra and that is not a cleverly disguised mule.

By Distribution, I can know

(11) That is not a cleverly disguised mule.

But Dretske and Nozick deny this.

> In relinquishing SPC, we are thus forced to relinquish certain other principles—[...] Distribution (or instead, Equivalence)—that are very compelling. A denial of SPC thus ramifies into costs that are extremely high.

Nozick denies we can know (11) — one's belief in (11) isn't Sensitive. Therefore Nozick must either deny that we can know (9) (which would involve abandoning his account of knowledge) or else deny the (intuitive) conjunction of Distribution and Equivalence.

2.2 The argument generalises. Take any ordinary proposition p and some proposition, q, known to be entailed by p, such that one's belief in q isn't Sensitive. We thus know *a priori* that p is equivalent to $(p \& q)$. By Equivalence, if one knows p then one is in a position to know $(p \& q)$. Then, by Distribution, one is in a position to know q. However, as one's belief in q is not held Sensitively, Nozick denies that q is known; and so Nozick is forced to deny either Distribution or Equivalence.

2.3 Note, however, that Distribution is effectively a restricted form of SPC: SPC claims knowledge is closed under competent deduction, whereas Distribution suggests knowledge is closed under conjunction elimination — a form of competent deduction. So, given that Nozick rejects SPC, it would be no *major* surprise were he to reject Distribution.[4] Indeed, as it stands, Sensitivity doesn't respect Distribution, and so Nozick rejects Distribution.

However, it is not satisfactory to respond to Hawthorne's argument simply by rejecting Distribution. First, Distribution is extremely plausible: it's hard to see how knowing a conjunction doesn't put one in a position to know each conjunct. Nozick (1981: 228, 692, n. 63) himself admits the plausibility of Distribution, although he does reject

---

4 I recognise that for any valid principle of inference, V, there is a less restricted principle that is invalid, I. Being 'no *major* surprise' is, thus, a weak claim. *Mutatis mutandis* for ensuing uses of the phrase.

it. (Going further, Dretske (1970: 1009) says "it seems to me fairly obvious that if someone knows that P and Q, [...] he thereby knows that Q".) Therefore if Nozick's account of knowledge were Hawthorne's chief target, an argument depending solely on Distribution — and not, additionally, Equivalence — might suffice to undermine it. Second, rejecting Distribution does nothing to undermine Hawthorne's claim that a subject who knows (9), also knows (12). But (12) is in all relevant respects similar to the kind of proposition that motivates the rejection of SPC (i.e. (11)), as there is some intuitive pull to the idea that we cannot come to know (12) via our senses and deduction. Rejecting Distribution is therefore both implausible and fails to address a problem that Hawthorne poses for the intuitive motivation for rejecting SPC.[5]

2.4 It might seem, then, that Nozick ought to reject Equivalence (though Equivalence, like Distribution, is extremely plausible, and so any rejection thereof will have associated costs). Like Distribution, Equivalence is effectively a restricted form of SPC. SPC, recall, claims knowledge is closed under competent deduction, whereas Equivalence suggests knowledge is closed under *a priori* known biconditional elimination — a form of competent deduction. So, again, given that Nozick rejects SPC, it would be no *major* surprise were he to reject Equivalence. But Hawthorne notes that Nozick's *reasons* for rejecting SPC don't carry over to rejecting Equivalence (although they do carry over to Distribution); and Nozick (1981: 229, 690, n. 60) agrees. For example, Nozick's rejection of SPC is based on the fact that a subject may Sensitively believe *p* without Sensitively believing some *q*, which that subject knows to be entailed by *p*. And since, for Nozick, Sensitivity is a necessary condition for knowledge, it can easily be shown that SPC fails *for Nozick*.[6] However, Hawthorne notes, this situation cannot

---

5   Nozick (1981: 228–30, 692, n. 64) himself in fact accepts that we can know conjunctions such as (12). (12) is Sensitive: when it's false, there's, say, a horse before you (rather than a zebra), and you don't believe the whole conjunction.

6   This last 'for Nozick' qualification is important. There is no strict entailment from the fact that a (putative) necessary condition on knowledge, such as Sensitivity, is not closed under competent deduction, to the proposition that knowledge itself is not closed under competent deduction: it might be that the Sensitively believed *p* in question doesn't satisfy some other condition which the account in question posits as necessary for knowledge. Nonetheless, for Nozick SPC *does* fail. For more on this, see Vogel (1987), Warfield (2004), Brueckner (2004), Murphy (2006), and Holliday (2014).

readily arise when *p* and *q* are *a priori* equivalent. That is, we cannot get $(\sim p \rightarrow \sim B_S p)^7$ & $\sim(\sim q \rightarrow \sim B_S q)$ when *p* and *q* are *a priori equivalent*, except, perhaps, in some recherché cases.

I'll show, however, that, Sensitivity is (likely) unacceptable as it stands and should be modified for reasons independent of Hawthorne's argument. Moreover, my modification conflicts with Equivalence, thereby allowing Nozick to reject Equivalence in a principled way. So a plausible Sensitivity condition on knowledge *does* provide reason to reject Equivalence, just as Nozick's account of knowledge provides reason to reject Distribution. Therefore a plausible condition on knowledge does rule out Equivalence, even if, as Hawthorne notes, Nozick's original condition does not. Moreover, once Equivalence is rejected, Nozick is able, I'll show, to retain the attractive Distribution.

3. Modifying Sensitivity: A Reductio of Nozick's Account of Knowledge

3.1 Consider the following case for *reductio*.[8] Suppose you have a headache. Now consider the following (*ex hypothesi* true) proposition:

(P) I have a headache and I have all my limbs.

Suppose you form the belief, (P), based solely on your evidence of having a headache. (To form the belief, *(P)*, on this basis, is to display an epistemic failing: this is not an apposite method for forming beliefs of this general nature. But it is not incoherent to make the foregoing

---

7   '$B_S p$' designates: A subject, S, believes *p*.
8   Why a *reductio* (and not a (mere) *counterexample*)? The *reductio* operates as follows: assume (for *reductio*) Nozick's account of knowledge; such an assumption leads to absurdity (given the generalisability of the case); therefore, not-Nozick's account of knowledge. (It is the generalisability of the case which generates the absurdity, and thus elevates the case from a (mere) counterexample to a *reductio*.) As I note later (in 3.3), the dialectic of this chapter assumes that something like Sensitivity is necessary for knowledge. Given this assumption, and again as I note later (in 3.3), the obvious, and natural, first response to this *reductio* is to modify Sensitivity. The inspiration for this *reductio* comes, somewhat ironically, from a distinct case presented by Hawthorne (2004: 44); Hawthorne doesn't notice his case's ramifications. I elsewhere (chapter 6) use an argument similar to the *reductio* here to stake out a principled modification to Dretske's conclusive reasons condition on knowledge.

supposition. Next time you have a headache, try forming the belief, *(P)*, solely on that basis. You will see for yourself that it can be done.) This is not to stipulate that having a headache is the only evidence you have; just that it is the only evidence on the basis of which you form the belief, *(P)*. Thus, this leaves open that you have whatever evidence is necessary to have the conceptual or cognitive resources to form the belief, *(P)*, provided such evidence is not playing a basing role. (For more on the basing relation, which is left undeveloped here, see Korcz 2006.) Given your basing evidence, you will hold that belief Sensitively: in the closest world in which *(P)* is false (a world in which you fail to have a headache but retain all your limbs) you won't believe *(P)*. (Assume, uncontroversially, Nozick's *adherence* condition on knowledge — were *p* true, S would believe *p*[9] — is met in this case.) However, your belief in *(P)* does not constitute knowledge.[10]

---

9 See Nozick's (1981: 680–81, n. 8) account of the semantics of subjunctive conditionals for how to interpret the adherence condition. Discussion of Nozick's adherence condition has not been vast (but cf. Roush (2005), (2010), and her discussion of multi(ple)-premise closure), and many have thought that it is forgoable (by Nozick) as a necessary condition on knowledge (cf. Roush). Given this, and given a chief aim of this chapter is to make Sensitivity — and not adherence — as plausible as it can be, I ask the reader to assume the following. Either (1) in all cases of (intuitive) knowledge, the adherence condition is met (in advance of compelling counterexamples coming in, in which case see disjunct (2)). Or (2) the adherence condition is not a necessary condition on knowledge. This assumption enables me, in what follows (4.5–4.6), to talk of Nozick's adoption of CON and DIS *allowing* him to endorse Distribution and AC, respectively.

10 Isn't this case essentially the same as Kripke's (2011: 186) 'red barn' variation on the 'fake barns' case? No. First, note that one can — indeed, most epistemologists do — take the 'red barn' proposition in Kripke's case as involving a (complex) conjunctive predicate, rather than a conjunction. Insofar as this is the case, and insofar as my account treats these closely related parsings differently (cf. 4.8 *infra*), we have a difference between my *reductio* and Kripke's case. Second, and more importantly, insofar as one takes Kripke's case to involve a conjunction, my *reductio* and Kripke's case *do*, for Nozick, share the form: S knows that *(p & q)*, but doesn't know that *q*. However, even on this alternative, permissible parsing, we have an important difference between the two cases: in my *reductio*, the subject has *no basing evidence* for *q* (cf. n. 11), whereas in Kripke's case the subject *does* (albeit, as in my case, the belief in *q* isn't held Sensitively). It's a corollary of this that it's highly counterintuitive in my case that the subject knows *(p & q)*, whereas that's not so highly counterintuitive in Kripke's case. That's why my case, but not Kripke's, serves as a *reductio* of Nozick's account of knowledge *with respect to the belief in (p & q) considered alone*. That's not the moral of Kripke's case. Third, and relatedly, in my case *q* comes out false only in worlds more remote than worlds in which *p* comes out false, whereas this isn't so in Kripke's case.

The case is generalisable: stipulate that a subject's sole basing evidence is a headache, and construct a conjunctive proposition, which the subject believes on the basis of that evidence, in which the first conjunct is the statement that the subject has a headache and the second conjunct is a (*ex hypothesi* true) quotidian proposition for which the subject has no basing evidence,[11] which comes out false only in worlds more remote than worlds in which the subject fails to have a headache.[12]

3.2 A natural first response to my case, on behalf of Nozick, might be to draw on a suggestion from Christopher Peacocke (1986), namely to require for knowledge of a proposition that is inferred from lemmas that the lemmas should be, not only true (no false lemmas), but also known (no unknown lemmas). On the face of it, here is a way of applying this proposal to my case: *(P)* is inferred from two lemmas. Lemma 1: I have a headache (believed on the basis of the experience of having a headache). Lemma 2: I have all my limbs (believed on no basis). Proposition *(P)* is believed Sensitively. But in order for *(P)* to count as known according to the proposal, Lemma 1 should be known and Lemma 2 should be known. Lemma 1 is Sensitively believed, and so counts as known. But Lemma 2 is not Sensitively believed, and so does not count as known. Thus, the proposal, applied to the case where *(P)* is inferred from these two lemmas, does impose a more demanding condition than Nozick's original account, with the result that *(P)* does not count as known.

However, despite the attractive simplicity of this response, the proposal does not apply to my case as I presented it: my case does

---

11 Put somewhat metaphorically, the subject's belief *outstrips his evidence*. Indeed, this is a general problem for Sensitivity accounts of knowledge (*modulo* the adherence condition being met): a Sensitively held belief can outstrip one's evidence — cf. Martin's (1983) case in which a subject believes *p* Sensitively when his evidence, intuitively, only entitles him to believe (*p* or *q*). At a general level, any modification to Sensitivity must somehow *link* belief and evidence. My ensuing modifications to Sensitivity — modifications which do not accommodate Martin's case — are means of linking belief and evidence for conjunctions and disjunctions, respectively.

12 There is nothing special about headaches. Further *reductios* can be constructed, using other sources of evidence, that exhibit the same structure. Indeed, the reader unsatisfied with the *outré* nature of my *reductio* can substitute a preferred *reductio* (with an alternative source of evidence, but exhibiting the same structure) in its stead. A word of caution, however: my suspicion is that the less *outré* one's *reductio*, the more contestable will be the 'closeness result' constituting the required structure. In essence, my suspicion is that there is a trade-off in play between the benefit of being 'less *outré*' and the benefit of securing the 'closeness result'.

not involve a conjunction which is inferred from its conjuncts. (Or, the proposal does not apply unless it is stipulated that all conjunctions are to be treated by the proposal as if they were inferred from their conjuncts).[13]

3.3 So something has gone badly wrong with Nozick's account of knowledge (on which truth, belief, Sensitivity, and adherence are severally necessary and jointly sufficient) in relation to conjunctive propositions.[14] And we might think that the Sensitivity condition is to blame. But we needn't abandon Sensitivity *tout court*. (Note the dialectic between Hawthorne and Nozick: it's not that Hawthorne is, in his arguments under consideration in this chapter, denying that something like Sensitivity is necessary for knowledge. Thus to offer — as I come to do — principled modifications to the Sensitivity condition is not, to repeat, perforce to be a card-carrying Sensitivity theorist; it's simply to make Sensitivity as plausible as it can be.) Here's the obvious, and natural, fix. Supplement Sensitivity with an alternative (strengthened) necessary condition:

CON: If *p* is a conjunctive proposition, S knows *p* only if S believes each of the conjuncts of *p* Sensitively.[15]

---

13   Suppose, though, we adopt this proposal, with this stipulation. It imposes the same conditions for knowledge of a conjunction as my coming account (except that, as I come to note, my account does not require that the conjunction be believed Sensitively). And my account, I've noted, conflicts with Equivalence. That's a cost. So it needs to be considered whether this proposal (with this stipulation) generates counterexamples to Equivalence (as my account does, for example, in certain cases involving a conjunction and an *a priori* equivalent non-conjunctive proposition). On the face of it, this proposal might not seem to do so. Nevertheless, however that question turns out, I take the cost associated with this proposal's stipulation to be severe.
14   Take, as a default rule, the logical form of propositions to be determined by the logical form of the sentences semantically expressing them in this or that case (cf. n. 10 *supra* and 4.8 *infra*).
15   Note that Becker (2012: 95) raises, but does not develop or pursue, something in the region of CON. Finally, note that if Sensitivity is a necessary condition for knowledge, then the effect of this condition CON could also be achieved by a condition stating that:

DIST: If S knows a conjunction, then S knows each conjunct.

For if Sensitivity is necessary for knowledge, then DIST requires that each conjunct is believed Sensitively.

This supplementation straightforwardly enables us to avoid the *reductio*: in a world in which you're an amputee sitting alone basing your beliefs on your headache, you would still believe that you had all your limbs. Given you don't believe the second conjunct of *(P)* Sensitively, you cannot, on the modified account, know *(P)*.

A word about applying CON (which also goes, *mutatis mutandis*, for DIS, my coming proposal with respect to disjunctions): we suppose Sensitivity is a necessary condition on knowledge. We then test propositions for Sensitivity as we check for knowledge. If a conjunctive proposition comes to be checked thus, we filter it off from unmodified Sensitivity to CON. Iff that conjunctive proposition meets CON's necessary condition on knowledge, (modified) Sensitivity is met.

This observation enables me to be a little more precise about what I mean when I talk of 'modifying Sensitivity' (where Sensitivity states a putative necessary condition on knowledge). I do *not* mean that I am modifying what it is *to believe a proposition Sensitively*. That is just what it has always been: it is a matter of meeting the condition that if the proposition were not true, one would not believe it. What I am instead doing is modifying the *connection between Sensitivity and knowledge*. For a conjunction, it is not required for knowledge of the conjunction that the conjunction should be believed Sensitively. Rather, it is required that each conjunct should be believed Sensitively. (Again, the same goes, *mutatis mutandis*, for DIS.)

3.4 Can I do better than simply contending that CON is the 'obvious, and natural, fix'? Clearly, it would be better if I can. Here is one possible bolstering of CON: CON is true because belief in a conjunction *just is* belief in the conjuncts, and so knowledge of a conjunction *just is* knowledge of the conjuncts. Therefore, whatever account is plausible for knowledge of 'atomic' propositions, we can use that account to give an account of conjunctive propositions. Since a Sensitivity account is plausible for 'atomics', CON should be endorsed.

However, even assuming, *pro tem*, its validity, pretty quickly, two problems arise with the soundness of any such line of argument — a line of argument reliant, in its opening premise, on the following biconditional:

BEL CON*: S believes a conjunctive proposition, p iff S believes each of p's conjuncts.

First, and more sketchily, it might be objected that belief in a conjunction somehow involves (in addition to believing its conjuncts) the concept of CONJUNCTION, whereas belief in the conjuncts does not. Second, and less sketchily, 'lottery' issues become salient. Take some $p_1, ..., p_n$, where one's rational credence for each p_i is very very high and the p_is are independent. If we make n large enough, the conjunction can have a very low probability — presumably one incompatible with belief.

These two objections share the goal of breaking down BEL CON* in the right-left direction. That is, each is designed to falsify the thesis that belief in each conjunct is sufficient for belief in the conjunction in question. Insofar as they work — and I think they do — they belie any efforts to bolster CON by reliance on BEL CON*.

However, even prior to consideration of these objections, one might well have had instinctive doubts about a proposal seeking to bolster CON — a principle only stating *necessary* conditions on knowing a conjunction — by so ambitiously trying to reach the interim conclusion that knowledge of a conjunction *just is* knowledge of the conjuncts (cf. n. 24 *infra*). Indeed, one might wonder whether one needs an interim conclusion as strong as this to provide *some* bolstering of CON. Thus, one might — new proposal — less ambitiously seek to bolster CON by exploring weakening BEL CON* so as to be read in just the left-right direction:

BEL CON: S believes a conjunctive proposition, p only if S believes each of p's conjuncts.

I don't seek here to conclusively defend BEL CON (other than to note it is not counterexampled by the above objections to BEL CON*). It has some initial plausibility, however. Insofar as it is true, it could offer some extra support for CON beyond a bare appeal to its intuitiveness as a fix. Appeal could be made, that is, to BEL CON — a *grounding* principle concerning belief.

What, though, *can* be validly inferred from BEL CON? Specifically, can one infer that S knows a conjunctive proposition, p only if S *knows* each of p's conjuncts? It would seem not. (Likewise, even though I initially granted the validity of the original, more ambitious, proposal, I do not think one can infer that knowledge of a conjunction *just is* knowledge of the conjuncts, from the proposition that belief in a conjunction *just is* belief in the conjuncts.) All that can be validly inferred from BEL CON would appear to be that S knows a conjunctive proposition, p only if S *believes* each of p's conjuncts. (Likewise, all that can be validly inferred from BEL CON* would appear to be the immediately foregoing conditional *and* S knows each of p's conjuncts only if S *believes* the conjunctive proposition, p.) Thus, this new, less ambitious, proposal, with BEL CON as a first premise, does not promise to vindicate CON in the dramatic manner promised by the original, more ambitious, proposal.

Now, all of the foregoing is, concededly, fairly inchoate. Nonetheless, it seems we *can* conclude the following: insofar as BEL CON (and, indeed, BEL CON*) offers *some* (additional) reason to accept CON (beyond a bare appeal to its intuitiveness as a fix), further exploration of it, its truth, what it *supports*, and what can be validly inferred therefrom, by the Sensitivity theorist will be worthwhile (cf. Williamson 2000: 283).

4. Rejecting Equivalence

4.1 Recall Equivalence:

> *Equivalence.* If you know *a priori* that p and q are equivalent and you know p, then you are in a position to know q.

As I've just argued, CON is an independently motivated modification of Sensitivity. But if Sensitivity is modified with CON, we can see why Equivalence fails for Nozick. When you know a priori that p and q are equivalent and you know p, *and where q is a conjunctive proposition the second conjunct of which you do not believe Sensitively (on the basis of your evidence for p)*, then you are *not (confining yourself to your evidence for p)* in a position to know q.[16]

---

16 Of course, this response assumes that there can be distinct *a priori* equivalent propositions. Moreover, CON requires, *pace* Lewis and Stalnaker, that propositions are more finely individuated than necessary equivalence. Rejection of the Lewis-Stalnaker picture is independently motivated by consideration of necessary truths, such as those of mathematics and *a posteriori* symmetric supervenience. The non-identification of *a priori* equivalent propositions is also motivated by consideration of mathematical truths and cases of the contingent *a priori*. In any case, what

Moreover, supplementing Sensitivity with CON enables Nozick to maintain the attractive Distribution, since one can know a conjunction only if one Sensitively believes each conjunct. Nozick can thus accept Distribution but deny knowledge of (12) (since one doesn't Sensitively believe its second conjunct) which blocks the route to knowledge of (11).

4.2 Therefore, returning to Hawthorne's 'Equivalence and Distribution' pro-closure argument, the step from (9) to (12) is no longer legitimated. You can know (presumably on the basis of an experience as of a zebra): (9) that is a zebra. However, with Equivalence falsified, it doesn't follow that you can know: (12) that is a zebra and that is not a cleverly disguised mule. On the basis of your experience as of a zebra you won't believe the second conjunct of (12) Sensitively. With the route to (12) blocked there is now no route to Hawthorne's conclusion that you can know — *pace* Nozick — that is not a cleverly disguised mule.

With CON, we can follow Nozick in relinquishing SPC, not by relinquishing Distribution, but instead by relinquishing Equivalence, which fails when CON is added, as an alternative necessary condition, to a Sensitivity account as it needs to be. Given that this failure of Equivalence is independently motivated, the costs of denying SPC by rejecting Equivalence aren't as high as Hawthorne suggests (more on this later, in 5.1).[17]

Hawthorne's discussion brings out is that this fine-grained individuation is a commitment of those who wish to accept that we can know (9) without knowing (12).

17 The failure of Equivalence will be a general phenomenon; that is, it will occur outside the limited circumstance detailed in 4.1, if my Sensitivity account is adopted. More on this later (see 4.7–4.8 *infra*). For now, consider the following case (similar to Kripke's 'red barn' variation on the 'fake barns' case): suppose a red ball is before one, and if it failed to be red it would appear blue. One thus believes that is a red ball Sensitively. Suppose, though, that if the ball failed to be coloured it would appear grey (rather than colourless). One thus fails to believe that it is a coloured ball Sensitively. One thus knows *a priori* that, that the ball is red, and that the ball is red and coloured, are equivalent, and one knows that the ball is red. However,, by CON, one fails to (be in a position to) know that the ball is red and coloured: one fails to believe the second conjunct of the conjunction Sensitively. Note, however, that, independently of CON, one fails to know that the ball is coloured. That one fails to know the *conjunction* that the ball is red and coloured, then, is not obviously an *extra* cost of my Sensitivity account.

4.3 Next, note Hawthorne has a second, 'Equivalence and Addition', pro-closure argument (2004: 39–41) resting on Equivalence and a second principle:

> *Addition Closure* (AC). Necessarily, if S knows p and competently deduces (p or q) from p, thereby coming to believe (p or q), while retaining knowledge of p throughout, then S knows (p or q).

[...] Nozick grant[s] that I know:

> (6) I have a hand.

With AC I can then deduce:

> (7) Either I have a hand or I am not a brain in a vat.

This is *a priori* equivalent to:

> (8) It is not the case that: I lack hands and am a brain in a vat.

So from (6), by applications of AC and Equivalence, we can come to know (8). But according to Nozick we cannot know that we're not handless brains in vats.

4.4 As with Distribution and Equivalence, note that AC is also a form of SPC, claiming that knowledge is closed under disjunction introduction — a form of competent deduction. Given that Nozick rejects SPC it would be no *major* surprise if he were also to reject AC. However, as with Distribution, AC is extremely compelling. As Nozick (1981: 230, 692, n. 64) admits, rejection of AC "surely carries [things] too far. [...] Surely our knowledge that p does not stand in such splendid isolation from knowledge of other things so closely connected to p".[18] It would be a cost to Nozick if he were forced to reject it.

As it stands, however, Nozick does reject AC, since we can believe p Sensitively and yet fail to believe (p v q) Sensitively. For example, let p be (6) and let (p v q) be (7). Although, if I had no hands, I wouldn't believe

---

18 Dretske (1970: 1009) accepts that if one knows p one knows (p v q) — a principle which entails AC. Williamson (2000: 283), however, notes that knowing a proposition entails grasping that proposition, and grasping a complex proposition involves grasping its components. So given that knowing p is not sufficient for grasping q, Dretske's claim is subject to counterexample. AC, however, is not subject to such worries.

I had hands, it's not the case that if I were a handless BIV, I wouldn't believe I had hands or wasn't a BIV. Rather, if I lacked hands and were a BIV I would, *ex hypothesi*, believe I had hands and wasn't a BIV. Put differently: I know, hence Sensitively believe, that I have hands. Now suppose that I deduce and come to believe that either I have hands or I am not a BIV. If that disjunction were false — i.e., if I had no hands and was a BIV — I would still believe that it was true. The disjunctive belief is therefore not Sensitive; so Nozick rejects AC.

4.5 However, my introduction of CON to account for Sensitivity with respect to conjunctions makes salient, and suggests an answer to, the question: What is the appropriate account of Sensitivity for disjunctive propositions? We might think that, if Sensitivity with respect to a conjunction requires that we Sensitively believe each conjunct, then Sensitivity with respect to a disjunction requires only that we Sensitively believe some disjunct. We'd then need to add the following further modification to Sensitivity:

> DIS*: If p is a disjunctive proposition, S knows p only if S believes one of p's disjuncts Sensitively.

DIS* allows Nozick to say that a subject can know Hawthorne's disjunctions (e.g. (7)) and to endorse AC, just as CON allows Nozick to endorse Distribution.

4.6 DIS*, however, is not plausible in general. We can know a disjunction without knowing or believing either disjunct. For example, we can narrow down the epistemic possibilities: we can know that Danny is in the kitchen or he's in the lounge by knowing Danny isn't in the bedroom. Similarly, suppose one knows a city is in France; one can then know that city is in either the north of France or the south of France. DIS*, then, is too strong.

What these cases show is that we can come to know a disjunction without knowing either disjunct. But when we infer a disjunction from one of its disjuncts, we know a disjunction *in virtue* of knowing one of its disjuncts. In such a case, our evidence for the disjunction is our evidence for the disjunct from which it's inferred. So, in this event, in order to know the disjunction we need only believe the disjunct from which it's inferred Sensitively rather than the disjunction itself. This suggests:

DIS: If S infers $(p \lor q)$ from p, S knows $(p \lor q)$ on that basis only if S believes p Sensitively.

With DIS, Nozick can endorse AC. That is, we are countenancing a version of the principle Sensitivity that imposes a less demanding necessary condition on a disjunctive proposition when it is inferred from one of its disjuncts (see 3.3 *supra* for how to apply DIS). This will guarantee that modified Sensitivity does not present any obstacle to closure of knowledge under AC. Of course, this does not yet suffice to avoid Hawthorne's argument. Indeed, the validity of AC is a premise of Hawthorne's argument. However, as we saw above, Nozick should reject Equivalence; and he should reject the instance of Equivalence in this case too. Although Sensitivity can be met with respect to (7) (i.e. (H v ~BIV)), since one can Sensitively believe (6) (i.e. H), it's not the case that Sensitivity can be met with respect to (8) (i.e. ~(~H & BIV)) even though this is equivalent to (7). The reason for this is just as it is in Nozick's original rejection of SPC: one can know that one has hands via one's senses or via one's senses and deduction, but one cannot, in any such manner, know that one isn't a handless BIV.[19]

So by accepting DIS and endorsing AC, Nozick can once again reject Equivalence in a motivated way. The facts that lead to Nozick's original rejection of SPC are exactly the facts that should lead to his rejection of the transition from (7) to (8). Therefore Hawthorne's second

---

19 Although (7) and (8) are *a priori* equivalent, the Sensitivity condition does not apply to them equivalently. Because (7) has the logical form of a disjunction, and is inferred from its first disjunct, all that is required is that its first disjunct be believed Sensitively. Similarly, one can know: that is a zebra or it is not a cleverly disguised mule, without knowing that it is not a cleverly disguised mule, even though the latter is equivalent to the former. One can Sensitively believe the first disjunct of this disjunction but one cannot Sensitively believe the second disjunct. However, on my revised version of Sensitivity, such a state of affairs is sufficient for the Sensitivity condition to be met with respect to this disjunction. Finally, note that Roush (2010), who employs a Sensitivity condition, and who uses probability rather than counterfactuals, contends that, if one knows H, one knows ~(~H & BIV) (and, more generally, ~(~H & Whatever)). Crucially, this is because, for Roush (2005, 2010, 2012), Sensitivity does not operate as a necessary (or, indeed, a sufficient) condition on knowledge (and thus Roush does not need to forsake SPC; indeed she endorses it).

pro-closure argument does nothing to increase the costs that Nozick must face — once, that is, he accepts DIS.[20]

4.7 Let me close by noting two (additional) costs of my proposal. Cost 1: What's the appropriate account of Sensitivity for negations of propositions? Negations of atomic propositions are to be treated just like the propositions they negate. That is, Nozick's unmodified Sensitivity condition suffices as a necessary condition for knowledge of the negation of an atomic proposition. But what about the negations of molecular propositions? In particular, what about the De Morgan equivalents of conjunctions and disjunctions? As we've just seen, on my proposed modification of Sensitivity, one can know (7) but not (8) — a negated conjunction. As a result, we cannot treat disjunctions and their De Morgan equivalents alike. However, unmodified Sensitivity explains our failure to know (8), since if I lacked hands and were a BIV, I would still believe that it is not the case that I lack hands and am a BIV.

This might suggest that negations are subject to unmodified Sensitivity. But the *reductio* of Nozick's account of knowledge, which motivated CON, shows that we cannot apply unmodified Sensitivity to negations of disjunctions. If someone believes:

(P) I have a headache and I have all my limbs,

solely on the basis of their headache, we concluded that they wouldn't know *(P)* despite satisfying unmodified Sensitivity. Similarly, the same considerations show that we do not know the De Morgan equivalent of *(P)* — *viz.* It's not the case that I neither have a headache nor all my limbs — even though we satisfy unmodified Sensitivity.

This all suggests the following, then. First, we should treat negations of disjunctions as conjunctions: one can know them only if one believes the negation of each disjunct Sensitively. Second, we should treat negations of conjunctions as subject to unmodified Sensitivity. Finally, note there will be no problematic interactions between CON and DIS, as we can never move directly from a disjunction to a conjunction or vice

---

20 As with CON (3.5 *supra*), one might explore bolstering a defense of DIS by appeal to a *grounding* principle concerning belief. This time, however, the relevant biconditional seems plausible:

BEL DIS: If S infers $(p \vee q)$ from p, S believes $(p \vee q)$ on that basis iff S believes p.

versa. Overall, however, it must be conceded that these manoeuvres may appear somewhat *ad hoc*.

4.8 Cost 2: Consider the following case which brings out an upshot of my proposal. Jones gets to know Peter, a paediatrician, by observing him medically treating children, and forms the Sensitive belief that Peter is a paediatrician on the basis of such observation. Nevertheless, Jones, who is in other relevant respects normal, holds the strange misconception that everyone is some kind of physician. Jones therefore believes the following conjunction: Peter is a paediatrician and Peter is a physician. By CON Jones does not know this conjunction, since his belief in the second conjunct is not Sensitive. But what about if Jones holds a belief concerning Peter involving, not a conjunction, but a complex (conjunctive) predicate? Specifically, what about if Jones believes: $\lambda x[x$ is a paediatrician and x is a physician](Peter)? Jones believes this proposition Sensitively since if Peter did not satisfy the predicate: $\lambda x[x$ is a paediatrician and x is a physician], Jones would not believe that he did.

In sum, we here have a case where Jones *does not* know:

(A) Peter is a paediatrician and Peter is a physician.

But Jones *does* know:

(B) $\lambda x[x$ is a paediatrician and x is a physician](Peter).

Now it is clear that on some fine-grained and plausible way of individuating propositions (A) and (B) express distinct propositions, but how plausible is it to say Peter knows (B) but not (A)? Of course, the approach I have explored denies the general validity of Equivalence, but the link between (A) and (B) is, concededly, tight. Indeed, we usually do not distinguish between the two propositions.

(Perhaps, though, the cost of this case is not so bad. I have already allowed that Equivalence is not generally valid. I have also allowed that the very same proposition (a disjunction) needs to meet only a weaker Sensitivity condition, rather than the standard Sensitivity condition for knowledge, depending on whether the disjunction was arrived at by inference from one of its disjuncts. The relevant point here is that (B) is not in the form that allows *immediate* inference to 'Peter is a physician'. It is only when there is an inference from (p & q) to q, for a proposition that is not believed Sensitively and so not known, that it is important that CON should be applied to give the result that the conjunction (p & q) is not known either.)

Relatedly, consider the following case. Suppose that we have three birds: a male blackbird, a female bird that looks like a female blackbird but is of a different species, and a female sparrow. (Male blackbirds are black and easily recognizable, but females are brown and superficially similar to birds of other species.) Suppose S never makes mistakes identifying male blackbirds; but S would mistake the bird that looks like a female blackbird for a female blackbird; and S always mistakes female sparrows for male sparrows. Suppose that we pick a bird at random and show it to S; suppose we pick the male blackbird. And suppose, to simplify, that the picked-the-female-blackbird-lookalike world and the picked-the-female-sparrow world are equally close to the actual picked-the-male-blackbird world.

It seems that S knows, and Sensitively believes, that the bird is a male blackbird. If the bird had not been a male blackbird then it might have been the female blackbird lookalike or it might have been the female sparrow. So S might have believed that the bird is a female blackbird and might have believed that the bird is a male sparrow but, either way, S would not have believed that the bird is a male blackbird. However, it seems that S does not Sensitively believe that the bird is male. If the bird had not been male, it might have been the female sparrow, and so S might still have believed that the bird is male. Equally, it seems that S does not Sensitively believe that the bird is a blackbird. If the bird had not been a blackbird, it might have been the female blackbird lookalike, and so S might still have believed that the bird is a blackbird.

Nonetheless, as noted, when S sees a male blackbird, it seems that S comes to know, and Sensitively believe, that the bird is a male blackbird. Here is a preliminary way of summarising the point of the case: if the subject were to infer, from the seemingly known premise 'That is a male blackbird' either 'That is a male bird' or 'That is a blackbird', then the inferred conclusion(s) would not be known.[21] What do I say

---

21 This case bears obvious similarities to Kripke's 'red barn' case (cf. nn. 10 and 17 *supra*). Note that Adams and Clarke (2005: 214–16) attempt to rescue Nozick from Kripke's case by appeal to methods: the subject in Kripke's case, for Adams

about this case? The proposition believed by S — that the bird is a male blackbird — could involve a conjunction:

(A*) The bird is male and the bird is a blackbird,

which, by CON, S *does not* know. Or it could instead (more naturally) involve a complex predicate:

(B*) λx[x is male and x is a blackbird](the bird),

which S *knows*. In sum, the paediatrician/physician case told us that Equivalence is to be given up in these cases where we have alternative, though closely related, parsings of a single sentence;[22] and now the male blackbird case tells us, moreover, that we can know a proposition involving a (complex) conjunctive predicate without knowing *any* of the corresponding propositions involving the simple predicates — and without knowing the equivalent conjunctive proposition. Overall,

---

and Clarke, comes to know that a red barn is before her by the 'red barn (look) method' — a method the subject also employs, for Adams and Clarke, to come to know that a barn is before her. A similar *thin slicing of methods* approach could be used, *mutatis mutandis*, to dissolve the force of the male blackbird case against Nozick (cf. Becker 2012: 94). Adams and Clarke are aware of the objection that they have "slic[ed] methods too thinly or without principle merely to rescue Nozick", and make a somewhat terse effort to address this objection. Myself, I am sympathetic to this objection (hence my presentation of the male blackbird case in the main text), though I do not presently have an argument defending my sympathies (cf. Goldman's (1983: 84) 'Dack the dachshund' case). (While Nozick's (1981: 179) treatment of his 'grandmother' case would suggest visual perception being the operative, and intuitive, method in cases such as these, it would be mistaken to take this to be Nozick's final, considered view. Nozick (1981: 179–85, 188–96) goes on to consider, with some sympathy, (much) more narrow individuations of methods.) For present purposes, I do not need to commit on this debate. All I need to commit on is the following. Either (1) Adams and Clarke's (and others') thin slicing of methods is apposite, and consequently the cost of Cost 2 for my proposal is diminished (though not eliminated). Or (2) It is not apposite, and the cost of Cost 2 remains undiminished. As my project is not to provide a bullet-proof defense of Sensitivity, I can remain neutral between (1) and (2). (Nozick (193), meanwhile, explicitly states that "[s]ince [he has] not [...] specified precisely how to identify a method and tell when it is held fixed, there is some leeway in [his] account", and does not take this to be problematic "provided [...] discussion of [problem] cases [does] not exploit the leeway [...] inconsistently.")

22 The sentence, in that case, could either be 'Peter is a paediatrician and Peter is a physician' (with the conjunction parsing being more natural), or 'Peter is a paediatrician and a physician' (with the complex predicate parsing being more natural).

however, it must (again) be conceded that these upshots are a cost of my proposal.²³

5. Conclusion

5.1   Where, then, does this leave us? Let me summarise the dialectic thus: (1) Hawthorne raises an objection to Sensitivity, namely that it cannot satisfy Equivalence and Distribution or Equivalence and AC. (2) Nozick explicitly rejects both Distribution and AC; and that's a cost of his account. (3) Hawthorne's argument shows that a Sensitivity account which respects Distribution and AC cannot respect Equivalence. So a dilemma arises: either reject both Distribution and AC or reject Equivalence. (4) I note that a Sensitivity account ought to reject Equivalence in any case (the *reductio* of section 3), and so Nozick picked the wrong horn of the dilemma: Sensitivity is free to respect Distribution and AC. Of course, rejecting Equivalence is itself a cost. (5) However, the best way for the Sensitivity theorist to go is problematic. As well as giving up on Equivalence, Sensitivity has to engage in manoeuvring which might appear *ad hoc* in the special cases of De Morgan's equivalents, and also has to give up on providing similar treatments of different parsings of 'conjunctive claims' (but cf. n. 23 *supra*).

No grand conclusion is warranted, to the effect that, once the Sensitivity theorist picks the right horn of Hawthorne's dilemma, there are no associated costs. We can, though, conclude that the costs to the Sensitivity theorist are somewhat more bearable once it is recognised that those costs are being incurred for principled reasons (the *reductio*

---

23   Here is an approach which promises to avoid cost 2 by effectively giving the same treatment for conjunctive propositions and propositions involving conjunctive predicates. Supplement CON with:

CON*: If p is a proposition of the form $\lambda x[Fx \text{ and } Gx](a)$, S knows p only if S believes the proposition $\lambda x[Fx](a)$ Sensitively and S believes the proposition $\lambda x[Gx](a)$ Sensitively.

Beyond the obvious cost of further complicating one's account of knowledge (by further modifying Sensitivity), I do not at present know if there are further (perhaps severe) costs of endorsing CON*. (Insofar as CON requires bolstering beyond an appeal to its intuitiveness as a fix (cf. 3.4 *supra*), so too does CON*.) Finally, note that Becker's (2012: 95, n. 13) 'large shrimp' case is relevantly similar to the cases I discuss here in 4.8.

of section 3). To that extent, then, we can conclude that Hawthorne's pro-closure arguments are not knock-down.[24]

---

24 Note in closing that Nozick (1981: 227–28, 230) also rejects the plausible claim that knowledge is closed under universal instantiation and existential generalization. What I say about conjunctions and disjunctions may apply, *mutatis mutandis*, to quantified statements too. If we take universal statements to be conjunctions and existential statements to be disjunctions, the natural application is that to know the universal statement 'for all x, F(x)' one must believe all its instances Sensitively, and to know the existential statement 'for some x, F(x)' one must believe (at least) one of its instances Sensitively (subject to DIS's proviso). The application to universal statements threatens to be the more problematic application. (Though note one pseudo-problem: as we are only here considering necessary conditions for knowledge, it is no problem that knowing universal statements requires more than believing all its instances Sensitively. In particular, it is no problem that it also requires a *that's all* belief to be held Sensitively.) Consider: the subject might not be able to express all the instances. Indeed, it might be that no natural language has names for all the objects quantified over (e.g. if the domain is very large). This worry can be defused by keeping clear that belief is a dispositional mental state, not an action. Therefore, actual limitations on the part of the subject or natural language need not preclude Sensitive belief provided the subject has an appropriate set of dispositions.

8. Safety

Beginning from Sosa's (1999) safety condition on knowledge, I engage with Comesaña's (2005) example of unsafe knowledge. I propose a modified safety condition, test it against examples, and respond to a series of objections. I argue that, while further modifications may be required, it is plausible that (some version of) safety is a necessary condition on knowledge.

0.1   My purpose in this chapter is to (begin to) defend *safety* as a necessary condition on knowledge. First, I introduce Ernest Sosa's (1999) safety condition.[1] Second, I set up and grapple with Juan Comesaña's (2005) putative counterexample to safety as a necessary condition on knowledge; Comesaña's case forces us to consider Sosa's updated (2002) safety condition. From such grappling a principled modification to Sosa's (2002) safety condition emerges. Safety is safe from this, and like, attacks.

1. Safety Introduced

1.1   Sosa (1999: 378) offered the following first pass at a safety condition on knowledge (time designations are suppressed throughout):

---

[1]   Timothy Williamson (2000: ch.5) also operates with a (distinct) safety condition on knowledge.

> Call a belief by S that p "safe" iff: S would not believe that p without it being so that p. (Alternatively a belief by S that p is safe iff: as a matter of fact, though perhaps not as a matter of strict necessity, S would not believe that p without it being so that p.)[2]

By such a condition's lights, on its supporters' views, we're not prevented from having quotidian knowledge, and nor are we prevented from having knowledge of the falsity of an array of sceptical hypotheses. So far, so good, one might think, for safety.

1.2 Note that safety — a reliability notion — is a squarely *externalist* condition on knowledge. It does not inquire one jot, for example, into a putative knower's recognition of certain epistemically salient facts about the basis, or bases, on which he adopts a particular belief. Rather, for a belief to be safe is simply for a particular modal relation to hold between a subject's belief that p and the fact that p.

1.3 Before coming to Comesaña's putative counterexample to safety, note one (familiar) modification to safety:

> A belief that p by S is safe iff S would not believe that p *on the same basis* without it being so that p. (Comesaña 2005: 397 (My emphasis))

(Or: S B(p) on basis e → p.)

This modification — as Comesaña points out (2005: 403, n. 4) — is incorporated by Sosa's (2002) updated condition on knowledge, a condition which we'll be focusing on, and modifying, in the remainder of this chapter.[3]

---

2   Or: S B(p) → p (and not the stronger: □ [S B(p) → p]). Read 'S B(p)' as: 'A subject, S, believes that p'. Following Sosa, we can read '→' as "*subjunctively implies*": if p → q, "its being so that p offers some guarantee, even if not an absolute guarantee, that it is also the case that q" (Sosa 2002: 284, n. 4). If one formulates safety in terms of a subjunctive conditional one will operate with an account of the semantics of subjunctive conditionals not rendering true-true subjunctives trivially true — cf. Nozick (1981: 680–81, n. 8). Assuming the truth of the relevant subjunctive conditional, any plausible semantics therefor will have the relevant material conditional not coming out false at the actual world.

3   I assume that all cases considered herein involve beliefs formed on the same basis in the actual and relevant counterfactual circumstances (cf. Williamson 2009: 307).

2. Comesaña's Putative Counterexample: HALLOWEEN PARTY

2.1 Comesaña (2005: 397) asks us to consider the following case:

> There is a Halloween party at Andy's house, and I am invited. Andy's house is very difficult to find, so he hires Judy to stand at a crossroads and direct people towards the house (Judy's job is to tell people that the party is at the house down the left road). Unbeknownst to me Andy doesn't want Michael to go to the party, so he also tells Judy that if she sees Michael she should tell him the same thing she tells everybody else (that the party is at the house down the left road), but she should immediately phone Andy so that the party can be moved to Adam's house, which is down the right road. I seriously consider disguising myself as Michael, but at the last moment I don't. When I get to the crossroads, I ask Judy where the party is, and she tells me that it is down the left road.

And Comesaña's gloss thereon:

> In this case, after I talk to Judy I know that the party is at the house down the left road, and yet it could very easily have happened that I had the same belief on the same basis (Judy's testimony) without it being so that the belief is true. That is, in this case I know that p but my belief that p is not safe — I have unsafe knowledge.

2.2 Ahead of grappling with HALLOWEEN PARTY let's note Sosa's updated (2002: 275–76) safety(-related)[4] principle — a principle motivated in response to cases demonstrating that *outright tracking*[5] isn't necessary for knowledge. Let's introduce it first — laden with heretofore unexplained Sosa-terminology — and explain the terminology by way

---

4   I say 'safety(-*related*)' as it does not, unlike the first pass set out at 1.1 *supra*, take the explicit form of a *definition* of safety. It rather takes the explicit form of a (disjunctive) necessary condition on knowledge, though it *should also* be taken as stating a (disjunctive) necessary and sufficient condition for *safe acceptance* — cf. n. 13 *infra*. (The same goes, *mutatis mutandis*, for my modification of this principle to come.) Note, moreover, that it employs the more general notion of acceptance rather than belief. (This will not matter, however, for present purposes, as throughout we assume the form of acceptance in question is belief.)
5   "One tracks the truth, outright, in believing that p IFF one would believe that p iff it were so that p: i.e., would believe that p if it were so that p, and only if it were so" (Sosa 2002: 267). Thus outright tracking combines a safety requirement and an *adherence* requirement.

of applying it to HALLOWEEN PARTY, the case in hand. Here's the updated principle:

> S knows that p on the basis of an indication I(p) only if either (a) I(p) indicates the truth outright and S accepts that indication as such outright, or (b) for some condition C, I(p) indicates the truth dependently on C, and S accepts that indication as such not outright but *guided* by C (so that S accepts the indication as such *on the basis* of C).[6]

The *indication*, I(p), in HALLOWEEN PARTY, is Judy's testimony to me that the party is down the left road.[7] Disjunct (a) doesn't hold: Judy's testimony doesn't indicate the truth outright as Judy's testimony indicates the truth dependently on the fact *that-I-do-not-appear-to-Judy-Michael'ly* (C).[8] What is it for an indication to "[indicate] the truth outright"? This happens iff I(p) → p. That leads us to disjunct (b). The first conjunct of the conjunctive condition contained in disjunct (b) is true. What is it for an indication to "[indicate] the truth dependently on C"? This happens iff C obtains and [C&I(p)] → p, but ~[I(p) → p]. The second conjunct of the conjunctive condition contained in disjunct (b), however, is false: *ex hypothesi* I don't accept Judy's testimony as true, conditional on the fact that-I-do-not-appear-to-Judy-Michael'ly. As the case is set up, I'll believe Judy's testimony whether or not I appear to her Michael'ly. I therefore don't accept the indication "*guided* by", or "*on the basis* of", C. (If I *do* accept Judy's testimony as true conditional on the

---

6   Sosa (2007: 105) adds the following disjunct to (b) in his most recent condition on (animal) knowledge based on an indication: "[...] *or else* [...] *C is constitutive of the appropriate normalcy of the conditions for the competence exercised by S in accepting I(p)*" (footnote omitted). The candidate C in HALLOWEEN PARTY (to come) does not satisfy this disjunct. Sosa defends this (2007) condition on (animal) knowledge yet now disavows (2007: 92–93) that safety is a necessary condition on (animal) knowledge: the addition of this disjunct must disqualify the principle in question from counting as a *safety* principle. Finally, for more on the basing relation – which features in both the antecedent and consequent of Sosa's (2002) principle – see Korcz (2006).

7   Sosa (2002) wavers on this. Transposing things to HALLOWEEN PARTY: at times Sosa takes the indication (or: safe *deliverance*) to be what Judy's testimony *causes* in me, but at other times he takes it to be *Judy's testimony to me itself*. Comesaña – and I will follow suit – goes with the latter interpretation (though I do not think this is crucial). Also, note it is, crucially, 'Judy's testimony *to me*'. For ease of prose I omit the 'to me' hereinafter, but please read it in.

8   Because we are interested in Judy's testimony *to a particular subject*, and that subject is me, the C on which I focus is as stated, and not the more general: that-Judy-is-not-appeared-to-Michael'ly.

fact that-I-do-not-appear-to-Judy-Michael'ly, HALLOWEEN PARTY becomes a straightforward case of safe knowledge.)

Therefore Sosa's updated (2002) safety principle — as Comesaña notes (2005: 399) — cuts no ice against HALLOWEEN PARTY. By its lights we still have unsafe knowledge.

2.3 Let's now grapple with HALLOWEEN PARTY. We need to modify Sosa's (2002) safety principle.[9] My modified principle aims to capture a pre-theoretic notion of beliefs which are safe from the danger of being false, just as other objects can be safe from myriad dangers. Moreover, the modification is motivated by scrupulous attention to the externalism which underpinned safety's first formulation. Earlier, we noted the squarely externalist nature of safety's initial formulation: it's merely the positing of a modal relation between a subject's belief and a fact. So we might be suspicious of the internalist flavour to 2.2's updated safety principle: 2.2's principle requires — *modulo* no outright indication of truth — that the putative knower accept the indication in question "*guided* by" and "*on the basis* of C". I take it that, in order to do this, the putative knower *in HALLOWEEN PARTY* (*viz*. me) must, at the very least, *recognise* (or: *be aware of*) the condition under which the indication in question indicates the truth (Sosa 2002: 271). (As a result the internalism in question here is *access internalism about grounds* (Pryor 2001: 106–08): one must have access to the conditions for a ground (or indication) counting as justified (or safe).) Otherwise there is no principled reason for the putative knower in HALLOWEEN PARTY (*viz*. me) to accept Judy's testimony guided by, or on the basis of, the fact that-I-do-not-appear-to-Judy-Michael'ly.[10]

---

9   As a closely related alternative to my proposal (to come) one might develop an explicitly time-sensitive notion of safety (cf. Sainsbury (1997: 907–19), Peacocke (1999: 310–28), and Williamson (2000: 124)). Relatedly, Bogardus (2014) thinks HALLOWEEN PARTY (and like cases) err as counterexamples by positing *epistemic risk* prior to the formation of the belief in question (cf. n. 27 *infra*).

10 I restrict my claim here *to HALLOWEEN PARTY* (and like cases). (Compare: if disjunct (a) *were* to hold, even though S *would* know p *on the basis* of an indication I(p), I would not take any internalism to be implicated thereby. This is because I take there to be a fundamental difference (in this regard) between accepting an indication outright (disjunct (a)) and not outright (disjunct (b)) — cf. disjunct (b)(ii) to come.) The form of acceptance required by 2.2's safety principle — *modulo* no outright indication of truth — could, in some cases, be cashed out simply in terms

But why — *modulo* no outright indication of truth — require this for knowledge? It seems that this further requirement, as to the putative knower's recognition-based acceptance in HALLOWEEN PARTY, is more aptly viewed as a requirement — *modulo* no outright indication of truth — not on knowledge *simpliciter*, but on knowing that one knows.

2.4 So the challenge is to set out a modified — more externalist — version of Sosa's updated (2002) safety principle. We need two novel pieces of terminology. First, a schema introducing the notion of a *safe condition*:

(C_{SAFE}) A condition, C, is safe iff C obtains,[11] and if C were the case in the way described in the thought experiment under consideration, then C would hold in all[12] close possible worlds.

We'll refer to a safe condition as (a) C_{SAFE}. Just as we can talk of the safety of a subject's belief that p — where that is cashed out as a modal relation between a subject's belief that p and the fact that p — so we can talk of the safety of a condition, C — where that is cashed out in terms of how far into modal space C holds, conditional on C being the case in the way described in the thought experiment under consideration. That is, in the thought experiments to come, we suppose the candidate C is the case

---

of a modal relation between a subject's acceptance that p and the fact that p (Sosa 2002: 272). But, insofar as my restricted claim is right, we've departed from a purely externalist safety condition. Cf. Sosa's later comments on 'guidance' (2002: 282).

11 This functions, in part, to prevent necessarily false conditions from being trivially safe conditions. According to standard semantics for subjunctive conditionals, necessarily false antecedents make (vacuously) true subjunctive conditionals. Sosa's account of dependent indication (see 2.2 *infra*) itself requires that C obtains, but I prefer an independent obtention requirement on C_{SAFE}s themselves. Finally, by 'obtain' I take it that Sosa means 'obtain *in the actual world*'. That is, in engaging with these thought experiments (which may, though need not of course, be actual cases), we *suppose* C obtains *in the actual world*, and not in some (remote) possible world which may have *bizarre metaphysics*. This is one reason why the following, admittedly cleaner, safe condition schema will not do: A condition C is safe at a world w iff C holds in all close possible worlds to w.

12 One might explore alternative formulations, for example replacing 'all' with 'all or nearly all' — cf. Pritchard's (2005b) safety account. It has, though, been noted by Greco (2007) that Pritchard's account may have especial difficulties with the *lottery problem* (cf. n. 22 *infra*). It should be noted that Pritchard (2009) has since attempted to amend his account of safety in an effort to respond to Greco's (and others') objections. I don't attempt to adjudicate on this debate here. Finally, to be explicit, we are here measuring closeness to the world represented in the thought experiment.

in the way described in the thought experiment under consideration, and then, given an intuitive ordering of worlds, check whether that condition, C, holds in all close possible worlds. In what follows, I want to suggest that it's intuitive to add a disjunct to Sosa's safety principle (thereby weakening it) making reference to the safety of candidate *conditions*.

Now here's our modified safety principle:

S knows that p on the basis of an indication I(p) only if EITHER (a) I(p) indicates the truth outright and S accepts that indication as such outright, OR (b) either (i) for some condition C, I(p) indicates the truth dependently on C, and S accepts that indication as such not outright but *guided* by C (so that S accepts the indication as such *on the basis* of C),[13] or (ii) for some non-trivial condition C_{SAFE}, I(p) indicates the truth dependently on C_{SAFE}, and S accepts that indication not-as-such outright.[14]

Now our second piece of terminology. Call a C_{SAFE} meeting the requirements of disjunct (b)(ii) (*viz.* it is non-trivial and I(p) indicates the truth dependently on it) *relevantly-safe* — (a) $C_{R\text{-}SAFE}$.[15] And a condition is trivial iff it is, or entails, the putatively known proposition; non-trivial otherwise (cf. Comesaña 2005: 403, n. 7). In HALLOWEEN PARTY this non-triviality requirement thus rules out conditions such as: that-the-party-is-down-the-(bumpy)left-road. Note that the (putatively relevantly-safe) condition that-I-do-not-appear-to-Judy-Michael'ly *does*

---

13 What is now called 'disjunct (b)(i)' must be retained. Though — *modulo* no outright indication of truth — such 'guidance' is no longer *necessary* for *safety*, it is still (stand-alone) *sufficient* therefor (cf. n. 4 *supra*): if I *do* accept Judy's testimony as true guided by the condition that-I-do-not-appear-to-Judy-Michael'ly, HALLOWEEN PARTY, we've seen, becomes a straightforward case of safe knowledge (and, arguably, second-order knowledge), even if that *condition* does not, suppose, obtain safely.

14 That is, S *does* accept the indication *outright*, but *not-as-such* outright, as the indication in question, if disjunct (b)(ii) is to be satisfied, is *not*, *ex hypothesi*, an outright indication of truth. Finally, it is worth noting that disjunct (b)(i) *can* (though of course need not) be satisfied by a C_{SAFE}. Mutual exclusivity would still be maintained between (b)(i) and (b)(ii) due to the different forms of acceptance involved in satisfaction of the two disjuncts. (For the mutual exclusivity of disjuncts (a) and (b) ((b)(ii) in particular), see 2.5 *infra*.)

15 This second novel piece of terminology is necessary. For example, that-2+2=4 is, and that-my-washing-machine-is-functioning can be, a C_{SAFE}. Without more, these conditions aren't relevant to our inquiry. We need to isolate a proper subset of C_{SAFE}s — $C_{R\text{-}SAFE}$s — in which we're particularly interested.

not entail that Judy's testimony that the party is down the left road is true: Judy's testimony could still have been false for any number of reasons (albeit such reasons obtain, *ex hypothesi*, only in distant possible worlds).

However, consider the condition: [p v ~I(p)]. The disjunction as a whole neither is, nor entails, p; and I(p) indicates the truth dependently on the disjunction (by disjunctive syllogism). Objection:[16] to allow this as a $C_{R\text{-}SAFE}$ would be to trivialise the notion of $C_{R\text{-}SAFE}$s: *for any p* one could construct a $C_{R\text{-}SAFE}$ consisting of the disjunction of p and the negation of an indication that p. One should combat this by making it sufficient for triviality that a *disjunct* of the condition is, or entails, p. Reply: while this objection draws attention to an interesting class of condition, it ignores the fact that being C_{SAFE} is a prerequisite for being $C_{R\text{-}SAFE}$. However, it will follow that on any occasion in which [p v ~I(p)] *is* C_{SAFE} it will also be $C_{R\text{-}SAFE}$. To the extent that this is a problematic result — something on which I do not here commit — we will need to modify our definition of triviality in line with this objection.

2.5   This modified safety principle is a move towards the externalism which motivated Sosa's initial (1999) formulations of safety, and dispenses with the internalist flavour of Sosa's subsequent (2002) formulations. (Recall: 2.2's principle requires — *modulo* no outright indication of truth — that the putative knower accept the indication in question *"guided* by" and *"on the basis* of C". My modified safety principle rejects this requirement.) My claim here is only this: insofar as one is interested in defending safety as a necessary condition on knowledge, why not see how far one can get with a more externalist account thereof? After all, as noted, initial formulations of safety were (purely) externalist.

Does this modified safety principle, however, handle HALLOWEEN PARTY? Do we get the result that I gain knowledge of the whereabouts of the party from Judy's testimony — chiming with our intuitions — with the belief on which such knowledge is based rendered safe by dint of fulfilment of disjunct (b)(ii)? To answer these questions we first,

---

[16] I close the chapter, in 2.7–2.10 *infra*, with four numbered objections to my *fully interpreted* safety principle. This objection, as with the subsequent objection in 2.5, bears on the antecedent matter of *correctly interpreting* my safety principle.

obviously, assess this (more externalist) safety condition's success in handling HALLOWEEN PARTY. But our enquiry should not rest there. We'll then move on to consider its plausibility (in general) by considering some objections thereto.

And so to HALLOWEEN PARTY itself and the candidate condition that-I-do-not-appear-to-Judy-Michael'ly. It's plausible that if this C were the case in the way described in HALLOWEEN PARTY — at which point in time, *ex hypothesi*, crucially my *decision has been made* not to disguise myself as Michael — Judy won't be appeared-to-Micheal'ly by me in any close possible worlds. I take it we should read such a decision into HALLOWEEN PARTY; otherwise how do we explain my move from "seriously considering disguising myself as Michael" to — "at the last moment" — not doing so? (cf. Raz 1999: 65)[17] To be sure, there are remote worlds in which, even after the decision has been made not to disguise myself as Michael, I end up disguising myself as Michael.[18] However, provided we stick to the case as set up, these "disguising myself as Michael"-worlds will not be close enough to threaten the safety of my true belief that the party is down the left road.

It is the element of *prior decision* — reached, I take it, as a result of deliberation on the reasons for or against the action in question, with decisions themselves terminating that deliberation and being reasons[19] — which distinguishes HALLOWEEN PARTY from the ensuing cases we'll consider. At a more general level, a condition will be C_{SAFE} if[20] there is some (*non-luck-infected*)[21] factor — whether a mental act, as in HALLOWEEN PARTY, or not — which pre-dates the putatively

---

17 Comesaña (2005: 399) reads such a decision in. This suggests a candidate (complementary) $C_{R\text{-}SAFE}$: that-I-*decide*-not-to-appear-to-Judy-Michael'ly (see 2.9 *infra*).
18 There are also worlds — I take it they are remote, if it were the case that-I-do-not-appear-to-Judy-Michael'ly in the way described in HALLOWEEN PARTY — in which I *don't decide* not to dress as Michael. I am not, by diktat, holding *that decision* fixed *across all worlds*.
19 These remarks are taken from Raz (1978: 135, 1999: 65–72). For Raz (1999: 66), "a decision is always, for the agent, a reason for performing the act he has decided to perform and for disregarding further reasons and arguments. It is always both a first-order and an exclusionary reason". Consistently with this, "in most cases the refusal to reopen the case is not absolute". (67) Cf. also Raz (2002: ch.1).
20 I am not committed to the 'only if' claim.
21 I leave this notion intuitive, but for an extended analysis of epistemic luck, see Pritchard (2005). It is omitted in what follows, as only non-luck-infected factors can secure the holding of conditions in all close possible worlds.

safe condition, and serves to *secure* that condition's holding in all close possible worlds. This candidate condition is therefore C_{SAFE}. Moreover, we saw in 2.2 that Judy's testimony indicates the truth dependently on this (non-trivial) C_{SAFE}. It's therefore a relevantly-safe condition: it's $C_{R\text{-}SAFE}$. We thus have disjunct (b)(ii) of 2.4's modified safety principle being met. We, untroublingly, have safe knowledge in HALLOWEEN PARTY.

There is, however, a complication here relating to how an indication can indicate the truth dependently on a C_{SAFE}. Or, put differently: how a C_{SAFE} can be a $C_{R\text{-}SAFE}$. Objection: for Sosa, we've seen, an indication indicates the truth dependently on a condition iff C obtains and $[C\&I(p)] \rightarrow p$, but $\sim[I(p) \rightarrow p]$. However if C is a C_{SAFE}, (*a fortiori*) obtains, and $[C\&I(p)] \rightarrow p$, that seems to entail that: $[I(p) \rightarrow p]$. Reply: however this is not so. Though there is, at root, one question to be determined in HALLOWEEN PARTY — *viz*. do I possess knowledge? — two "contexts of thought or discussion" are "relevant" (Sosa 2002: 271) at different stages of enquiry into that question. At the first stage of enquiry — determining whether the condition in question is C_{SAFE} — schema (C_{SAFE}) *makes salient* the way in which the condition came about in the thought experiment under consideration. At the second stage of enquiry — determining whether the condition in question satisfies disjunct (b)(ii) — the foregoing feature of the condition is *not* rendered salient: Sosa's formulation of when an indication indicates the truth dependently on a condition, of course, makes no reference to C_{SAFE}s. It is only by recognising these two different contexts within a single project of enquiry that we can pay due deference to the initial intuitive pull towards thinking of HALLOWEEN PARTY as a case of unsafety — recognising, that is, that I *could very easily* (in some context of thought or discussion) have disguised myself as Michael. This will be a general feature of applying my safety principle.[22]

Thus, in HALLOWEEN PARTY we assess whether the condition that-I-do-not-appear-to-Judy-Michael'ly satisfies disjunct (b)(ii) *not* building in information about precisely how that condition came about in the thought experiment (i.e. via a prior decision). Given this, the foregoing entailment does not hold and, plausibly: $\sim[I(p) \rightarrow p]$. To fail to adopt this

---

22 To recognise the foregoing is not, I take it, to perforce become an *epistemic contextualist* — see Rysiew (2007).

approach, Judy's testimony would end up indicating the truth outright (*modulo* my reading of HALLOWEEN PARTY). (More generally, to fail to adopt this approach, condition (b)(ii) of my safety principle would be unsatisfiable, with my proposal boiling down to Sosa's updated principle.) While the result would still be safe knowledge, by my reckoning something important would be lost in describing the case this way. Overall, this complication demonstrates the fine line between outright and dependent indications of truth (cf. Sosa 2002: 270–71).

2.6 Now, as a preamble to considering objections, let's distinguish between two epistemological projects one might undertake. First, one might attempt to defend safety as a necessary condition on knowledge. This is my project in this chapter. Second, and more ambitiously, one might attempt to give a *reductive analysis* of knowledge, with safety as a component part — perhaps: all and only safe true beliefs count as knowledge. For familiar reasons, any such reductive analysis fails to have the resources to account for knowledge of necessary truths: such an account cannot allow for failure to know (some) necessary truths, because all necessary truths count as safe. (And for less familiar problems with such a reductive analysis, see Manley (2007: 408).) More prosaically, insofar as Becker's (2006) case, in which a person (safely) believes that the earth revolves around the sun solely on the basis of his adherence to a religion in which the sun is worshipped, is non-knowledge such a reductive analysis would fail on this score too. Note, however, that such an analysis is not vulnerable to Roush's (2005: 122–23) FAIRY GODMOTHER case of putative safe non-knowledge, in which a fairy godmother — let's say, of nomological necessity — renders true, for any p, S's belief that p, however faulty S's mode of reasoning in coming to believe that p. Recall (from n. 2), our formulation of safety using a subjunctive conditional was: $S\,B(p) \to p$. It wasn't the stronger: $\Box\,[S\,B(p) \to p]$. As such, we can, without complication, rely on the non-obtaining of fairy godmothers in close possible worlds (cf. n. 11 *supra*'s remarks on thought experiments).

The more ambitious project of reductive analysis, however, is not my project here. Insofar, then, as other safety accounts *can* successfully undertake this more ambitious project, my project might seem unduly *unambitious*. But my project would only be *mistaken* should my safety condition not feature as a necessary component of the reductive analysis.

(For other accounts which *might* be thought to provide the basis for a reductive analysis — accounts which are not in competition with, and indeed may need to be supplemented by, my account — cf. *method safety/process reliabilism* and *virtue reliabilism*. Each of these alternative accounts is, however, vulnerable to objections — most notably, perhaps, the *generality problem*: the problem of identifying precisely which process it is whose reliability determines how justified your belief is.) Still, insofar as we follow Sosa (1999) in considering safety an advance on *sensitivity*,[23] and insofar as the sensitivity condition allowed for progress on the Gettier problem (1963), it would be troubling for my proposed safety condition if one could readily invent Gettier-style cases of safe (true beliefs which are) non-knowledge. Any putative Gettier-style cases — see objections 1 and 2 (to come) — of safe non-knowledge should be accommodated by my project.[24]

2.7 Objection 1 and Reply 1: Suppose Judy flips a coin in a situation like HALLOWEEN PARTY but absent the 'that-I-do-not-appear-to-Judy-Michael'ly' condition. Instead, if the coin comes up tails, she'll direct me down the left road to the party at Andy's; if it comes up heads, she'll direct me down the left road to Andy's, but will immediately phone Andy so the party can be moved to Adam's. Call this JUDY COIN-FLIP. Suppose the coin lands tails. Do I know that the party is at the house down the left road?[25] It seems that I don't know this. Is my safety condition met? Suppose the candidate $C_{R\text{-}SAFE}$ here is: that-Judy-is-not-appeared-to-heads'ly. Is this C *indeed* safe? If this C were the case in the way described in JUDY COIN-FLIP, would C hold in all close possible worlds? No. That the flipped coin lands tails in our case has no (strong) bearing on what way the coin lands in close possible worlds; in

---

23 Viz.: If p weren't true, S wouldn't believe that p via M. (Or: ~p → ~[S B(p) via M].) This is a (Nozick-inspired) refinement on Nozick's (1981: 172) "condition (3)".
24 I am content to classify the classic *lottery case* — in which one truly believes one's single ticket in, say, a million-ticket lottery loses — as unsafe non-knowledge: although the odds of winning the lottery are minuscule, there are close possible worlds in which one wins. Space prevents detailed defense of this classification.
25 This case is found in Comesaña (2005: 402). (I do not think things turn out materially different if the coin-flip takes place *after* I get Judy's testimony.) One could construct a similar case in which Judy tells the truth conditional on it being the case that-Judy's-one-ticket-wins-a-million-ticket-lottery, and her ticket in fact wins said lottery.

particular, that the flipped coin lands tails in our case does not make it the case that the coin lands tails in all close possible worlds. Therefore we don't have a case of safe non-knowledge. Rather, it's, untroublingly, unsafe non-knowledge.[26]

HALLOWEEN PARTY — as with nearly all thought experiments — is, of course, under-described. Clearly I am making mileage out of a prior decision in HALLOWEEN PARTY securing C's (*viz.* that-I-do-not-appear-to-Judy-Michael'ly) holding in all close possible worlds. But suppose — as Comesaña (2005: 402) does — that the decision not to disguise myself as Michael was formed — as is, concededly, left open by HALLOWEEN PARTY — on the basis of a coin-flip landing tails (or conditional on my one ticket winning a million-ticket lottery). Call this PARTYGOER COIN-FLIP. Suppose the coin lands tails (or I win said lottery). Now, it's not so that if C were the case in the way described in PARTYGOER COIN-FLIP, C would hold in all close possible worlds. Result (*pace* Comesaña 2005: 402): more of an intuitive pull to withhold knowledge. We have unsafe non-knowledge (as in JUDY COIN-FLIP).

Summary diagnosis: in all the cases we've considered so far there's *some* (however weak) initial intuitive appeal to ascribe knowledge — after all, all the cases have a source of knowledge (whether testimony or perception) operating successfully. As we fill in the cases it becomes clear that the relevant source only operates successfully dependently on some or other (non-trivial) condition being the case. And the relevant condition, in each thought experiment, might — it seems — very well not have been the case. Now we have an intuitive pull to withhold knowledge. As we fill in the cases further we discover — my contention — that our willingness to ascribe knowledge in this or that case is a function of whether or not the relevant condition, if it were the case in the way described in the thought experiment under consideration, holds in all close possible worlds. In other words, it's a function of whether the relevant condition, C, is *safe*.

---

26 I give a like diagnosis, *mutatis mutandis*, of Goldman's (1976) FAKE BARNS, Neta and Rohrbaugh's (2004) two cases, and Bogardus's (2012) case. (To the extent that denying Neta and Rohrbaugh's cases involve knowledge is a bullet, I am prepared to bite it — cf. n. 27 *infra*.) Though note the following putative difference between FAKE BARNS and Neta and Rohrbaugh's cases: the threat to knowledge in FAKE BARNS is *actual* — there really are fake barns around — whereas the threat in Neta and Rohrbaugh's (as in HALLOWEEN PARTY) is *purely counterfactual*.

Indeed, on the back of this summary diagnosis, I'm open to persuasion — *contra* my initial diagnosis of HALLOWEEN PARTY at 2.5 *supra* — that, in HALLOWEEN PARTY, the condition that-I-do-not-appear-to-Judy-Micheal'ly is *not* safe. More descriptive information about the case pointing in this direction could come to light. Moreover, orderings of modal space are contentious. If this condition is not, after all, safe, discovery that it is not safe will, I suggest, be matched by — will generate — an intuitive pull to withhold knowledge.[27] We would, untroublingly, have unsafe non-knowledge.

Throughout, I — following most leading proponents of safety — rely on an intuitive ordering of possible worlds and do not commit on any substantive account of orderings of possible worlds (such as Lewis's (1979)). Clearly, this leaves room for disagreement over whether a condition is safe (e.g. on account of context dependence and/or vagueness infecting the relevant subjunctive conditional which is being given a possible worlds analysis). But perhaps this is exactly what we should expect in hard cases (cf. Gendler and Hawthorne (2005) on the putative instability of knowledge-intuitions in hard cases). It must be conceded, however, that it is the very fact that modal orderings are contentious which leads some philosophers to give accounts of knowledge which do not use modal conditions at all.

2.8   Objection 2: My proposal trivialises the safety condition, for almost every true belief will, on this objection, turn out to be safe. Consider, for instance, PARTYGOER COIN-FLIP, and grant that the condition that-I-do-not-appear-to-Judy-Michael'ly is not C_{R-SAFE}. That doesn't by itself show that the belief in question isn't safe, for there may be other C_{R-SAFE}s relative to which the belief is safe. In this case, let the candidate condition be: that-the-party-is-at-Andy's-house. This condition is, on this objection, C_{R-SAFE}. That-the-party-is-at-Andy's-house doesn't *entail* that the party is at the house down the left road, and thereby counts as non-trivial. And Judy's testimony does indicate the truth dependently

---

27 For a contrasting strategy to that adopted in this chapter, see Williamson (2009: 305): "One may have to decide whether safety obtains by first deciding whether knowledge obtains, rather than vice-versa." Sloganistically, Williamson's is a 'knowledge first' strategy; mine (at least in hard cases) is a 'safety first' strategy.

on this condition. But we've classed PARTYGOER COIN-FLIP as a case of intuitive non-knowledge.[28]

Reply 2: But the condition that-the-party-is-at-Andy's-house is not (relevantly-)C_{SAFE}. It's not the case that, if this C were the case *in the way described in PARTYGOER COIN-FLIP*, the party would be at Andy's house in all close possible worlds. The party is only at Andy's house in PARTYGOER COIN-FLIP thanks to a coin-flip landing tails (or my winning said lottery). If, by contrast, this C is *stipulated to be* (relevantly-)C_{SAFE}, the case is changed beyond all recognition and I don't see that the resultant case would be a genuine Gettier-case. That is, suppose, for contrast, the party *is* at Andy's house in all close possible worlds. *Now* is my belief that the party is at the house down the left road a clear case of non-knowledge? I don't think so.[29, 30]

2.9 Objection 3: My proposal does not tell us *how to find* $C_{R\text{-}SAFE}$s. Perhaps we're better off with Sosa's original proposal that — *modulo* no outright indication of truth — the putative knower must accept the indication "*guided* by", or "*on the basis* of", C. (Sosa's original proposal, though, is, of course, vulnerable to Comesaña's HALLOWEEN PARTY counterexample.)

Reply 3: I agree that no algorithm for finding $C_{R\text{-}SAFE}$s is on offer. However: so what? I take it 2.4's safety principle states a (disjunctive) necessary condition on knowledge. It doesn't have epistemic pretensions to furthermore help us *identify* $C_{R\text{-}SAFE}$s. Identifying such conditions is for (common-sense, philosophical) judgment to do (though this is not to say

---

28 This objection would putatively generalise to Gettier-cases like Lehrer's (1965: 168–75) NOGOT AND HAVIT, in which the subject's belief that *someone* in his office owns a Ford is safe dependently on the putative $C_{R\text{-}SAFE}$: that-*Havit*-owns-a-Ford. Again: that-Havit-owns-a-Ford doesn't entail that someone in the subject's office owns a Ford; only that-Havit-*who-is-in-the-subject's-office*-owns-a-Ford entails that.

29 And in NOGOT AND HAVIT, the condition that-Havit-owns-a-Ford is, for all we're told in that case, not (relevantly-)C_{SAFE}. If it's *stipulated to be* a C_{SAFE}, it's less clear we have a genuine Gettier-case of non-knowledge — cf., *inter alia*, Klein (2008: 25–61) for the possibility of knowledge inferred from falsehoods. As noted in 2.6, though, I don't claim to have set out a 'Gettier-proof' safety condition.

30 Is the condition that-the-party-is-at-Andy's-house a candidate (complementary) $C_{R\text{-}SAFE}$ *in HALLOWEEN PARTY*? To answer this, we need more information about the likelihood of Michael himself (and any other potential 'Michael-disguiser', such that there be) talking to Judy at the crossroads.

such identification will always be easy). 2.4's safety principle is none the worse for leaving this epistemic task to judgment. Try plugging some non-trivial conditions into the relevant subjunctive conditional and then evaluate it. We might be pleasantly surprised — I conjecture — by the paucity of conditions — none? one? *just* more than one? — which turn out to be $C_{\text{R-SAFE}}$s in this or that case.[31]

2.10 Objection 4: Whether a condition counts as (relevantly-)safe depends on how the condition and the facts that pre-date the condition are described. In JUDY COIN-FLIP, for example, the condition that-Judy-is-not-appeared-to-heads'ly does not seem to be safe, and (as a result) it is a case of unsafe non-knowledge. But what prevents us from describing the relevant condition as the condition that-Judy-is-not-appeared-to-heads'ly-given-the-fact-that-the-coin-lands-tails? This fact pre-dates the condition and, on this objection, guarantees that the condition holds in all close possible worlds. Using such a description, JUDY COIN-FLIP would come out as a case of either safe non-knowledge (which is troubling for my project) or safe knowledge (which is counterintuitive).

Reply 4: Objection 4 describes, not two different descriptions of one condition, but rather two different conditions — two ways of picking out different features of the world. Given a way close worlds are, we can fully expect two different conditions — two ways of picking out different features of the world — to differ in whether or not they're (relevantly-)safe.[32] As it happens, here, on a correct construal of the new condition, it shares the property of the condition in JUDY COIN-FLIP of failing to be safe (and so failing to be relevantly-safe), and thus the difficulties that would have arisen had we had a case of safety do

---

31 Some $C_{\text{R-SAFE}}$s — in the event of there being more than one in a particular case — will, however, be *explanatorily superior* to others.

32 Beyond the claim that if one has two ways of picking out different features of the world one has two different conditions, I don't commit on more substantive individuation criteria for conditions — that is, criteria for telling one numerically distinct condition from another. More specifically, I don't commit on whether Leibniz's law — the principle of the Indiscernibility of Identicals — holds for the *modal* property of (relevant-)safety (or the *logico-linguistic* property of logical form considered in the next paragraph). (Even more plainly, I don't need to commit on the status of the principle of the Identity of Indiscernibles.)

not arise. (On a mistaken construal, we'll see, the new condition has different properties.)

Let me explain. The logical form of the new condition is, abbreviating, the following conditional: T ⊃ ~APP H.[33] According to our safe condition schema (of 2.4 *supra*), to be safe a condition must 'obtain', and 'hold' in all close possible worlds. To do this, a conditional must be non-vacuously true throughout these worlds. And, while this conditional will not be false in any close possible worlds, it will go vacuously true — the coin will land heads — in some. We cannot, by diktat, stipulate that the coin lands tails in all close possible worlds: we are beholden to modal space. This condition, thus, is not safe. (If, mistakenly, one took non-falsity in all close possible worlds to be sufficient for a conditional to be a safe condition, this conditional, while safe, will not be *relevantly-safe* — consider the close worlds in which it goes vacuously true.)

Having said all this, let me concede that it *may be* that whether a condition counts as (relevantly-)safe *can depend* on how the condition is described. Return, for example, to HALLOWEEN PARTY. Suppose, with me, that the condition that-I-do-not-appear-to-Judy-Micheal'ly is relevantly-safe. But now also suppose that Judy happens to be the tallest person invited to Andy's party. On one plausible way of individuating conditions, the condition that-I-do-not-appear-to-the-tallest-person-invited-to-Andy's-party-Micheal'ly is the *same condition* as the one we've classed as relevantly-safe — it picks out the same features of the world — *just newly described*. Equally plausibly, though, the newly described condition may fail to be (relevantly-)safe (cf. n. 31 *supra*). However, even if all this is so: so what? A given belief will count as *safe* if there is *some description* of a condition under which the condition in question counts as relevantly-safe.[34]

---

33 T = the-coin-lands-tails; ~APP H = Judy-is-not-appeared-to-heads'ly.
34 I do not lay myself open to trivialisation by this 'some description' test; the 'relevantly' qualifier will pose a demanding test for such descriptions.

3. Conclusion

3.1 I haven't conclusively demonstrated that (2.4's) safety is a necessary condition on knowledge. I have, though, dismissed some cogent objections thereto.

9. Safety: An Application

In this final chapter, I bring epistemology to the practical domain of law. As Comesaña (2005) presented a putative counterexample to the necessity of Sosa's (1999, 2002) safety condition, so I present a putative counterexample to the necessity of the safety condition that Pardo (2010) employs in his work on knowledge and jury verdicts. My aim is not, of course, to falsify the thesis that safety is necessary for knowledge, but rather to advance discussion of the safety condition in philosophy of law (see Pardo, 2011). Towards the end, connections are drawn with my proposal in Chapter Eight.

0.1   Michael Pardo (2010: 38) recently intriguingly argues that "the goal or aim of legal proof is knowledge (or something approximating knowledge) rather than less epistemically demanding goals."[1] Pardo (52) continues, "[L]egal verdicts require more than truth and justification […] [T]ruth and justification also need to be connected in an appropriate way." I do not want to contest (directly) this central claim of Pardo's. My aim here is principally to show some difficulties for the account of (legal) knowledge with which Pardo (nn. 61 and 81) evidently operates, on which *safety* is a necessary condition. Highlighting these difficulties, however, puts pressure on Pardo's central claim.

---

1   As Pardo (57) notes, this claim of his takes place against the backdrop of a vast epistemological literature devoted to analyzing whether, and in what respect, knowledge is more valuable than less epistemically demanding achievements. For a comprehensive overview, see Pritchard and Turri (2007/2012). For an illuminating recent proposal, see Goldman and Olsson (2009). Finally, while Pardo (46) notes interesting issues about the relationship between *systemic* and *case-specific* epistemic considerations, Pardo's principal focus—and I follow suit—is on specific cases.

The plan: first, I set out and probe Pardo's *Fake Cabs* case — a case that demonstrates Pardo's commitment to safety as a necessary condition on (legal) knowledge. Second, I present a putative legal counterexample to safety as a necessary condition on (legal) knowledge. I close by presenting Pardo with a trilemma.

1. Pardo's Fake Cabs Case

1.1   Pardo (52) presents the following case:

> *Fake Cabs*: The plaintiff files a lawsuit against the defendant, who owns and drives the only taxicab in town, claiming she was hit by the defendant's cab while crossing the street. She saw the cab drive away but did not see the driver. A video camera at the intersection filmed the accident, and it shows what appears to be a cab (but not the driver) hitting the plaintiff, exactly as she claimed. Now, suppose the car in the video really is the defendant's, but also that — unknown to the jury — along with his real cab there are hundreds of other cars in the town that look identical to his cab. The jury finds for the plaintiff based on the video.

And Pardo's (52) gloss thereon:

> The verdict is true and justified (that is, there is sufficient evidence before the jury and no evidence regarding the fake cabs), and [...] there is a straight-forward causal connection between the true conclusion and the evidence. But there is still something problematic about the verdict — the jury would have formed the same conclusion if it had been one of the hundreds of other identical-looking cars on the video. The fortuitous circumstances — that it just happened to be the defendant's cab — render the relationship between the conclusion's truth and justification accidental in a way that undermines knowledge. It also [...] makes the verdict problematic.

So far, so good. But what feature does Pardo take to *explain* the verdict's problematicalness?:

> The verdict is problematic primarily because it is unsafe — that is, in a number of similar possible worlds the jury would have reached the same result and been in error.[2] (n. 61)

---

2   Plausibly, the verdict is also (what might be called) insensitive.

Pardo thus evidently operates with an account of (legal) knowledge on which safety is a necessary condition.³

1.2 Let us put Pardo's notion of unsafety on display alongside a cognate notion of safety. First, we can extract a general notion (pertaining to a subject S's actual belief in a proposition p):

UNSAFETY*: In a number of similar possible worlds, S would have believed p, and been in error.

SAFETY*: It is not the case that in a number of similar possible worlds, S would have believed p, and been in error.⁴

For familiar reasons,⁵ these theses need to be refined as follows:

---

3 Now that *Fake Cabs* has been introduced and preliminarily grappled with, note that the case from which *Fake Cabs* is derived — *Fake Barns* — originates in Goldman (1976) (with Goldman crediting Carl Ginet with the case). *Fake Cabs* is the first of several thought experiments in this chapter. The success of the thought experiments does not depend on their being empirically likely. (But consider the more prosaic presentation in Duff, Farmer, Marshall and Tadros (2007: 91), of a case of a defendant convicted accurately on the basis of evidence that though apparently sufficient at trial, turned out to be tainted or unreliable. Such cases that bear similarities to *Fake Cabs* are by no means far-fetched.) Rather, by abstracting from the untidiness of real-life cases, they serve interestingly to put pressure on concepts germane to the project of inquiry and to elicit intuitive judgments thereon. The sharpened conceptual awareness arising from consideration of these thought experiments can then serve to hone normative claims about the goal or aim of legal proof *in verdicts in concrete legal systems*.

In *Fake Cabs* the relationship between truth and justification is accidental in a knowledge-undermining way. Following the seminal paper by Gettier (1963), we can refer to such verdicts as being *Gettierised*. (Importantly, my thought experiment in section 2, *Insecure Mafia*, is *not* a Gettierised verdict; it is central to *Insecure Mafia* that knowledge is *not* undermined.) Objection: Pardo's claim that legal verdicts ought to be non-Gettierised is utopian: with sufficient ingenuity we can 'tweak' the facts of any otherwise unproblematic verdict to Gettierise it. Reply: Pardo is claiming that legal verdicts ought to be non-Gettierised; not (*contra* the objection) non-Gettierisable — where non-Gettierisable verdicts are verdicts with a guarantee that the facts cannot be tweaked to Gettierise them.

4 Safety has received many different formulations — and defenses as a necessary condition on knowledge — in the epistemological literature; cf., notably, Williamson (2000: ch.5); and Sosa (2002). Pardo's 'in a number of similar possible worlds' locution is regrettably imprecise. We might read 'a number of' as 'some'. If we do so, Pardo's SAFETY* would be equivalent to: In **no** similar possible worlds is it the case that S would have believed p, and been in error. The formulations extracted from Pardo are not ideal, but aim to stay close to Pardo's n. 61.

5 See the famous 'granny' case in Nozick (1981).

UNSAFETY: In a number of similar possible worlds, S would have believed p *on the same basis*, and been in error.

SAFETY: It is not the case that in a number of similar possible worlds, S would have believed p *on the same basis*, and been in error.

Second, to focus the discussion, let us put Pardo's restricted notion of jury unsafety on display alongside a cognate notion of jury safety:

JURY UNSAFETY: In a number of similar possible worlds the jury would have reached the same result *on the same basis*, and been in error.

JURY SAFETY: It is not the case that in a number of similar possible worlds the jury would have reached the same result *on the same basis*, and been in error.[6]

Given certain plausible assumptions — notably, a jury forming a belief in the relevant legal proposition semantically expressed by its verdict[7] — a counterexample to jury safety as a necessary condition on (legal) knowledge serves as a counterexample to safety as a necessary condition on knowledge.

1.3 We can see the intuitive appeal of Pardo's analysis by 'tweaking' the facts of *Fake Cabs*. Consider:

Fake Cabs*: As *Fake Cabs*, but the video camera filming the accident is operated by Sam Spade, a private investigator, hired to investigate the defendant's conduct, with perfect discriminative abilities in picking out the defendant's cab.[8]

This tweak now makes the jury's verdict safe: now it is not the case that in a number of similar possible worlds — say, worlds in which the defendant's cab hits the plaintiff at a slightly different angle and/

---

6   One could construct like restricted notions for other legal fact finders.
7   I prescind from the difficult question of what is it for a jury (a group of minded individuals) to form a belief (whether it is, for example, just a matter of all — or a majority of — the individuals forming beliefs with the same content).
8   Similar tweaks are given to *Fake Barns* in the epistemological literature — e.g., cloud occlusion of the fake barns, binoculars trained rigidly on the real barn, etc.

or velocity — the jury's finding for the plaintiff would be in error. And now (*modulo* no other knowledge-thwarting luck in the offing) the problematicalness of the verdict vanishes and it becomes a candidate for knowledge. We can play out this tweak — namely, rendering an unsafe verdict safe — in a number of similar cases to comparable effect. So I take the point to generalize. Pardo's explanation of the problematicalness of the verdict in *Fake Cabs* seems on the right lines, and safety seems a good candidate to be a necessary condition on (legal) knowledge.

2. Legal Counterexample to Safety as a Necessary Condition on Knowledge

2.1 Consider:

> *Insecure Mafia*: The chief prosecution witness, Amoruso, an honest and reliable citizen, is ready truthfully to provide damning evidence against the guilty defendant, Baggio, a member of the Mafia — such evidence guaranteeing a guilty verdict. However, Insecure Mafia, the Mafia's rival, has reason to believe that Baggio's brother, Carbone, may be a member of the jury and is certain that Carbone, if on the jury and presented with damning evidence against Baggio, will successfully obstruct a guilty verdict. So as not to lose face (by dint of a rival mafioso going scot-free *and being seen to do so*), Insecure Mafia devises the following plan: should Carbone appear on the jury on the first day of trial, Insecure Mafia will overnight switch Baggio for Twin Baggio (an unrelated exact lookalike of Baggio) — Twin Baggio becomes the defendant — and will inform only Carbone of the switch (who is no longer motivated to obstruct the guilty verdict). Baggio has no incentive to reveal the switch, and Twin Baggio is paid handsomely by Insecure Mafia in return for his silence. Amoruso would then, unawares, untruthfully provide the same damning evidence against Twin Baggio, thereby guaranteeing an unjust guilty verdict against Twin Baggio and saving Insecure Mafia's face — at least it would *seem like* a rival mafioso had been sent down. Carbone, however, is not on the jury. At the final hurdle in the tests for jury membership — Carbone having passed ninety-nine of the one hundred tests — it emerges, quite by chance, that

Carbone is Baggio's brother, and Carbone is dismissed. So the plan is not initiated, and the case proceeds normally. Amoruso provides true damning evidence against Baggio, and the jury convicts Baggio on the basis of Amoruso's testimony.[9]

Plausibly, in this case, the jury knows that the defendant is guilty[10] — therefore, *modulo* Pardo's central claim, the goal or aim of legal proof has been realized. And yet, plausibly, in a number of similar possible worlds the jury would have reached the same result *on the same basis* (Amoruso's testimony), and would have been in error. That is, in this case the jury knows that the defendant is guilty, but its verdict is not jury-safe. The jury has unsafe (legal) knowledge.

2.2 Objection (premise 1): the jury knows *that Baggio is guilty* (by Amoruso's testimony). And this knowledge *is* safe — the jury would not easily have been in error. However, according to this objector (premise 2), the jury does not know *that Baggio is the defendant*; *modulo* the details of *Insecure Mafia*, the jury would easily have been in error, and if the man in the dock — the defendant — had not been Baggio, the jury would still have believed he was Baggio, and so on. Therefore, inductively (conclusion), the jury does not, after all, know that *the defendant* is guilty — no unsafe (legal) knowledge.[11]

---

9   *Insecure Mafia* is inspired by Comesaña's (2005) *Halloween Party* case (though there are salient differences). Neta and Rohrbaugh (2004) also concoct two putative cases of unsafe knowledge, one of which involves a lottery. One may construct (more streamlined) variations on *Insecure Mafia* involving, for example, lotteries (e.g., where the switch is dependent on a lottery result); but my sense is that lottery cases lend an otherworldly nature to these cases. In any event, cases of this general form seem capable of being invented.

10 How does *Insecure Mafia* (knowledge) differ from *Fake Cabs* (non-knowledge)? One idea is that the threat to knowledge in *Fake Cabs* is *actual* — there really are fake cabs around the video camera — whereas the threat in *Insecure Mafia* is *purely counterfactual* — Carbone is not on the jury.

11 Consider: there is an opaque box into which I shall put either a frog, Kermit, or a donkey, Eeyore. I introduce you (an honest and reliable citizen) and a third party to Kermit but not to Eeyore. You think that I shall put Kermit in the box because I tell you, but only you, that I will. As it happens, I flip a coin to decide which animal to put in the box. The coin lands heads up, meaning, suppose, that I do in fact put Kermit in the box. Now you, pointing at the box, say to the third party, 'The animal in this box is smaller than a bread bin.' Does the third party know this claim? Objection (premise 1'): the third party does *safely* know *that Kermit is smaller than a bread bin* (by perception and my testimony). However (premise 2'), the third party does not know *that Kermit is the animal in the box*. So, inductively (conclusion'), the third party does not know that *the animal in the box* is smaller than a bread bin.

Reply: the proponent of *Insecure Mafia* should deny premise 2 and affirm that the jury *does* (unsafely) know that Baggio is the defendant. How so? The proponent must, plausibly, say it is a perceptual-*cum*-testimonial analogue of the jury's (unsafe) knowledge that the defendant is guilty in *Insecure Mafia* itself.[12]

3. Conclusion

3.1 This all suggests the following trilemma for Pardo (and how intuitively problematic he views the outcome in *Insecure Mafia* will have a bearing on which limb he takes and in what fashion): (1) retain his central claim that (safe) knowledge[13] is the goal or aim of legal proof *and deny that Insecure Mafia is a case of knowledge*;[14] (2) retain his central claim that (safe) knowledge is the goal or aim of legal proof *and deny that Insecure Mafia is a case of unsafety*;[15] or (3) withdraw his central claim that (safe) knowledge is the goal or aim of legal proof. Each option has its drawbacks.[16]

No unsafe knowledge. And, the objector would press, *Insecure Mafia* is relevantly similar (though obviously disanalogous in some ways): 'I/my' is Insecure Mafia; Kermit is Baggio; Eeyore is Twin Baggio; 'you' is Amoruso; the third party is the jury; the coin flip is the jury tests; the animal in the box is the defendant; and 'is smaller than a bread bin' is 'is guilty'.

12 Reply to n. 11's objection: the proponent of *Insecure Mafia* should deny that n. 11's case is relevantly similar to *Insecure Mafia*. Premise 2' *is true*, but only because — unlike, *mutatis mutandis*, *Insecure Mafia* — the third party receives no knowledge-conferring evidence that Kermit is the animal in the box. If the third party *does* receive such knowledge-conferring evidence (e.g., testimony from you after my coin flip), the cases become relevantly similar, but premise 2' becomes false.

13 By '(safe) knowledge' I mean knowledge on which safety is a necessary condition.

14 In Chapter Eight, I proposed a different safety condition which could be used to argue that *Insecure Mafia* is a case of unsafe non-knowledge (see section 2.7 of Chapter Eight especially). (Perhaps, though, plausibly, for a world to be relevantly similar, Carbone needs to be dismissed — as in the actual world, according to *Insecure Mafia*. One might analogise the facts leading to Carbone's dismissal with the element of *prior decision* in *Halloween Party* (see section 2.5 of Chapter Eight), such that that-Carbone-is-dismissed is a *relevantly-safe condition*. I reject the analogy: the facts leading to Carbone's dismissal are designed to be 'luck-infected' in a way that the prior decision in *Halloween Party* is not.)

15 This option involves constructing a (plausible and motivated) modified safety condition on which the jury's verdict in *Insecure Mafia* comes out safe. For an explicitly time-sensitive safety condition that could be put to such use, cf. Sainsbury (1997); Peacocke (1999: 310–28); and Williamson (2000: 124).

16 Pardo (2011) has replied to me.

Conclusion

We have explored the viability of allowing immediate justification and basic knowledge. While the existence of such a category of knowledge/justification strikes many as plausible, we observed (in Part One of the book) that to allow it is to face several problems. Good responses can be offered to most of these problems, but the objection discussed in Chapter Five was strong. In the Interim Review, I suggested several genuinely promising ways to respond to the objection. While I attempted to develop them, I concluded that, at this stage, I cannot take myself to have fully vindicated them. This led me to the following conditional verdict: If it really is the case that the justification to believe the quotidian proposition depends epistemically (constitutively) on the antecedent justification to believe that the source K is reliable, then (as I said in the Introduction) it is at best unclear whether this is even Cohenian basic knowledge. On the other hand, if there is not the constitutive epistemic dependence then we should say that it is Pryorian (and thus Cohenian) basic knowledge, and that the challenge to dogmatism is not compelling. While it would be optimal to enter a categorical — and not provisional — verdict, I still hope to have made some progress by my elaboration and scrutiny of several possible responses to Chapter Five's objection (in addition to the proposals I made in Chapters One to Four).

We then considered (in Part Two of the book) certain conditions which some philosophers have claimed are necessary for knowledge — *viz.* conclusive reasons, sensitivity and safety. While not decisively defending the (conclusive reasons or) sensitivity condition as a necessary condition on knowledge, several principled modifications thereto emerged as we concluded that two recent forceful arguments in favour of a plausible knowledge-closure principle were not knock-down successes. This conclusion with respect to knowledge-closure, we noted, was of relevance to the prospects for basic knowledge: rejection of knowledge-closure, and perhaps also of justification-closure, may provide a means of defending such a category of knowledge from the argument(s) in Chapter Five. Finally, we noted that a modified safety condition may well be a necessary condition on knowledge (and proceeded to attempt to advance discussion of the safety condition in philosophy of law).

Many avenues for further research open up. (Clearly, the most pressing challenge is to attempt to convert the provisional verdict entered on the viability of basic knowledge into something more categorical.) Let me mention just two from each part of the book, and then one more tying together Parts One and Two (though there are, of course, many more such avenues in practice).

Focusing on dogmatism about justification, according to which one can have immediate justification, Pryor (2000: 539) limits his dogmatism to "propositions we seem to perceive to be so, but *not* in virtue of seeming to perceive that other propositions are so, [which he calls] **perceptually basic** propositions, or propositions that our experiences **basically represent**." In this book I did not consider the *scope* of perceptually basic propositions (such that there be); and Pryor himself has yet to fully commit on this subject. This large and important issue — the issue of the possible contents of perceptual representation (see Siegel 2005/2010) — is one which I'd like to consider further.

For our second avenue for further research from Part One, recall that in the Interim Review we considered the possibility of some kind of putative default justification against sceptical hypotheses. It would seem that different philosophers will want to say very different things about such default justification. It would be a useful project to gain a deeper understanding of the different substantive things philosophers have said about such default justification — in particular, determining to what extent the different substantive notions of default justification are compatible with one another (see, for example Burge 1993, 2003, Wright 2004, and Davies 2004).

Next, taking Part Two, in Chapter Seven we made several principled modifications to a sensitivity condition (and, in Chapter Six, to a conclusive reasons condition). It would be an interesting project — our first avenue from this part — to consider whether further work could result in a sensitivity condition bulletproof to counterexample as a necessary condition on knowledge across the board. A corollary of any such project would involve an extension of the scope of application of any such condition beyond the principal scope of application of our project in Chapter Six, *viz.* atomic propositions, conjunctions, disjunctions, and (some) negations. Indeed — and relevantly to a defense of dogmatism — such a project might be extended to investigate whether justification to believe might itself be *characterised* by a sensitivity condition

Also — our second avenue from this part — Chapters Eight and Nine looked at the safety condition, with Chapter Nine in particular considering an application of epistemological work to a practical domain — law. An increasing number of theorists are considering possible applications of some of the conditions considered in Part Two for law (see, for an example involving sensitivity, Enoch, Spectre and Fisher (2012)). Such projects deserve serious consideration — in particular, questions must be asked whether domains such as law raise especial problems for engaging in applied epistemology.

To close, let me detail a research challenge firmly tying Part Two (specifically Chapter Eight — and Nine) back to Part One. It is a pretty stern challenge, particularly as the two bodies of literature on Parts One and Two of the book typically operate independently from one another. The rewards of successfully completing such a challenge, however, have the potential to be great: to provide a unified account of basic knowledge would be no small philosophical achievement.

Martin Smith (2009) has (in effect) intriguingly attempted to connect issues from Part One of the book — in particular, transmission failure — with issues from Part Two of the book — in particular, safety. (It will be seen that the notion of *antecedence* — whether temporal or epistemic — does not feature in Smith's account of transmission failure.) Insofar as Smith's arguments go through (cf. Tucker (2013b) for criticism of Smith) — and I do not commit on this here — my tentative defense of safety as a necessary condition on knowledge could be put to work in providing an analysis of transmission failure.

Smith (2009) applies several novel distinctions in developing his account of transmission failure in terms of safety. It is best to put the nub of Smith's contention on display up front — laden with heretofore unexplained Smith-terminology — and then to explain Smith's contention by explaining Smith's terminology. Smith's terminology is best explained with the aid of an example — the 'zebra' case (considered, *en passant*, previously in this book). Here is the heart of Smith's claim:

> Suppose one safely believes that P is true, notices that Q is a deductive consequence of P and proceeds to infer that Q is true too. If one's belief that Q is safe purely in virtue of its content, then presumably it cannot be said to be safe in virtue of the inference from P. One's belief that Q would have been safe irrespective of whether one inferred Q from P — it would have been safe even if it were held as an article of faith. Safety, we might say, is not always transmitted by deductive inference. When knowledge is not transmitted, this may be due to the safety condition […] All that I am claiming here is that a failure to transmit safety is a sufficient condition for a failure to transmit knowledge. Even if an inference transmits safety, it may yet fail to transmit knowledge because of a failure to transmit some other necessary precondition. (Internal footnote omitted) (Smith 2009: 171–72)

(Smith appears to assume, without argument, that safety is a necessary condition on knowledge.) Let 'P' be 'the animals are zebras' and let 'Q' be 'the animals are not disguised mules'. (Moreover, suppose one believes P on the basis, B, 'the animals are black and white, striped and equine'.) Suppose one infers Q from P in this case. In such a case Smith contends that one's belief that Q is safe *purely in virtue of its content*. What does this come to? In essence, it comes to one's belief that Q being safe *purely in virtue of the modal profile* of Q. In essence, here, the point is that one's belief that the animals are not disguised mules is true purely in virtue of the fact that worlds in which the animals *are* disguised mules are *very remote*. It follows that if this belief is safe *purely* in virtue of its content, then it is not safe *in virtue of the inference*. (Plausibly if P is safe, that which is deductively inferred from P — Q — is also safe. Smith endorses this, and he would put this as safety always being *preserved* — if not always being *transmitted* — by deductive inference. His point is that in the 'zebra' case the inference, as contrasted with content, is playing no *explanatory role* — the *in virtue of* relation — in the safety of that which is inferred. As Smith puts it, the belief that Q in this case "would have been safe even if it were held as an article of faith".) In this last respect, Smith would contrast his diagnosis of the 'zebra' case — transmission failure — from many quotidian inferences — no transmission failure. And Smith notes that:

> A belief may be safe purely in virtue of its content even though it was deductively inferred from a belief that is safe *in virtue of its basis*. The zebra inference, of course, provides one example of this phenomenon. (My emphasis) (2009: 171)

(A belief safe *in virtue of its basis* is one safe in virtue of the *modal relationship* between the basis and the believed proposition.) In sum, for Smith, failure of an inference to *transmit safety* — failure of an inferred belief to be safe in virtue of the inference — is a sufficient condition for an inference to fail to *transmit knowledge*; a sufficient condition, that is, for *transmission failure*. (Since safety is preserved by deductive inference, this promises an account of transmission failure that is consistent with the preservation of knowledge by deductive inference.)

Now Smith's account of transmission failure in terms of safety has been boiled down here to its bare essentials. Nonetheless, I hope its broad outline is now apparent, and, moreover, that it is at least initially plausible. To repeat, insofar as it can be fully vindicated (something on which I don't presently commit), we would have an explanation of a phenomenon considered in Part One of the book — transmission failure — in terms of a phenomenon considered in Part Two of the book — safety.

Indeed, we can draw an analogy between Smith's position and Wright's position. When we have transmission failure on Wright's account, it is because of epistemic circularity. The inferred proposition is in good order epistemically, but *not* in virtue of the inference. Rather, the inferred proposition is in good order epistemically because of justification by default. So there will always be preservation (of justification) despite the failure of transmission of justification. Safety purely in virtue of content is the analogue of justification by default.

(The analogy will be tighter, and Smith's account of transmission failure of *knowledge* can carry over to transmission failure of *justification*, insofar as safety is accorded a justificatory role. Smith rejects according safety such a role on the basis that safe beliefs must be true, while justified beliefs need not be; and he accordingly prefers to explain transmission failure of justification in terms of his own non-factive notion of *reliability*. Even insofar as safe beliefs must be true (cf. Chapter Seven, n. 2), something on which I believe I can remain neutral, I think that this is compatible with safety being accorded a justificatory role. To carve out space for such a role we can appeal to our previously introduced distinction between *prima-* and *ultima-facie* justification. The view would be that *prima facie* justified (dogmatist) beliefs need not be safe, and so need not be true; but *ultima facie* justified (dogmatist) beliefs must be safe, and therefore true.)

As a result of the analogy with Wright, we can predict that the problem of easy knowledge would be solved by appeal to transmission failure. It seems that looking at a red table and doing some simple inference is too easy to be a way of coming to know that there is no tricky red lighting. But 'there is no tricky red lighting' is safe purely in virtue of content: it would be safe if it were believed as an article of faith.

Bibliography

Adams, F. and Clarke, M. 2005. "Resurrecting the Tracking Theories." *Australasian Journal of Philosophy* 83: 207–21, https://doi.org/10.1080/00048400500111030

Alston, W. 1989. *Epistemic Justification*. (Ithaca: Cornell University Press).

Armstrong, D. 2004. *Truth and Truthmakers*. (Cambridge: Cambridge University Press), https://doi.org/10.1017/cbo9780511487552

Bach, K. "Statements and Beliefs Without Truth-aptitude." Manuscript available at http://userwww.sfsu.edu/~kbach/Minimalism.htm

Becker, K. 2006. "Reliabilism and Safety." *Metaphilosophy* 37: 691–704, https://doi.org/10.1111/j.1467-9973.2006.00452.x

—. 2012. "Methods and How to Individuate Them." In: K. Becker and T. Black (eds.), 81–97, https://doi.org/10.1017/cbo9780511783630.008

Becker, K. and Black, T. (eds.), 2012. *The Sensitivity Principle in Epistemology*. (Cambridge: Cambridge University Press), https://doi.org/10.1017/cbo9780511783630

Beebe, J. 2010. "Constraints on Skeptical Hypotheses." *The Philosophical Quarterly* 60: 449–70, https://doi.org/10.1111/j.1467-9213.2009.635.x

Black, T. 2008. "Solving the Problem of Easy Knowledge." *The Philosophical Quarterly* 58: 597–617, https://doi.org/10.1111/j.1467-9213.2008.554.x

Black, T. and Murphy, P. 2007. "In Defense of Sensitivity." *Synthese* 154: 53–71, https://doi.org/10.1007/s11229-005-8487-9

Blome-Tillmann, M. 2006. "A Closer Look at Closure Scepticism." *Proceedings of the Aristotelian Society* CVI: 383–92, https://doi.org/10.1111/j.1467-9264.2006.00154.x

Bogardus, T. 2014. "Knowledge Under Threat." *Philosophy and Phenomenological Research* 88: 289–313, https://doi.org/10.1111/j.1933-1592.2011.00564.x

Boghossian, P. and Peacocke, C. (eds.), 2000. *New Essays on the A Priori*. (Oxford: Oxford University Press), https://doi.org/10.1093/0199241279.001.0001

Brueckner, A. 2004. "Strategies for Refuting Closure for Knowledge." *Analysis* 64: 333–35, https://doi.org/10.1093/analys/64.4.333

Burge, T. 1993. "Content Preservation." *The Philosophical Review* 102: 457–88, https://doi.org/10.2307/2185680

—. 2003. "Perceptual Entitlement." *Philosophy and Phenomenological Research* 67: 503–48, https://doi.org/10.1111/j.1933-1592.2003.tb00307.x

Carter, A. 2012. "Recent Work on Moore's Proof." *International Journal for the Study of Skepticism* 2: 115–44, https://doi.org/10.1163/221057011x560974

Casullo, A. and Thurow, J. (eds.), 2013. *The A Priori in Philosophy*. (New York: Oxford University Press), https://doi.org/10.1093/acprof:oso/9780199695331.001.0001

Chandler, J. 2010. "The Transmission of Support: A Bayesian Re-analysis." *Synthese* 176: 333–43, https://doi.org/10.1007/s11229-009-9570-4

Cohen, S. 1988. "How to be a Fallibilist." *Philosophical Perspectives* 2: 91–123, https://doi.org/10.2307/2214070

—. 1999. "Contextualism, Skepticism, and the Structure of Reasons." *Philosophical Perspectives* 13: 57–89, https://doi.org/10.1111/0029-4624.33.s13.3

—. 2002. "Basic Knowledge and the Problem of Easy Knowledge." *Philosophy and Phenomenological Research* 65: 309–29, https://doi.org/10.1111/j.1933-1592.2002.tb00204.x

—. 2005. "Why Basic Knowledge is Easy Knowledge." *Philosophy and Phenomenological Research* 70: 417–30, https://doi.org/10.1111/j.1933-1592.2005.tb00536.x

—. 2010. "Bootstrapping, Defeasible Reasoning, and *A Priori* Justification." *Philosophical Perspectives* 24: 141–59, https://doi.org/10.1111/j.1520-8583.2010.00188.x

Coliva, A. 2010. "Moore's Proof and Martin Davies's Epistemic Projects." *Australasian Journal of Philosophy* 88: 101–16, https://doi.org/10.1080/00048400802587317

—. (ed.), 2012. *Mind, Meaning and Knowledge: Themes from the Philosophy of Crispin Wright*. (Oxford: Oxford University Press), https://doi.org/10.1093/acprof:oso/9780199278053.001.0001

Comesaña, J. 2005. "Unsafe Knowledge." *Synthese* 146: 395–404, https://doi.org/10.1007/s11229-004-6213-7

—. 2007. "Knowledge and Subjunctive Conditionals." *Philosophy Compass* 2: 781–91, https://doi.org/10.1111/j.1747-9991.2007.00076.x

Conee, E. and Feldman, F. 2008. "Evidence." In: Q. Smith (ed.), 83–104.

Copi, I. 1961. *Introduction to Logic*. (New York: Macmillan).

Cross, T. 2010. "Skeptical Success." *Oxford Studies in Epistemology* 3: 35–62.

Dancy, J., Sosa, E. and Steup, M. (eds.), 2010. *A Companion to Epistemology*. (Malden, MA: Wiley-Blackwell), https://doi.org/10.1002/9781444315080

Davies, M. 2000. "Externalism and Armchair Knowledge." In: P. Boghossian and C. Peacocke (eds.), 384–414, https://doi.org/10.1093/0199241279.003.0016

—. 2003. "The Problem of Armchair Knowledge." In: S. Nuccetelli (ed.), 23–55.

—. 2004. "Epistemic Entitlement, Warrant Transmission and Easy Knowledge." *Aristotelian Society Supplementary Volume* 78: 213–45, https://doi.org/10.1111/j.0309-7013.2004.00122.x

—. 2009. "Two Purposes of Arguing and Two Epistemic Projects." In: I. Ravenscroft (ed.), 337–83, https://doi.org/10.1093/acprof:oso/9780199267989.003.0015

DeRose, K. 1995. "Solving the Skeptical Problem." *The Philosophical Review* 104: 1–52, https://doi.org/10.2307/2186011

—. 2011. "Insensitivity is Back, Baby!" *Philosophical Perspectives* 24: 161–87, https://doi.org/10.1111/j.1520-8583.2010.00189.x

Dodd, D. and Zardini, E. (eds.), 2014. *Scepticism and Perceptual Justification*. (Oxford: Oxford University Press), https://doi.org/10.1093/acprof:oso/9780199658343.001.0001

Dretske, F. 1970. "Epistemic Operators." *The Journal of Philosophy* 67: 1007–23, https://doi.org/10.2307/2024710

—. 1971. "Conclusive Reasons." *Australasian Journal of Philosophy* 49: 1–22, https://doi.org/10.1080/00048407112341001

—. 2000. "Entitlement: Epistemic Rights Without Epistemic Duties?" *Philosophy and Phenomenological Research* 60: 591–606, https://doi.org/10.2307/2653817

—. 2005a. "The Case against Closure." In: M. Steup and E. Sosa (eds.), 13–25.

—. 2005b. "Reply to Hawthorne." In: M. Steup and E. Sosa (eds.), 43–46.

Duff, A., Farmer, L., Marshall, S., and Tadros, V. 2007. *The Trial on Trial, Vol. 3: Towards a Normative Theory of the Criminal Trial* (Oxford: Hart), https://doi.org/10.5040/9781472564153

Enoch, D., Spectre, L., and Fisher, T. 2012. "Statistical Evidence, Sensitivity, and the Legal Value of Knowledge."*Philosophy and Public Affairs* 40: 197–224, https://doi.org/10.1111/papa.12000

Fantl, J. 2012. "Knowlege How." In: E. Zalta (ed.), *The Stanford Encyclopedia of Philosophy*, available at: http://plato.stanford.edu/entries/knowledge-how/

Field, H. 1994. "Disquotational Truth and Factually Defective Discourse." *Philosophical Review* 103: 405–52, https://doi.org/10.2307/2185788

Fumerton, R. 2000/2010. "Foundationalist Theories of Epistemic Justification." In: E. Zalta (ed.), *The Stanford Encyclopedia of Philosophy*, available at: http://plato.stanford.edu/entries/justep-foundational/

Gendler, T. and Hawthorne, J. 2005. "The Real Guide to Fake Barns: A Catalogue of Gifts for your Epistemic Enemies." *Philosophical Studies* 124: 331–52, https://doi.org/10.1007/s11098-005-7779-8

—. (eds.), 2007. *Oxford Studies in Epistemology, Vol. 2.* (Oxford: Oxford University Press).

Gettier, E. 1963. "Is Justified True Belief Knowledge?" *Analysis* 23: 121–23, https://doi.org/10.2307/3326922

Goldberg, S. (ed.), 2007. *Internalism and Externalism in Semantics and Epistemology.* (Oxford: Clarendon).

Goldman, A. 1976. "Discrimination and Perceptual Knowledge." *The Journal of Philosophy* 73: 771–91, https://doi.org/10.2307/2025679

—. 1979. "What is Justified Belief?" In: G. Pappas (ed.), 1–23, https://doi.org/10.1007/978-94-009-9493-5_1

—. 1983. "*Philosophical Explanations* by Robert Nozick." *The Philosophical Review* 92: 81–88, https://doi.org/10.2307/2184523

Goldman, A., and E. Olsson. 2009. "Reliabilism and the Value of Knowledge." In: A. Haddock, A. Millar, and D. Pritchard, (eds.), 19–41, https://doi.org/10.1093/acprof:oso/9780199231188.003.0002

Greco, J. 2007. "Worries about Pritchard's Safety." *Synthese* 158: 299–302, https://doi.org/10.1007/s11229-006-9040-1

Greenough, P. and Pritchard, D. (eds.), 2009. *Williamson on Knowledge.* (Oxford: Oxford University Press), https://doi.org/10.1093/acprof:oso/9780199287512.001.0001

Haddock, A., Millar A., and Pritchard, D. (eds.), 2009. *Epistemic Value.* (Oxford: Oxford University Press), https://doi.org/10.1093/acprof:oso/9780199231188.001.0001

Harman, G. 1986. *Change in View: Principles of Reasoning.* (Cambridge, MA: MIT Press).

—. 2010. Epistemological self-profile, originally entitled "Epistemology as Methodology." In: J. Dancy, E. Sosa, and M. Steup (eds.), 152–56.

Hawthorne, J. 2002. "Deeply Contingent A Priori Knowledge." *Philosophy and Phenomenological Research* 65: 247–69, https://doi.org/10.1111/j.1933-1592.2002.tb00201.x

—. 2004. *Knowledge and Lotteries.* (Oxford: Clarendon), https://doi.org/10.1093/0199269556.001.0001

—. 2005. "The Case for Closure." In: M. Steup and E. Sosa (eds.), 26–42.

—. 2007. "A Priority and Externalism." In: S. Goldberg (ed.), 201–18.

Hawthorne, J. and Stanley, J. 2008. "Knowledge and Action." *The Journal of Philosophy* 105: 571–90, https://doi.org/10.5840/jphil20081051022

Heller, M. 1999. "Relevant Alternatives and Closure." *Australasian Journal of Philosophy* 77: 196–208, https://doi.org/10.1080/00048409912348941

Hempel, C. 1945. "Studies in the Logic of Confirmation." *Mind* 54: 1–26, 97–121, https://doi.org/10.1093/mind/liv.213.1, https://doi.org/10.1093/mind/liv.214.97

Holliday, W. 2014. "Epistemic Closure and Epistemic Logic I: Relevant Alternatives and Subjunctivism." *Journal of Philosophical Logic* 44: 1–62, https://doi.org/10.1007/s10992-013-9306-2

Hudson, H. 2007. "Safety." *Analysis* 67: 299–301, https://doi.org/10.1093/analys/67.4.299

Huemer, M. 2001. *Skepticism and the Veil of Perception*. (Lanham: Rowman & Littlefield).

—. 2006. "Phenomenal Conservatism and the Internalist Intuition." *American Philosophical Quarterly* 43: 147–58.

—. 2007. "Compassionate Phenomenal Conservatism." *Philosophy and Phenomenological Research* 74: 30–55, https://doi.org/10.1111/j.1933-1592.2007.00002.x

Jackson, F. 1987. *Conditionals*. (Oxford: Blackwell).

Klein, P. 1995. "Skepticism and Closure: Why the Evil Genius Argument Fails." *Philosophical Topics* 23: 213–36, https://doi.org/10.5840/philtopics19952315

—. 2004. "Closure Matters: Academic Skepticism and Easy Knowledge." *Philosophical Issues* 14: 165–84, https://doi.org/10.1111/j.1533-6077.2004.00026.x

—. 2008. "Useful False Beliefs." In: Q. Smith (ed.), 25–61, https://doi.org/10.1093/acprof:oso/9780199264933.003.0003

Korcz, K. 2006. "The Epistemic Basing Relation." In: E. Zalta (ed.), *The Stanford Encyclopedia of Philosophy*, available at: http://plato.stanford.edu/entries/basing-epistemic/

Kripke, S. 2011. "Nozick on Knowledge." In: *Philosophical Troubles: Collected Papers, Vol. 1*. (Oxford: Oxford University Press), 161–224, https://doi.org/10.1093/acprof:oso/9780199730155.003.0007

Kvanvig, J. 2006. "Closure Principles." *Philosophy Compass* 1: 256–67, https://doi.org/10.1111/j.1747-9991.2006.00027.x

Lasonen-Aarnio, M. 2008. "Single Premise Deduction and Risk." *Philosophical Studies* 141: 157–73, https://doi.org/10.1007/s11098-007-9157-1

Lehrer, K. 1965. "Knowledge, Truth and Evidence." *Analysis* 25: 168–75, https://doi.org/10.1093/analys/25.5.168

Lewis, D. 1979. "Counterfactual Dependence and Time's Arrow." *Nous* 13: 455–76, https://doi.org/10.2307/2215339

—. 1996. "Elusive Knowledge." *Australasian Journal of Philosophy* 74: 549–67, https://doi.org/10.1080/00048409612347521

Luper-Foy, S. (ed.), 1987. *The Possibility of Knowledge*. (Totowa, NJ: Rowman and Littlefield).

McDowell, J. 1982. "Criteria, Defeasibility, and Knowledge." *Proceedings of the British Academy* 68: 455–79.

—. 1986. "Singular Thought and the Extent of Inner Space." In: P. Pettit and J. McDowell (eds.), 137–68.

McGlynn, A. 2014. "On Epistemic Alchemy." In: D. Dodd and E. Zardini (eds.), 173–89, https://doi.org/10.1093/acprof:oso/9780199658343.003.0009

Manley, D. 2007. "Safety, Content, Apriority, Self-Knowledge." *The Journal of Philosophy* 104: 403–23, https://doi.org/10.5840/jphil2007104813

Markie, P. 2005. "Easy Knowledge." *Philosophy and Phenomenological Research* 70: 406–16, https://doi.org/10.1111/j.1933-1592.2005.tb00535.x

Martin, R. 1983. "Tracking Nozick's Skeptic: A Better Method." *Analysis* 43: 28–33, https://doi.org/10.1093/analys/43.1.28

Moore, G. 1939. "Proof of an External World." *Proceedings of the British Academy* 25: 273–300.

Moretti, L. 2012. "Wright, Okasha and Chandler on Transmission Failure." *Synthese* 184: 217–34, https://doi.org/10.1007/s11229-010-9771-x

Moretti, L. and, T. 2013. "Transmission of Justification and Warrant." In: E. Zalta (ed.), *The Stanford Encyclopedia of Philosophy*, available at: http://plato.stanford.edu/entries/transmission-justification-warrant/

Moser, P. (ed.), 2002. *The Oxford Handbook of Epistemology*. (Oxford University Press USA), https://doi.org/10.1093/0195130057.001.0001

Moyal-Sharrock, D. and Brenner, W. (eds.), 2005. *Investigating On Certainty: Essays on Wittgenstein's Last Work*. (Basingstoke: Palgrave Macmillan), https://doi.org/10.1057/9780230505346

Murphy, P. 2006. "A Strategy for Assessing Closure." *Erkenntnis* 65: 365–83, https://doi.org/10.1007/s10670-006-9009-y

Neta, R. and Rohrbaugh, G. 2004. "Luminosity and the Safety of Knowledge." *Pacific Philosophical Quarterly* 85: 396–406, https://doi.org/10.1111/j.1468-0114.2004.00207.x

Nozick, R. 1981. *Philosophical Explanations*. (Cambridge, MA: Belknap/Harvard University Press).

Nuccetelli, S. (ed.), 2003. *New Essays on Semantic Externalism and Self-Knowledge.* (Cambridge, MA: MIT Press).

Nuccetelli, S. and Seay, G. (eds.), 2007. *Themes from G. E. Moore: New Essays in Epistemology and Ethics.* (Oxford: Oxford University Press).

Okasha, S. 2004. "Wright on the Transmission of Support: a Bayesian Analysis." *Analysis* 64: 139–46, https://doi.org/10.1093/analys/64.2.139

Olsson, E. 2003/2012. "Coherentist Theories of Epistemic Justification." In: E. Zalta, ed., *The Stanford Encyclopedia of Philosophy,* available at: http://plato.stanford.edu/entries/justep-coherence/

Pappas, G. (ed.), 1979. *Justification and Knowledge.* (Dordrecht: D. Reidel), https://doi.org/10.1007/978-94-009-9493-5

Pardo, M. 2010. "The Gettier Problem and Legal Proof." *Legal Theory* 16: 37–57, https://doi.org/10.1017/s1352325210000054

—. 2011. "More On The Gettier Problem And Legal Proof: Unsafe Nonknowledge Does Not Mean That Knowledge Must Be Safe." *Legal Theory* 17: 75–80, https://doi.org/10.1017/s135232521100005x

Peacocke, C. 1986. *Thoughts: An Essay on Content.* (Oxford: Blackwell).

—. 1999. *Being Known.* (Oxford: Clarendon), https://doi.org/10.1093/0198238606.001.0001

—. 2003. *The Realm of Reason.* (Oxford: Oxford University Press), https://doi.org/10.1093/0199270724.001.0001

Pérez Otero, M. 2013. "Purposes of Reasoning and (a New Vindication of) Moore's Proof of an External World." *Synthese* 190: 4181–200, https://doi.org/10.1007/s11229-013-0256-6

Pettit, P. and McDowell, J. (eds.), 1986. *Subject, Thought and Context.* (Oxford: Clarendon).

Plantinga, A. 1993. *Warrant: The Current Debate.* (New York: Oxford University Press), https://doi.org/10.1093/0195078624.001.0001

Pollock, J. 1986. *Contemporary Theories of Knowledge.* (Totowa, NJ: Rowman & Littlefield).

Pritchard, D. 2005a. "Wittgenstein's *On Certainty* and Contemporary Anti-scepticism." In: D. Moyal-Sharrock and W. Brenner (eds.), 189–224, https://doi.org/10.1057/9780230505346_11

—. 2005b. *Epistemic Luck.* (Oxford: Clarendon), https://doi.org/10.1093/019928038x.001.0001

—. 2009. "Safety-Based Epistemology: Whither Now?" *Journal of Philosophical Research* 34: 33–45, https://doi.org/10.5840/jpr_2009_2

Pritchard, D. and Turri, J. 2007/2012. "The Value of Knowledge." In: E. Zalta, (ed.), *The Stanford Encyclopedia of Philosophy,* available at: http://plato.stanford.edu/entries/knowledge-value/

Pryor, J. 2000. "The Skeptic and the Dogmatist." *Nous* 34: 517–49, https://doi.org/10.1111/0029-4624.00277

—. 2001. "Highlights of Recent Epistemology." *British Journal for the Philosophy of Science* 52: 95–124, https://doi.org/10.1093/bjps/52.1.95

—. 2004. "What's Wrong with Moore's Argument?" *Philosophical Issues* 14: 349–78, https://doi.org/10.1111/j.1533-6077.2004.00034.x

—. 2012. "When Warrant Transmits." In: A. Coliva (ed.), 269–303, https://doi.org/10.1093/acprof:oso/9780199278053.003.0011

—. 2013. "Problems for Credulism." In: C. Tucker (ed.), 89–132, https://doi.org/10.1093/acprof:oso/9780199899494.003.0005

—. "Uncertainty and Undermining." MS available at: http://www.jimpryor.net/research/papers/Uncertainty.pdf

Putnam, H. 1981. *Reason, Truth, And History*. (Cambridge: Cambridge University Press), https://doi.org/10.1017/cbo9780511625398

Ravenscroft, I. (ed.), 2009. *Minds, Ethics, and Conditionals: Themes from the Philosophy of Frank Jackson*. (Oxford: Oxford University Press), https://doi.org/10.1093/acprof:oso/9780199267989.001.0001

Raz, J. 1978. "Reasons for Action, Decisions, and Norms." In: J. Raz (ed.), *Practical Reasoning*. (Oxford: Oxford University Press).

—. 1999. *Practical Reason and Norms*. (2nd edn.) (Oxford: Oxford University Press), https://doi.org/10.1093/acprof:oso/9780198268345.001.0001

—. 2002. *Engaging Reason*. (Oxford: Oxford University Press), https://doi.org/10.1093/0199248001.001.0001

Reisner, A. and Steglich-Petersen, A. (eds.), 2011. *Reasons for Belief*. (Cambridge: Cambridge University Press), https://doi.org/10.1017/cbo9780511977206

Roush, S. 2005. *Tracking Truth*. (Oxford: Oxford University Press), https://doi.org/10.1093/0199274738.001.0001

—. 2010. "Closure on Skepticism." *Journal of Philosophy* Volume CVII: 243–56, https://doi.org/10.5840/jphil2010107518

—. 2012. "Sensitivity and Closure." In: K. Becker and T. Black (eds.), 242–68, https://doi.org/10.1017/cbo9780511783630.019

Rysiew, P. 2007. "Epistemic Contextualism." In: E. Zalta (ed.), *The Stanford Encyclopedia of Philosophy*, available at: http://plato.stanford.edu/entries/contextualism-epistemology/

Sainsbury, M. 1997. "Easy Possibilities." *Philosophy and Phenomenological Research* 57: 907–19, https://doi.org/10.2307/2953809

Schaffer, J. 2003. "Perceptual Knowledge Derailed." *Philosophical Studies* 112: 31–45, https://doi.org/10.1023/a:1022590626235

Schiffer, S. 2004. "Skepticism and the Vagaries of Justified Belief" *Philosophical Studies* 119: 161–84, https://doi.org/10.1023/b:phil.0000029355.63475.9d

Siegel, S. 2005/2010. In: E. Zalta (ed.), *The Stanford Encyclopedia of Philosophy*, available at: http://plato.stanford.edu/entries/perception-contents/

Silins, N. 2005. "Transmission Failure Failure." *Philosophical Studies* 126: 71–102, https://doi.org/10.1007/s11098-005-4541-1

—. 2007. "Basic Justification and the Moorean Response to the Skeptic." In: T. Gendler and J. Hawthorne (eds.), 108–40.

Smith, M. 2009. "Transmission Failure Explained." *Philosophy and Phenomenological Research* 79:164–89, https://doi.org/10.1111/j.1933-1592.2009.00270.x

Smith, Q. (ed.) 2008. *Epistemology: New Essays* (Oxford: Oxford University Press) https://doi.org/10.1093/acprof:oso/9780199264933.003.0005

Sosa, E. 1999. "How Must Knowledge be Modally Related to What is Known?" *Philosophical Topics* 26: 373–84, https://doi.org/10.5840/philtopics1999261/229

—. 2000. "Skepticism and Contextualism." *Philosophical Issues* 10: 1–18, https://doi.org/10.1111/j.1758-2237.2000.tb00002.x

—. 2002. "Tracking, Competence, and Knowledge." In: P. Moser (ed.), 264–86, https://doi.org/10.1093/0195130057.003.0009

—. 2007. *A Virtue Epistemology, Vol. 1.* (Oxford: Clarendon), https://doi.org/10.1093/acprof:oso/9780199297023.003.0002

—. 2009. *Reflective Knowledge, Vol. 2.* (Oxford: Clarendon), https://doi.org/10.1093/acprof:oso/9780199217250.001.0001

Stalnaker, R. 1984. *Inquiry*. (Cambridge, MA: Bradford Books).

Steup, M. and Sosa, E. (eds.), 2005. *Contemporary Debates in Epistemology*. (Wiley-Blackwell).

Stine, G. 1976. "Skepticism, Relevant Alternatives, and Deductive Closure." *Philosophical Studies* 29: 249–61, https://doi.org/10.1007/bf00411885

Tucker, C. 2010. "When Transmission Fails." *The Philosophical Review* 119: 497–529, https://doi.org/10.1215/00318108-2010-012

—. 2013a. *Seemings and Justification: New Essays on Dogmatism and Phenomenal Conservatism*. (Oxford University Press USA), https://doi.org/10.1093/acprof:oso/9780199899494.001.0001

—. 2013b. "The Dangers of Using Safety to Explain Transmission Failure: A Reply to Martin Smith." *Episteme* 9: 393–406, https://doi.org/10.1017/epi.2012.24

Van Cleve, J. 2011. "Sosa on Easy Knowledge and the Problem of the Criterion." *Philosophical Studies* 153: 19-28, https://doi.org/10.1007/s11098-010-9647-4

—. (ed.), 2013c. *Seemings and Justification: New Essays on Dogmatism and Phenomenal Conservatism*. (Oxford: Oxford University Press), https://doi.org/10.1093/acprof:oso/9780199899494.001.0001

Vogel, J. 1987. "Tracking, Closure, and Inductive Knowledge." In: S. Luper-Foy (ed.), 197–215.

—. 1999. "The New Relevant Alternatives Theory." *Philosophical Perspectives* 13: 155–80, https://doi.org/10.1111/0029-4624.33.s13.8

Warfield, T. 2004. "When Epistemic Closure Does and Does Not Fail: A Lesson From the History of Epistemology." *Analysis* 64: 35–41, https://doi.org/10.1093/analys/64.1.35

Wedgwood, R. 2011. "Primitively Rational Belief-Forming Processes." In: A. Reisner and A. Steglich-Petersen (eds.), 180–200, https://doi.org/10.1017/cbo9780511977206.011

—. 2013. "*A Priori* Bootstrapping." In: A. Casullo and J. Thurow (eds.), 226–46, https://doi.org/10.1093/acprof:oso/9780199695331.003.0011

White, R. 2006. "Problems for Dogmatism." *Philosophical Studies* 131: 525–57, https://doi.org/10.1007/s11098-004-7487-9

Williams, J. and Sinhababu, N. 2015. "The Backward Clock, Truth-Tracking, and Safety." *Journal of Philosophy* 112: 46–55, https://doi.org/10.5840/jphil201511213

Williamson, T. 2000. *Knowledge and Its Limits*. (Oxford: Oxford University Press), https://doi.org/10.1093/019925656x.001.0001

—. 2009. "Replies to Critics." In: P. Greenough and D. Pritchard (eds.), 279–384, https://doi.org/10.1093/acprof:oso/9780199287512.003.0017

Wittgenstein, L. 1969. *On Certainty*. (Oxford: Blackwell).

Wright, C. 1985. "Facts and Certainty." *Proceedings of the British Academy* 71: 429–72.

—. 1991. "Scepticism and Dreaming: Imploding the Demon." *Mind* 100: 87–116, https://doi.org/10.1093/mind/c.397.87

—. 2002. "(Anti)-Sceptics Simple and Subtle: Moore and McDowell." *Philosophy and Phenomenological Research* 65, 330–48, https://doi.org/10.1111/j.1933-1592.2002.tb00205.x

—. 2003. "Some Reflections on the Acquisition of Warrant by Inference." In: S. Nuccetelli (ed.), 57–78.

—. 2004. "Warrant for Nothing (And Foundations for Free?)." *Aristotelian Society Supplementary Volume* 78: 167–212, https://doi.org/10.1111/j.0309-7013.2004.00121.x

—. 2007. "The Perils of Dogmatism." In: S. Nuccetelli and G. Seay (eds.), *Themes from G. E. Moore: New Essays in Epistemology and Ethics* (Oxford: Oxford University Press), 25–48.

—. 2008. "Internal-External: Doxastic Norms and Defusing of Sceptical Paradoxes." *The Journal of Philosophy* 105: 501–17, https://doi.org/10.5840/jphil2008105930

—. 2011. "Frictional Coherentism? A Comment on Chapter 10 of Ernest Sosa's *Reflective Knowledge*." *Philosophical Studies* 153: 29–41, https://doi.org/10.1007/s11098-010-9684-z

—. 2014. "On Epistemic Entitlement II: Welfare State Epistemology." In: D. Dodd and E. Zardini (eds.), 213–47, https://doi.org/10.1093/acprof:oso/9780199658343.003.0011

Zalabardo, J. 2005. "Externalism, Skepticism, and the Problem of Easy Knowledge." *The Philosophical Review* 114: 33–61, https://doi.org/10.1215/00318108-114-1-33

Index

Adams, F. 21, 177, 178
Alston, W. 12, 57
Armstrong, D. 114
Bach, K. 44–45

basic knowledge 1, 6–12, 22, 25, 29–31, 33, 55, 57, 77–78, 82–85, 89, 125, 132–133, 135, 141, 207–209
Bayesian 79, 96, 127–129
Becker, K. 21, 161, 167, 178–179, 191
Beebe, J. 84
Black, T. 21, 24
Blome-Tillmann, M. 24
Bogardus, T. 185, 193
Brueckner, A. 163
Burge, T. 11, 35, 131, 208

Carter, A. 11
Chandler, J. 121
Clarke, M. 21, 177, 178
closure of warrant under known entailment 31–32
Cohen, S. 6–12, 17, 19, 29, 35, 55–58, 65, 70, 77–78, 80–84, 86–88, 90, 92–93, 117, 122, 129, 132, 133, 147
   Cohenian 7, 8, 9, 132, 133, 207
coherentism 13–21
Coliva, A. 11
Comesaña, J. 21–22, 181–185, 187, 189, 192–193, 195, 199, 204
conditions on knowledge 1, 21–22, 24–25, 126, 139–141, 143, 150, 159–160, 163–165, 168, 174, 181–183, 188, 191, 195, 198, 201–202, 207–210
   conclusive reasons 1, 21, 22, 23, 24, 126, 127, 135, 139, 140, 141, 142, 143, 146, 147, 149, 150, 151, 152, 153, 154, 155, 156, 157, 158, 161, 164, 207, 209
   safety 1, 21, 22, 24, 25, 135, 139, 140, 141, 142, 181, 182, 183, 184, 185, 186, 187, 188, 189, 190, 191, 192, 194, 195, 196, 197, 198, 199, 200, 201, 202, 203, 205, 207, 208, 209, 210, 211, 212
   sensitivity 1, 21, 22, 23, 24, 81, 126, 127, 135, 139, 140, 141, 142, 147, 152, 159, 160, 161, 162, 163, 164, 165, 166, 167, 168, 170, 171, 173, 174, 175, 176, 178, 179, 192, 207, 208, 209
Conee, E. 98
cornerstone 30
credence 39, 79, 120–121, 128, 130–131, 169
Cross, T. 21, 114

Davies, M. 3–4, 11, 30–31, 34–35, 38–39, 42, 50, 52, 77–83, 94, 99, 101, 103, 128–129, 208
defeasible justification 6, 118
De Morgan 175, 179
DeRose, K. 21, 147
distribution 161–165, 171–173, 179

dogmatism 5, 10–12, 22–23, 30–32, 55, 77, 81, 103, 117–119, 122–123, 125–128, 131–136, 139–140, 207–209
  dogmatism about justification 23, 118, 120, 121, 123, 126, 127, 130, 131, 140, 208
  dogmatism about knowledge 22, 23, 118, 120, 122, 123, 126, 127, 135
doxastic justification/warrant 2, 61, 124
Dretske, F. 21, 23, 35, 41, 57, 101, 107, 135, 140, 141, 143–158, 159–164, 172–173
  Dretskean 146, 152, 153, 156, 158
Duff, A. 201

easy knowledge, problem of 11, 13, 17–22, 24, 29–31, 55, 57–60, 64–65, 69–70, 72–73, 76, 81, 83, 94, 117, 119, 134–135, 212
Enoch, D. 209
entitlement 3, 34–35, 37, 40–45, 51–52, 131
epistemic antecedence 4–8, 13, 32, 67, 108–110, 112, 114–115
epistemic circularity 4, 10–11, 29, 31–32, 35, 42, 67, 81, 94, 99, 101, 103–104, 107, 116, 125–126, 132, 211
epistemic dependence 5, 67, 115, 130, 133, 207
epistemic project of deciding what to believe 78
epistemic project of settling the question 30–31, 86, 134
equivalence 159–164, 167, 170–172, 174–177, 178–179
equivalence principle 159–160
evidence 3, 11, 17, 20, 32, 37–38, 45, 52, 56–57, 62, 64, 82, 84, 87–94, 95–107, 109–111, 113–116, 117–120, 125, 128–129, 146–150, 154–155, 164–166, 170, 173, 200–201, 203–205

external world 2, 4, 12, 29–31, 33, 39, 49, 56, 71, 80, 82, 85, 95, 99, 109, 114, 128–129, 134

Fantl, J. 1
Farmer, L. 201
Feldman, F. 98
Fisher, T. 209
foundationalism 9, 13–18, 21
Fumerton, R. 13

Gendler, T. 194
Gettier, E. 61, 192, 195, 201
  Gettier-case 195
  Gettierisable 201
  Gettierisation 61, 122
  Gettierised 201
  Gettier problem 192
Ginet, C. 57, 201
global sceptical hypothesis 30, 36, 84, 88, 89
Goldman, A. 57, 61, 178, 193, 199, 201
Greco, J. 186

Harman, G. 3
Hawthorne, J. 22, 57, 58, 71, 97, 116, 118, 122, 126, 129, 141, 143–147, 149–158, 159–164, 167, 171–175, 179–180, 194
Heller, M. 107, 147
Holliday, W. 163
Hudson, H. 22
Huemer, M. 5

immediate justification 4–5, 8–14, 29, 31, 33, 55, 77, 125, 207–208
inference 1–3, 19, 21–22, 24, 31, 34, 48–50, 55, 58–60, 62–63, 65–66, 68–76, 85, 89, 93–94, 98–99, 104–105, 114–115, 126, 144, 162, 176, 177, 210–212

Jackson, F. 78
jury verdicts 199
justification by default 131–132, 211

justification-closure 23, 123, 124, 126–127, 131, 135, 140, 208
justification; warrant 1, 1–6, 4–11, 8, 10–11, 13–20, 17, 19–20, 23–24, 24, 29–31, 30, 33–34, 33–42, 40–41, 44, 44–52, 55, 58–76, 78–80, 87, 93, 94, 96–116, 97, 117–118, 117–123, 125, 126–132, 129–130, 132–134, 135, 140, 143, 146, 152, 199–201, 207–209, 211, 212

Klein, P. 57, 65, 97, 107–108, 146, 195
knowledge 1, 6–10, 17, 19–20, 22–25, 30, 42, 56–58, 60–61, 64, 65, 66–67, 69, 71, 73–76, 77–80, 83–93, 100–102, 104, 107–108, 110–111, 114–115, 118, 118–119, 122–123, 125–126, 132–135, 139–142, 143–144, 146–149, 153–155, 158, 161–172, 174–175, 176, 179–180, 183–188, 190–196, 199–205, 207–208, 210–212
knowledge-closure 1, 22–23, 57–58, 79, 107, 123, 124, 126–127, 135, 139–140, 143, 159, 208
Korcz, K. 61, 165, 184
Kripke, S. 135, 157, 165, 171, 177
Kvanvig, J. 24

Lasonen-Aarnio, M. 124
law 40, 155, 196, 199, 208–209
legal proof 139, 199, 201, 204–205
Lehrer, K. 195
Lewis, D. 83, 147, 170, 194

Manley, D. 191
Markie, P. 11
Marshall, S. 201
McDowell, J.
  McDowellian 18
McGlynn, A. 4
Moore, G. E. 2–3, 29, 33, 39, 80, 85, 125, 128, 133
Moore's 'Proof' 29, 33, 80, 85, 125
Moretti, L. 4, 121
Murphy, P. 21, 163

Neta, R. 193, 204
non-evidential warrant 3, 35, 37–38, 41–42, 45, 48–49
Nozick, R. 21, 23, 57, 107, 135, 145, 152, 159–167, 170–175, 177–179, 182, 192, 201

Okasha, S. 121
Olsson, E. 15, 199
Otero, P. 11

Pardo, M. 199–205
Peacocke, C. 35, 152, 166, 185, 205
perceptual justification 6, 30–31, 118, 125, 131
Piazza, T. 4
Plantingan 61
Pollock, J. 35, 57
Pritchard, D. 37, 186, 189, 199
propositional justification/warrant 2, 61–66, 124, 129–130
Pryor, James 5–9, 10–11, 13–14, 16, 29, 35, 38–39, 57, 61, 78, 87, 99, 101, 109, 118, 120, 128, 131–132, 144, 185, 208
  Pryorian 8, 9, 10, 132, 133, 207
Putnam, H. 152

Raz, J. 189
reliability 12, 56, 131–132, 182, 192, 212
Rohrbaugh, G. 193, 204
Roush, S. 21, 165, 174–175, 191
Rysiew, P. 80, 190

scepticism 3, 29, 32, 38, 91, 121
Schaffer, J. 156
Schiffer, S. 40, 121
Siegel, S. 208
Silins, N. 35, 61–66, 97–99, 104, 111–112, 115–116, 128–130
Sinhababu, N. 141
Smith, M. 24, 25, 139, 141, 143, 209–212
Sosa, E. 13, 17–22, 56–57, 181–188, 190–192, 195, 199, 201

Spectre, L. 209
Stalnaker, R. 144, 170
Stanley, J. 71
Stine, G. 147
suppositional doubt 30, 39, 51, 79–80

Tadros, V. 201
temporal antecedence 5–6, 67
transmission failure 2, 4, 11, 13, 31–32, 35–36, 42, 46, 50, 59, 59–60, 63–64, 66–67, 80, 83, 94, 101–104, 106, 108–109, 111–116, 121, 125–126, 139, 141, 209–212
transmission of epistemic warrant (failure of) 1, 4, 29–30, 34, 39, 46, 48, 83, 103, 108
transmission of knowledge (failure of) 24
Tucker, C. 5, 62, 108, 116, 209
Turri, J. 199

unearned warrant 3, 10, 50, 52, 100, 131, 133

Van Cleve, J. 56
visual experience 2–4, 6, 10–11, 33, 35, 45, 47–50, 96, 103, 109, 111, 119, 133
Vogel, J. 22, 163

Warfield, T. 163
Wedgwood, R. 10, 12
White, R. 35, 121, 124, 128–129, 131–132
Williams, J. 141
Williamson, T. 6, 97, 100, 110, 116, 122, 144, 158, 161, 170, 172, 181–182, 185, 194, 201, 205
Wittgenstein, L. 37, 40, 45, 52
Wright, C. 2–4, 10–12, 15–16, 18–20, 23, 29–31, 33–53, 66, 71, 79, 82, 85, 95, 97, 99–101, 103, 112, 119, 121, 125, 131, 133–134, 208, 211–212

Zalabardo, J. 5–6, 30–31, 55, 58–61, 65–74, 76

This book need not end here…

At Open Book Publishers, we are changing the nature of the traditional academic book. The title you have just read will not be left on a library shelf, but will be accessed online by hundreds of readers each month across the globe. OBP publishes only the best academic work: each title passes through a rigorous peer-review process. We make all our books free to read online so that students, researchers and members of the public who can't afford a printed edition will have access to the same ideas.
This book and additional content is available at:
https://www.openbookpublishers.com/product/537

Customize

Personalize your copy of this book or design new books using OBP and third-party material. Take chapters or whole books from our published list and make a special edition, a new anthology or an illuminating coursepack. Each customized edition will be produced as a paperback and a downloadable PDF. Find out more at:
https://www.openbookpublishers.com/section/59/1

Donate

If you enjoyed this book, and feel that research like this should be available to all readers, regardless of their income, please think about donating to us. We do not operate for profit and all donations, as with all other revenue we generate, will be used to finance new Open Access publications.
https://www.openbookpublishers.com/section/13/1/support-us

Like Open Book Publishers

Follow @OpenBookPublish

Read more at the OBP Blog

You may also be interested in:

Knowledge and the Norm of Assertion
An Essay in Philosophical Science

By *John Turri*

https://www.openbookpublishers.com/product/397

Metaethics from a First Person Standpoint
An Introduction to Moral Philosophy

By *Catherine Wilson*

https://www.openbookpublishers.com/product/417

Foundations for Moral Relativism
Second Expanded Edition

By *J. David Velleman*

https://www.openbookpublishers.com/product/416

Beyond Price
Essays on Birth and Death

By *J. David Velleman*

http://www.openbookpublishers.com/product/349

www.ingramcontent.com/pod-product-compliance
Lightning Source LLC
Chambersburg PA
CBHW050556170426
43201CB00011B/1720